Essentials of the Laws of the Belt and Road Countries

Greece, Hungary, Norway

Edited by

Guiguo WANG

Alan Yuk-Lun LEE

Priscilla Mei-Fun LEUNG

ZHEJIANG UNIVERSITY PRESS
浙江大学出版社

图书在版编目（CIP）数据

"一带一路"沿线国法律精要＝Essentials of the Laws of the Belt and Road Countries. 希腊、匈牙利、挪威卷：英文/王贵国,李鋈麟,梁美芬主编.—杭州:浙江大学出版社,2017.8(2018.9 重印)
ISBN 978-7-308-17228-8

Ⅰ.①一… Ⅱ.①王…②李…③梁… Ⅲ.①法律－研究－希腊－英文②法律－研究－匈牙利－英文③法律－研究－挪威－英文 Ⅳ.①D910.4

中国版本图书馆 CIP 数据核字（2017）第 187160 号

"一带一路"沿线国法律精要：希腊、匈牙利、挪威卷（英文版）
Essentials of the Laws of the Belt and Road Countries：Greece，Hungary，Norway
王贵国　李鋈麟　梁美芬　主编

出 品 人	鲁东明
总 编 辑	袁亚春
丛书主持	陈佩钰　张　琛
责任编辑	陈佩钰（yukin_chen@zju.edu.cn）
文字编辑	祁　潇
责任校对	黄静芬
封面设计	城色设计
出版发行	浙江大学出版社
	（杭州市天目山路 148 号　邮政编码 310007）
	（网址:http://www.zjupress.com）
排　　版	浙江时代出版服务有限公司
印　　刷	虎彩印艺股份有限公司
开　　本	710mm×1000mm　1/16
印　　张	19.75
字　　数	475 千
版 印 次	2017 年 8 月第 1 版　2018 年 9 月第 2 次印刷
书　　号	ISBN 978-7-308-17228-8
定　　价	88.00 元

Introduction to International Academy of the Belt and Road

Founded in January 2016, International Academy of the Belt and Road (IABR) is the first research institution concerning the Belt and Road Initiative in Hong Kong, and is committed to setting up an international platform for academic and professional communication. Experts of countries along the Belt and Road Initiative from various areas, such as law, economics, finance, investment, politics and international relations, are invited to share their views and conduct research on relevant issues in the implementation of the Belt and Road Initiative. The IABR has held several international forums on the Belt and Road, and compiled *Essentials of the Laws of the Belt and Road Countries* Series and *Dispute Resolution Mechanism for the Belt and Road Initiative*. The IABR aims at providing expert services to corporations and institutions involved in the Belt and Road Initiative.

Professor Guiguo Wang serves as the President of the Academy, while Dr Alan Yuk-Lun Lee and Dr Priscilla Mei-Fun Leung serve as Vice Presidents. The IABR has an International Advisory Board with 26 experts and scholars, 42 fellows and 7 associate fellows from all over the world. The IABR endeavours to contribute to education and training of specialists so that Hong Kong could take full advantage of its unique position to develop international economy and keep world peace.

Preface

The Belt and Road ("B&R") Initiative, since it was officially announced by the Chinese Government in 2013, has generated much excitement not only within China but also internationally. The "Belt" refers to a transnational economic cooperation initiative among the countries along the ancient Silk Road from central China to central Asia and then to Western Europe with Amsterdam as the finishing point—the "Silk Road Economic Belt"; the "Road" indicates an economic cooperation initiative among countries along a new maritime Silk Road from China, South-east Asia, India, Sri Lanka, Yemen, Egypt, Greece, Italy to the Netherlands (Amsterdam)—the "Maritime Silk Road". As such, the B&R Initiative mainly focuses on the connectivity and cooperation among countries in Eurasia and some African countries. The National Development and Reform Commission, Ministry of Foreign Affairs and Ministry of Commerce of China with the authorisation of the State Council of China released the official document "Vision and Actions on Jointly Building Silk Road Economic Belt and 21St-Century Maritime Silk Road" in March 2015, which outlines the direction and rough contents of the B&R Initiative. An official B&R Initiative website was launched in March 2017. Yet, none of these official documentations indicates what specific countries are covered under the B&R Initiative, which implies that the B&R Initiative is an open-ended concept. Having said that, it is clear that the B&R Initiative aims at promoting economic cooperation among the countries concerned. It is equally clear that with or without a precise coverage, the B&R Initiative includes a large number of countries with different cultures, history, traditions, religions, and political and legal systems.

By its nature, implementation of the B&R Initiative involves cross-border movement of people, goods and services, capital and technology, a process which unavoidably entails interactions among the concerned countries. What norms should be observed in transacting business in these countries? Do as the Romans do, according to Western culture. As for the traditional Chinese culture such as the *Book of Rites(Liji Quli I)* , "When crossing the boundaries (of a state) , one should ask what its prohibitory norms are; having fairly entered it, one should ask about its customs; before entering a house, one should ask about the names to be avoided whilst in it. " Knowing the prohibitory norms, customs and names to be avoided of each country along the B&R is of utmost importance for the successful implementation of the initiative. It is precisely for this reason that this book series— *Essentials of the Laws of the Belt and Road Countries*—has been prepared.

This book series had its origin in a workshop that was held by the International Academy of the Belt and Road in Hong Kong, where some of its authors were present. The consensus of the workshop was that mutual understanding among the B&R countries over their legal traditions, constitutional and governance frameworks, laws on trade transactions and other immediately relevant areas such as financial regulation, employment law and environmental law was crucially important for implementing the B&R Initiative. It is only through a proper understanding of commonalities and differences between these nations that we could develop a meaningful framework for carrying out the related trade, investment and other activities.

The authors were provided with terms of reference for the chapter construction. Each country study would begin with an overview of its legal system relating to cross-border commercial transactions. The substantive parts of each chapter deal with customs systems, foreign trade law, law on foreign direct investments, monetary and banking law, laws relating to construction and infrastructure, labour management and treatment, environment and dispute resolution—both judicial and non-judicial (ADR) .

It is also part of the terms of reference that the authors should focus not only on the black letters of the laws but also on how these laws in fact operate in the market place. The authors were given a fair amount of leeway in examining each of these aspects in order that they could highlight those areas where their own nations would have a particular interest. The result is a happy blend of not only different writing styles but also different aspects of law in action.

A distinctive feature of this highly globalised world is coexistence of multilateral and bilateral economic cooperative schemes. As a result, trade and investment barriers have been removed or reduced with the development of both multilateral and bilateral cooperative programmes. These schemes not only regulate trade, investment and finance and banking at the international level but also directly impact on law-making and law enforcement at the national level. For this reason, we decided to have chapters devoted to two such associations—the European Union and ASEAN. These chapters provide support to the study of countries belonging to these associations and explain the interrelations that exist in terms of laws and legal processes between the central authorities and member states. A study of how EU and ASEAN authorities guide, coordinate and encourage a unified legal order for the promotion of trade and economic cooperation is also critical to the B&R Initiative which can learn from relative successes and lessons of the existing regional organisations.

When the B&R Initiative was first introduced, the United States and Japan were not among the B&R countries. Yet, as they are important countries for international economic cooperation, the B&R Initiative is an open concept and there are signs that the two countries may eventually take part in the B&R Initiative, we decided to include them in this book series.

We believe that, by providing an overview of the laws and legal structures that shape business relationships of the countries along the B&R, this book will contribute in a meaningful way to the implementation of the B&R Initiative.

Guiguo WANG

Alan Yuk-Lun LEE

Priscilla Mei-Fun LEUNG

18 April 2017

About the Editors

Guiguo Wang is University Professor and Scholar of "1000 Talents", Zhejiang University, in Hangzhou, China; Eason-Weinmann Chair of International and Comparative Law, School of Law, Tulane University, in New Orleans, USA; President of International Academy of the Belt and Road (Hong Kong, China); Chairman of the Hong Kong WTO Research Institute; Chairman of the National Committee (Hong Kong, China) and Titular Member of the International Academy of Comparative Law; former Dean of School of Law, City University of Hong Kong in Hong Kong, China and former Director of the Centre for Judicial Education and Research, City University of Hong Kong in Hong Kong, China; and Vice President of the Chinese Society of International Economic Law.

Professor Wang has an arbitration experience for more than 20 years. He is now President of Hangzhou International Arbitration Court and is an arbitrator of China International Economic and Trade Arbitration Commission; Beijing Arbitration Commission; Hong Kong International Arbitration Centre; Panel of Arbitrators of Korean Commercial Arbitration Board and Chinese Arbitration Association of Taiwan, China.

Professor Wang, holder of the JSD degree from Yale Law School and LLM degree from Columbia Law School, is the first person from the Chinese mainland to obtain the JSD degree from Yale Law School since 1949. Having obtained the JSD degree from Yale, he worked in several world-renowned law firms in countries and regions such as the United States, Canada and Hong Kong of China.

Professor Wang used to be an official at the Department of Law and Treaties, Ministry of Foreign Affairs of China. At the recommendation of the Chinese Foreign Ministry, he became the first Chinese recipient of the United Nations Institute for Training and Research fellowship which enabled him to participate in the seminars offered by the International Court of Justice and to study at The Hague Academy of International Law, the United Nations and the World Bank in 1980.

In the summer of 2010, Professor Wang served as a special lecturer at The Hague Academy of International Law and gave a series of lectures on "Radiating Impact of WTO on Its Members' Legal System: The Chinese Perspective".

Professor Wang has published more than 20 books and over 100 journal articles in established journals in China and other countries. His *Legal Order of International Trade* published by the Law Press in 1987 is one of the earliest treatises on the GATT. Professor Wang's main works include: *Sino-American Economic Exchanges: The Legal Contributions* (1984); *International Banking and Financial Law* (1988); *Contemporary Legal Prescriptions for International Investment* (1988); *China's Investment Law: The New Directions* (1988); *International Economic Law* (1992); *Wang's Business Law of China* (4th Ed., 2003); *The Law of the WTO* (2003); *International Trade Law* (2004); *The Law of the WTO: China and the Future of Free Trade* (2005); *International Monetary and Financial Law* (3rd Ed., 2007); *International Investment Law* (2nd Ed., 2008); "Radiating Impact of WTO on Its Members' Legal System: The Chinese Perspective", *Collected Courses of The Hague Academy of International Law*, vol. 349 (2010); *International Investment Law: A Chinese Perspective* (in English) (2015); *International Law Perspective of the Belt and Road Initiative* (co-ed.) (2016); *Dispute Resolution Mechanism for the Belt and Road* (co-ed.) (2016).

Dr Yuk-Lun Lee is a Justice of Peace. He graduated from Lincoln University, USA in 2009 with an honorary doctorate of Management, and was elected as the academician of Canadian Chartered Institute of Business Administration(CCIBA). In 2014, he obtained his Master of Business Administration at the University of Wales Newport, UK. Now, Dr Lee is studying for the collaborative PhD degree programme with Fudan University (APRU) and Stanford University.

Dr Lee is also keen in charity affairs, and is chairman (2017/2018) of Tung Wah Group of Hospitals, founding chairman of Phoenix Charitable Foundation, honorary permanent president of Hong Kong Commerce and Industry Associations, China. He also serves as chairman of Pico Zeman Asset Management Limited and Volk Favor Food Company Limited, Vice President of the International Academy of the Belt and Road (IABR), committee member of All-China Federation of Returned Overseas Chinese, committee member of CPPCC Beijing Committee, Director of China Overseas Friendship Association and member of Board of New Asia College of the Chinese University of Hong Kong, China.

Dr Priscilla Mei-Fun Leung has taught at the School of Law, City University of Hong Kong for 24 years and is specialised in Chinese Law, Hong Kong Basic Law and conflicts of law amongst the Chinese mainland, Hong Kong and Taiwan.

Dr Leung is the Chairman of the Judicial and Legal Affairs Committee of the Legislative Council in Hong Kong. She is Associate Professor at the School of Law, City University of Hong Kong; Barrister-at-Law; Arbitrator(CIETAC) and received the Ten Outstanding Young Persons Award of the Year 2000.

Dr Leung has published different articles and books on the above areas both in English and Chinese, including the China Law Reports series(English), the China International Economic and Trade Arbitration Commission Awards series(English) and *Hong Kong Basic Law: Hybrid of Chinese Law and Common Law* (published in 2007 in English). Her publications also include *Comparative Studies of Family Law between Chinese Mainland, Taiwan and Hong Kong* published by the Joint Publishing House in June 2003(Chinese), *Legal Reform of China*(co-ed) in 1994.

Contents

Greece ·· (1)

  About the Editors ·· (3)

  Introduction ·· (4)

  Chapter 1 Customs System and Law ································· (9)

  Chapter 2 Foreign Trade System and Law ······················· (23)

  Chapter 3 Foreign Direct Investment System and Law ·············· (36)

  Chapter 4 Monetary and Banking System and Law ··············· (46)

  Chapter 5 Laws Relating to Construction of Infrastructure ··········· (56)

  Chapter 6 Laws Relating to Labour Management and Treatment ·········· (63)

  Chapter 7 Environmental Law ···································· (75)

  Chapter 8 Laws Relating to Dispute Resolution Concerning Foreign Entities ···
  ··· (81)

Hungary ·· (97)

  About the Authors ·· (99)

  Introduction ·· (100)

  Chapter 1 Customs System and Law ······························ (105)

  Chapter 2 Foreign Trade System and Law ······················· (119)

  Chapter 3 Foreign Direct Investment System and Law ············ (132)

  Chapter 4 Monetary and Banking System and Law ··············· (146)

  Chapter 5 Laws Relating to Infrastructure Construction in Hungary ······ (160)

  Chapter 6 Law Relating to Labour Management and Treatment in Hungary ···
  ··· (175)

  Chapter 7 Environmental Law in Hungary ······················· (194)

Chapter 8   Laws Relating to Resolution of Disputes Concerning Foreign Entities
.... (205)

Norway .... (222)

About the Authors .... (224)

Introduction .... (225)

Chapter 1   Customs System and Law .... (231)

Chapter 2   Foreign Trade System and Law .... (238)

Chapter 3   Foreign Direct Investment System and Law .... (248)

Chapter 4   Monetary and Banking System and Law .... (256)

Chapter 5   Laws Relating to Construction of Infrastructure .... (265)

Chapter 6   Laws Relating to Labour Management and Treatment .... (274)

Chapter 7   Environmental Law .... (283)

Chapter 8   Laws Relating to Dispute Resolution Concerning Foreign Entities ...
.... (288)

Greece

Dr Nikolaos I. Theodorakis

About the Authors

Dr Nikolaos Theodorakis is a lecturer and fellow at the University of Oxford, lecturing on public international law and international economic law. He recently acted as a consultant for the United Nations. Prior to his current appointments, Dr Theodorakis taught and conducted research at the University of Cambridge, Harvard Law School and Columbia Law School and gained professional experience at the US Committee on Capital Markets Regulation, the Kluge Centre at the US Library of Congress and the UK Ministry of Justice. Dr Theodorakis has received awards from several bodies, and his research has been widely published, including the monograph *Transparency in Investor – State Dispute Settlement: Law, Practice, and Emerging Tools against Institutional Corruption*, published by Harvard University in 2015.

Introduction

Greece is a Parliamentary Republic. The President is the Head of State and is e-lected by the Parliament every five years. The Prime Minister is the Head of Government. The Ministerial Council, consisting of the Prime Minister, Ministers, Deputy Ministers and Ministers without portfolio is the collective decision-making body that comprises the Government of Greece, which is the executive branch. [1]

Although the President of the Republic has limited political power, as most power lies with the government, his duties include formally appointing the Prime Minister, on whose recommendation he also appoints or dismisses other members of government. He represents the state in its relations with other states, proclaims referendums and more.

Greece is the 45th largest economy in the world with a nominal gross domestic product(GDP) of USD 235. 6 billion per year. [2] It is also the 51st largest state in the world by purchasing power parity, at USD 291. 9 billion per year. It is currently the 13th largest economy in the 28-member European Union. [3]

In terms of the main sectors of activity, Greece's economy is mostly based on services (82. 8 percent). Industrial sectors follow(13. 3 percent) along with the agricultural sector (3. 9 percent). [4] Tourism is its main industry with several million tourists visiting the country every year. In fact, it is the 16th most visited country in the world.

The Greek Merchant Navy is the largest in the world, with Greek-owned vessels accounting for 15 percent of global deadweight tonnage as of 2013. Over the past years there has been an increased demand for international maritime transportation between Greece and Asia, which has resulted in significant investment in the shipping industry.

---

[1]   http://www. mfa. gr/usa/en/about-greece/government-and-politics/.

[2]   http://databank. worldbank. org/data/download/GDP. pdf.

[3]   http://appsso. eurostat. ec. europa. eu/nui/show. do.

[4]   https://www. cia. gov/library/publications/the-world-factbook/geos/gr. html.

Legislative branch

Legislative power is exercised by Parliament and the President of the Republic. General elections are held every four years unless the Parliament is dissolved earlier. The electorate consists of all Greek citizens who are 18 years of age. Each new Government, after a general election or after the previous government's resignation, has to appear before Parliament and request a vote of confidence.

The State is structured by the Constitution. The Constitution of Greece is the fundamental Charter of the State. It has been voted by the Fifth Revisional Assembly and enforced in 1975. It was amended in 1986, in 2001 and in 2008 by the Greek Parliament. It includes the main rules concerning the structure of the State, the exercise of its powers by the authorities as well as a list of human rights.

The Hellenic Parliament is the supreme democratic institution that represents the citizens through the elected body of Members of Parliament(MPs), whose core activity is legislative work and the exercise of control over Government. Currently, the Hellenic Parliament consists of 300 deputies. They are elected through direct, universal, secret and simultaneous ballot for a term of four years. The Parliament is headed by the Speaker.

Judicial branch

The judicial branch is divided into civil and administrative courts. Civil courts judge civil and penal cases, whereas administrative courts judge administrative cases, namely disputes between the citizens and the State. The Council of State (*Symvoulio tis Epikrateias*) is the Supreme Administrative Court of Greece. *Areios Pagos* is the Supreme Civil and Criminal Court. The Court of Audit (*Elegktiko Synedrio*) has jurisdiction on the audit of the expenditures of the State, local government agencies and other legal entities.

These high courts are composed of professional judges, graduates of the National School of Judges. The way the judges are gradually promoted, until they become members of the Supreme Courts, is defined by the Constitution and the existing laws. The presidents and the vice-presidents of the three Supreme Courts are chosen by the Cabinet of Greece among the serving members of each of the Supreme Courts.

Sometimes, the Supreme Courts take contradictory decisions or they judge differently the constitutionality of a legal provision. When this happens, the Supreme Special Court is in charge, whose composition and jurisdiction is regulated by Article 100 of the Constitution. The court is not permanent and only convenes on an ad hoc basis. When the Supreme Special Court sits, it comprises 11 members: the Presidents of the three Supreme Courts, four members of the Court of Cassation and four members of the Council of State.

Greece and the EU

Accession negotiations between Greece and the European Union were initiated in July 1976 and brought to a conclusion in May 1979, with the signing of the Accession Deed in Athens (*Zappeion Megaron*). The Greek Parliament ratified the Accession Deed of Greece to the European Community on 28 June 1979. The Accession Treaty entered into force two years later, on 1 January 1981. [1]

Greece is strategically located at the north-eastern corner of the Mediterranean Sea, forming the southern tip of the Balkan Peninsula in south-east Europe. With regard to its specific participation in the European Union:

European Parliament

There are 21 members of the European Parliament who are from Greece.

Council of the EU

In the Council of the EU, national ministers meet regularly to adopt EU laws and coordinate policies. Council meetings are regularly attended by representatives from the Greek government, depending on the policy area being addressed.

Presidency of the Council of the EU

The Council of the EU doesn't have a permanent, single-person president. Instead, its work is led by the country holding the Council presidency, which rotates every six months. During these six months, ministers from that country's government chair and help determine the agenda of Council meetings in each policy area, and fa-

---

[1]   http://www. mfa. gr/en/foreign-policy/greece-in-the-eu/greeces-course-in-the-eu. html.

cilitate dialogue with the other EU institutions.

Dates of Greek presidencies:

Jul-Dec 1983/Jul-Dec 1988/Jan-Jun 1994/Jan-Jun 2003/Jan-Jun 2014.

European Commission

The Commissioner nominated by Greece to the European Commission is currently Dimitris Avramopoulos, who is responsible for Migration, Home Affairs and Citizenship. The Commission is represented in each EU country by a local office, called a "representation".

European Economic and Social Committee

Greece has 13 representatives on the European Economic and Social Committee. This advisory body—representing employers, workers and other interest groups—is consulted on proposed laws, to get a better idea of the possible changes to work and social situations in member countries.

Committee of the Regions

Greece has 12 representatives on the Committee of the Regions, the EU's assembly of regional and local representatives. This advisory body is consulted on proposed laws, to ensure these laws take account of the perspective from each region of the EU.

Permanent representation to the EU

Greece also communicates with the EU institutions through its permanent representation in Brussels. As Greece's "embassy to the EU", its main task is to ensure that the country's interests and policies are pursued as effectively as possible in the EU.

Greece and the Eurozone

Greece was accepted into the Economic and Monetary Union of the European Union by the European Council on 19 June 2000, based on a number of criteria (inflation rate, budget deficit, public debt, long-term interest rates, exchange rate) using

1999 as the reference year.

Greece has been majorly involved in the eurozone crisis that hit in 2009. Over the past years, the scenario of Greece exiting the eurozone ("Grexit") has been extensively discussed. Yet, since the beginning of the sovereign-debt crisis in the EU, Greece maintained that the right approach is to address the root causes of the problem, namely the competitiveness gap between the various eurozone member states. All partners must work together, creditors and debtors, thereby improving the intra-eurozone balance of payments.

Greece is an advocate of bridging the gap through balanced growth and support for employment. This will be achieved, according to Greece, by a solid fiscal and financial framework, which is the prerequisite of any future growth and stability. [1] Greece believes that the EU should complement the above progress by intensifying efforts to deliver on the commitments made in the European Council's Compact for Growth and Jobs, including through the European Semester process and the Europe 2020 Strategy, the EU's primary growth tool for the coming decade.

---

[1]   http://www. mfa. gr/en/foreign-policy/greece-in-the-eu/the-euro-area-debt-crisis. html.

Chapter 1   Customs System and Law

1.1   General principles

Upon the establishment of the Single Internal Market, on 1 January 1993, the customs control among the EU member states was abolished and the movement of goods and services was freely implemented, subject only to the value-added tax (VAT) liability control.

The intra-community trade is designated as purchases and sales, while the terms import and export refer only to the extra-community trade. VAT is a general, broadly based consumption tax assessed on the value added to goods and services. It applies to most goods and services that are bought and sold for use or consumption in the Union. The applicable EU legislation since 1 January 2007 has been Directive 2006/112/EC(VAT Directive). This Directive provides exemptions for(i)intra-community supply of goods and for(ii)exportation. [1]

Article 146 of the VAT Directive provides an exemption for exports to countries outside the EU, since the goods are consumed outside the EU. EU legislation makes a very clear distinction between customs legislation, which applies to the importation phase, and sector-specific legislation, which regulates the placing of certain products on the EU market. The EU customs code covers all the customs matters relating to trade with non-EU countries. It ensures that customs procedures in all EU member states are consistent and transparent. The implementing provisions provide the rules and processes to enforce the Customs Code. [2] The Union Customs Code (UCC), adopted in Regulation No (EU) 952/2013, will repeal the existing customs code on 1

---

[1]   http://eur-lex. europa. eu/legal-content/EN/TXT/? uri = URISERV%3Al31057.

[2]   The main legislation regarding importation of goods into the EU territory is enshrined in the Community Customs Code(CC)(Council Regulation(EEC) No 2913/92 of 12 October 1992 establishing the Community Customs Code [OJ L 302,19. 10. 1992,p. 1]) and its implementing provisions(CCIP)(Commission Regulation (EEC) No 2454/93 of 2 July 1993 laying down provisions for the implementation of Council Regulation(EEC) No 2913/92 establishing the Community Customs Code [OJ L 253,11. 10. 1993,p. 1]).

May 2016.

The Union Customs Code was adopted on 9 October 2013 as Regulation (EU) No. 952/2013 of the European Parliament and of the Council. It entered into force on 30 October 2013 and repealed the Regulation(EC) No. 450/2008 of 23 April 2008 laying down the Community Customs Code(OJ L 145,4.6.2008,p.1). Its substantive provisions will apply only on 1 May 2016, once the UCC-related Commission acts (Delegated and Implementing Acts) are adopted and in force and by not later than 1 May 2016.

The UCC is part of the modernisation of customs and will serve as the new framework regulation on the rules and procedures for customs throughout the EU. The UCC and the related delegated and implementing acts seek to:[1]

- streamline customs legislation and procedures;
- offer greater legal certainty and uniformity to businesses;
- increase clarity for customs officials throughout the EU;
- simplify customs rules and procedures and facilitate more efficient customs transactions in line with modern-day needs;
- complete the shift by Customs to a paperless and fully electronic environment;
- reinforce swifter customs procedures for compliant and trustworthy economic operators (Authorised Economic Operators).

In line with the Articles 290 and 291 of the Treaty on the Functioning of the European Union (TFEU), shaping of the provisions within the Acts is done through proper involvement of the member states and the business community.

1. 2　Operator Registration and Identification number registration

The importer does not need to pre-notify the importation of his products into the EU, except for dual-use goods and goods that require a specific licence, nor must it get any kind of authorization to import those goods. The only obligation on the importer is to request a registration number, called the Economic Operator Registration and Identification number (EORI number), which will be needed later on in the process. [2]

---

[1] http://ec.europa.eu/taxation_customs/customs/customs_code/union_customs_code/ucc/index_en.htm.

[2] See Articles 4k-4t CCIP.

This request is made to EU customs authorities. In most cases, the customs a-
gent acting for the importer will in fact get an EORI number for the importer. Customs agents must also have an EORI number.

The EORI number is a unique identifier for every economic operator, company
and individual, who engages in activities covered by EU customs legislation. Importers active outside the EU will be assigned an EORI number the first time the carrier
of their goods lodges a customs declaration, an entry summary declaration(ENS)or
an exit summary declaration(EXS). ①

The EORI number is used for communication with the EU customs authorities
and serves the following purposes:

• avoiding multiple registration within the EU. As an EORI number is valid
throughout the EU, no additional registration is required when the person initiates a
customs procedure in another member state;

• allowing for automated risk analysis with regard to persons mentioned in
any declaration lodged with customs (e. g. carrier, consignee);

• facilitating the verification of whether the person lodging a customs declara-
tion(or on whose behalf it is lodged)holds any required authorisation or licence in
the case of sensitive goods, such as medicines or agricultural products.

An importer established in the EU has to register in the member state where it
is established(i. e. where it has its registered office, headquarters, or permanent business establishment), while an importer not established in the EU(i. e. which does
not even have a permanent business establishment in the EU)has to request an EO-
RI number in the member state in which it intends to first lodge a customs declaration.

In sum, from a customs perspective, importers wishing to place a product on
the EU market have no other obligation before goods reach EU territory. ②

That being said, they can benefit from trade facilitation measures later on in the
process if they are registered as a so-called authorised economic operator (AEO).

Importers established in the EU that meet specific qualifying criteria may apply

① http://ec. europa. eu/taxation_customs/customs/procedural_aspects/general/eori/index_en. htm.
② By contrast, carriers need to lodge an entry summary declaration("ENS")and notify customs authorities of the arrival of goods.

for and receive AEO certification. ①The aim of bestowing AEO status is to enhance security in the international supply chain through granting recognition to reliable traders. In turn, such traders benefit from administrative simplification. Further, certain trade facilitation measures can be used if the imports take place on a regular basis.

1.3　Lodging an entry summary declaration(ENS)

The carrier② must lodge an ENS electronically before the goods are brought into the EU, according to timelines depending on the transportation mode. ③ An economic operator other than the carrier may lodge an ENS, but only with the knowledge and consent of the carrier under contractual arrangements. ④

The purpose of the ENS is to allow the customs authorities to perform automated risk analysis and to target those consignments that will be controlled for safety and security purposes on arrival (road, rail and internal waterways traffic) or following unloading (sea and air traffic). ⑤ Customs authorities wish to target such consignments at an early stage.

The ENS must be lodged at the customs office of entry, that is, the customs office with jurisdiction over the place where the goods are first brought into the EU (i. e. a port, an airport, a land or river border crossing, or a railway station). ⑥This customs office is responsible for performing risk analysis on the basis of the ENS prior to the arrival of the goods. ⑦

The carrier lodging the ENS is obliged to submit all data required for such declaration⑧ and is responsible for accuracy of the information given in the declara-

---

①　The following are the main qualifying criteria that must be satisfied: establishment in the EU; customs compliance; appropriate record-keeping; financial solvency; and, where relevant, appropriate security and safety standards.

②　The carrier is the person who brings the goods, or who assumes responsibility for the carriage of the goods, into the EU. See Article 181b CCIP.

③　See Article 184a CCIP.

④　See Article 183(6)and(7)CCIP.

⑤　See Articles 184d and 184e CCIP.

⑥　See Articles 4(4a)and 36a(2)CCIP.

⑦　See Article 184d CCIP.

⑧　The data to be provided for a standard ENS is detailed in Table 1 of Annex 30A CCIP. It mainly relates to the goods, the packaging of the goods, the means of transport, etc.

tion, authenticity of the documents presented① and compliance with all the obligations relating to the entry of the goods in question under the procedure concerned. ②

If the means of transport is diverted to a member state other than the member state where the declared customs office of first or subsequent entry is located, the operator of the active means of transport must lodge a "diversion request" with the member state where the declared customs office of first entry is located. In any other case of diversion, no action is needed, as the necessary exchange of data between the involved member states being arranged automatically. The specifications for that diversion process are made available by the member state concerned.

1. 4   After the entry of a product in EU territory

The presentation of goods occurs when the customs office of entry is notified by the carrier③that the goods have arrived and are available for controls. ④Two situations have to be distinguished:

• If the goods arrive by sea or air, this notification concerns only goods that are unloaded at that port or airport. ⑤Goods that are only unloaded temporarily to enable the unloading and loading of other goods are also exempted from such notification;

• For all other modes of transport, the notification must cover all goods on the means of transport.

Such notification must include all goods unloaded or, in cases other than air or sea, on the means of transport, including goods for which no ENS was lodged. From the moment goods have been presented, they are subject to a set of rules known as rules for temporary storage. ⑥

The presentation shall take place upon arrival of the goods into the EU customs territory. Where the legislation waives the requirement for goods to be presented, no

---

① For an ENS, no documents need to be attached.
② See Article 183(1), in conjunction with Article 199(1)CCIP.
③ Presentation can also be done by the carrier's representative or by the person who assumes responsibility for carriage of the goods following entry into EU territory.
④ See Article 4, No. 19 CC.
⑤ See Article 189 CCIP.
⑥ See Article 50 CC.

presentation/temporary storage is needed.

The act of presentation can be made in the following ways:

• If the goods remain on the means of transport(primarily road and rail transport) but the goods enter the customs territory, the act of presentation can consist of immediately lodging a customs declaration with the customs office of entry;

• For sea and air transport, goods remaining on board are declared at the place of unloading or transshipment;

• If the goods are to be unloaded and stored at the customs office of entry (primarily air and maritime transport), the person presenting the goods lodges a summary declaration with the customs office of entry.

1.5 Customs declaration

The importer also has certain additional obligations after the goods have entered EU territory but before they can be released for free circulation. These mainly consist of the filing of a customs declaration.

Once released for free circulation the goods can circulate freely within the European Economic Area (EEA), including the 28 EU member states, ① once the customs duties and other charges have been paid and any rules or import restrictions have been satisfied. ②

All goods imported into the EU must be declared to the customs authorities of the relevant country using the Single Administrative Document (SAD), which is the common import declaration form for all EU countries. The SAD can be presented to the customs authorities by the importer or a representative, either electronically (each EU country has its own system) or by delivery directly to the premises of the customs office. In the near future, SAD will only be processed electronically.

The main purpose of the SAD is to identify data about:

• the parties involved in the transaction (importer, exporter, representative, etc.);

• the goods (tariff code, weight, units), location and packaging;

• the means of transport;

---

① The EEA includes EU member states and certain European Free Trade Association countries(i. e. Iceland, Norway, Liechtenstein).

② See Articles 28 and 29 of the TFEU.

- country of origin, country of export and destination;
- commercial and financial details (incoterms, invoice value, invoice currency, exchange rate, insurance etc.);
- any documents associated to the SAD (import licences, inspection certificates, document of origin, transport document, commercial invoice, etc.);
- declaration and method of payment of import taxes (tariff duties, VAT, excises, etc.).

The SAD set consists of eight copies; the economic operator completes all or part of the sheets depending on the type of operation.

To export to the EU three copies of the SAD are used: the first is to be retained by the authorities of the EU country in which arrival formalities are completed; the second is used for statistical purposes by the country of destination; and the third is returned to the consignee after being stamped by the customs authority.

Overall, the customs declaration for release for free circulation includes the following steps: [1]

1. The customs agent of the importer lodges a customs declaration for release for free circulation at the customs office where the consignment is available for any controls. [2]

2. Through its IT system the customs office formally accepts the customs declaration. This means that it checks whether all required fields are filled in using the prescribed format. There is no material verification of the information provided.

3. Depending on each member state's risk management program, the customs office may then decide: [3]

—to examine documents for those goods (e. g. invoice, airway bill, certificate of origin);

—to physically examine the goods (e. g. to verify that the customs classification of the goods provided corresponds to the goods actually imported);

—to refrain from any examination at this stage.

4. If the goods are subject to import duties and other charges, they must be paid

---

① Electronic declaration via data-processing(i. e. electronic data interchange) is available for any type of customs declaration and is a simplified way of lodging the customs declaration.

② See Article 59 CC; Article 201 CCIP.

③ See Articles 68 – 71 and 73 CC.

or guaranteed. ①

5. If there are no prohibitions or restrictions preventing the release of the goods, the customs office then releases the goods for free circulation, which means that the goods can be placed on the EU market. ②

Importers wishing to place chocolate products on the EU market have no other obligation towards customs authorities before goods can be released for free circulation in the EU.

1. 6　Possible outcomes: Customs destinations

Once goods arrive at the customs office of entry to the EU, they are placed into temporary storage under customs supervision for no longer than 45 days for goods carried by sea, or 20 days in any other case. This temporary regime is meant to give customs authorities some time to gather information to:

- carry out customs supervision; ③ and
- levy import duties and taxes in case the goods disappear. ④

This temporary regime also helps the trader, who has additional time to decide what it wishes to do with the goods, e. g. schedule a pickup or opt for temporary storage in case a volatile market significantly shifts the prices of the goods. The trader can choose one of several possibilities, as listed below:

1. 6. 1　Release for free circulation

Goods are released for consumption once all the import requirements have been met:

- all applicable tariff duties, VAT and excise duties have been paid;
- all applicable authorizations and certificates(e. g. for quotas, health requirements, etc.) have been presented.

In practice, when a product is brought to the EU market, it is possible to declare it for release for free circulation immediately upon its arrival/presentation and thus avoid all the intermediate arrangements mentioned below. ⑤

---

①　See Article 74 CC.

②　See Articles 73 and 79 CC.

③　See Article 37 CC.

④　See Article 203 CC.

⑤　See Article 50 CC.

1. 6. 2   Transit procedure

When goods are moved between customs offices in different EU countries, customs clearance formalities can be transferred to the customs office of destination.

1. 6. 3   Customs warehousing

Imported goods can be stored in specially designated facilities, and duties, taxes and formalities can be suspended until the goods are assigned another approved customs treatment.

1. 6. 4   Inward processing

Goods can be imported into the EU, without being subject to duties, taxes and formalities, to be processed under customs control and then re-exported out of the EU. If the finished products are not finally exported, they become subject to the applicable duties and formalities.

1. 6. 5   Temporary importation

Goods can enter the EU without payment of import duties, provided they are intended for re-export without undergoing any change. The maximum period for temporary import is two years.

1. 6. 6   Entry into a free zone or warehouse

Free zones are special areas within the EU customs territory where goods can enter without payment of customs duties, VAT and excise duties, and without other import formalities until they are either assigned another approved customs treatment or re-exported. Under this procedure, goods may also undergo simple operations such as processing and re-packing.

1. 7   Classification of merchandise and assessment of duties

The classification of merchandise is a necessary element of the importation phase. The product to be imported is classified pursuant to specific rules and criteria, analysed below. The classification is primarily used to determine the duties due upon importation.

The Common Customs Tariff is the external tariff applying to goods being imported to the European Union. The rates of customs duties applying upon the imports of goods from third countries (countries outside the European Union) to the EU's customs territory are specified in the EU's Common Customs Tariff (Combined Nomenclature-Council Regulation No. 2658/87, as amended). The aforesaid Common Customs Tariff is modified every year and it is published on the last day of October of the year preceding its effective date.

The amount of the customs duties charged for each commodity being imported to the European Union is determined upon the customs clearance by the competent customs office of import on the basis of "Tariff Classification" of the commodity in the aforesaid "Common Customs Tariff", that is to say it is about finding the correct tariff subheading to which the commodity is subject and the customs duty rate corresponding to such subheading.

The Harmonised System (HS) is a nomenclature developed by the World Customs Organisation (WCO) comprising about 5,000 commodity groups, organized in a hierarchical structure by sections, chapters(2 digits), headings(4 digits) and subheadings(6 digits). [1]

The Combined Nomenclature of the EU integrates the HS Nomenclature and comprises additional 8-digit subdivisions and legal notes specifically created to address the needs of the Community.

Every product is classified under a tariff code that carries information on:
- duty rates and other levies on import and export;
- any applicable protective measures(e. g. anti-dumping);
- external trade statistics;
- import and export formalities and other non-tariff requirements.

1.8   Valuation for customs purposes

Most customs duties and VAT are expressed as a percentage of the value of the goods being imported. Customs authorities define the value of merchandise for customs purposes based on their commercial value at the point of entry into the EU. This includes commercial price, transport, insurance and other costs. This value does not always correspond to the price stated on the sales contract and may be subject to specific adjustments.

A Customs Value Declaration must be presented to the customs authorities where the value of the imported goods exceeds EUR 10,000. The Customs Value

---

[1]   http://www. wcoomd. org/en/faq/harmonized_system_faq. aspx.

Declaration must be drawn up using a prescribed form. ① This form must be presented with the Single Administrative Document.

The main purpose of this requirement is to assess the value of the transaction in order to determine the customs value(taxable value) and then to apply the tariff duties.

In certain cases the transaction value of the imported goods may be subject to an adjustment, which involves additions or deductions. For instance:

- commissions or royalties may need to be added to the price; and
- the cost of internal transport(from the entry point to the final destination in the Community Customs Territory) must be deducted.

The customs authorities must waive the requirement of all or part of the customs value declaration where:

- the customs value of the imported goods in a consignment does not exceed EUR 10,000, provided that the goods do not enter EU territory as split or multiple consignments from the same consignor to the same consignee; or
- the importations involved are of a non-commercial nature; or
- the submission of the particulars in question is not necessary for the application of the Customs Tariff of the European Communities or where the customs duties provided for in the Tariff are not chargeable pursuant to specific customs provisions.

1.9   Country of origin marking

1.9.1   The EU Generalised Scheme of Preferences and the Rules of Origin

The EU Generalised Scheme of Preference (GSP) defines the Rules of Origin that address the special needs of developing countries. This preferential treatment is non-reciprocal, which means that developing countries do not have the same obligations towards the EU. That said, the GSP schemes offered by the various donor countries and their rules of origin differ fundamentally. Goods complying with the conditions of the GSP of the USA, for example, will not necessarily comply with the

---

① Declaration of particulars relating to customs value, or D. V. 1 form, available at: http://exporthelp. europa. eu/update/requirements/ehir_eu12_02v002/eu/auxi/eu_gen_valuedec_dv1. pdf.

EU GSP. ①

Products originating from specific countries are, in principle, eligible for the GSP rules of origin. This means that such products will be subject to a preferential duty compared to the default duty payable under *erga omnes* obligations.

To qualify for preferential duty rates, products originating in the beneficiary countries of the EU's GSP must be accompanied by proof of origin. This can be either:

• a certificate of origin form A②issued by the competent authority in the beneficiary country. The exporter applying for the certificate should be prepared to submit documents proving the originating status of the products concerned. The certificate should be made available to the exporter as soon as the export has taken place (or is ensured). Nevertheless, exceptionally, a certificate can be made after exportation, under some conditions; or

• an invoice declaration drafted by the exporter③ for consignments valued at EUR 6,000 or less. When filling out an invoice declaration, the exporter should be prepared to submit documents proving the originating status of the products.

The exporter must sign the invoice declaration by hand. Any proof of origin remain valid for 10 months after issue.

These Rules follow the applicable provisions included in Articles 97k to 97v and in Annexes 17 and 18 of Regulation(EEC) 2454/93 implementing the Community Customs Code.

Rules applicable for certification of origin took effect after the 1 January 2017. As of this date, the proof of origin will be brought in the form of a statement on origin issued by exporters, who will be registered in the country of exportation. ④

1.10   Customs and security

The 2005 amendments are aimed at tightening security requirements for movement of goods across international frontiers. Economic operators are now required to

---

① http://eeas. europa. eu/delegations/myanmar/documents/page_content/gsp_guidance_en. pdf.
② Certificate of origin form A, available at:
http://trade. ec. europa. eu/doclib/docs/2009/june/tradoc_143726. pdf.
③ Invoice declaration, available at:
http://trade. ec. europa. eu/doclib/docs/2009/june/tradoc_143730. pdf.
④ See Cf. Articles 90 to 97i of Regulation(EEC) 2454/93 implementing the Community Customs Code.

provide the customs authorities with details of goods before they are imported into or exported from the EU. This will entail the setting up of a one-stop shop for importers and exporters. ①

The new concept of AEO simplifies trade. A member state may grant AEO status to any economic operator meeting common criteria. These criteria concern control systems, financial solvency and the operator's track record in complying with the rules.

Member states are required to use risk-analysis methods. Uniform Community criteria have been introduced for identifying risks for control purposes.

In November 2005 the Commission adopted a proposal, as part of the implementation of the Lisbon Strategy, aimed at modernising the Community Customs Code. This proposal is aimed at simplifying the legislation and administrative procedures governing imports and exports. Facilitating customs operations in this way reduces costs. In addition, the Commission proposed:

- streamlining structures and making terminology more consistent;
- streamlining the system of customs guarantees;
- extending the use of single authorisations (whereby an authorisation issued by one member state on completion of a procedure would be valid throughout the Community).

1. 10. 1   Key terms used in the act

- Binding origin information (BOI) and binding tariff information (BTI): They are written notices issued by the customs authorities. BOI notices concern the preferential or non-preferential origin of goods and are issued to a specific importer or exporter. BTI notices concern the classification of goods in the Combined Nomenclature or a secondary nomenclature such as TARIC.

- Customs value: the value of goods used to calculate the amount of customs duties.

- Customs declaration: an act whereby a person expresses the wish to place goods under a customs procedure.

- Customs warehousing: the customs procedure permitting the storage of goods.

---

① http://eur-lex. europa. eu/legal-content/HU/TXT/? uri = uriserv: 111010.

- Processing: inward processing permits the import of goods for working and subsequent re-export. Outward processing permits Community goods to be exported for working and then subsequently re-imported with total or partial relief from duties.

- Processing under customs control: processing under customs control permits import duties to be suspended on goods imported for working and these goods to be released for free circulation at a lower rate of duty.

- Free zone and free warehouse: free zones and free warehouses are part of the Community customs territory, but import duties on non-Community goods are suspended there. Community products are eligible for measures conditional, in principle, on their being exported.

Chapter 2   Foreign Trade System and Law

2. 1   Anti-dumping

Greece, as an EU member, follows the European legislation in the matter. The Greek antidumping committee works in close collaboration with the European authorities. The applicable law in the matter closely follows WTO legislation, in specific the Agreement on Implementation of Article VI of the General Agreement on Tariffs and Trade 1994 (the Anti-dumping Agreement).

A company is said to dump goods in the EU region, hence in Greece, if it exports a product to the EU at prices lower than the normal value of the product (the domestic price of the product or its cost of production) on its own domestic market. The European Commission is responsible for investigating allegations of dumping by exporting producers in non-EU countries. An investigation is set in motion when the Commission receives a complaint from the Community producers of the product concerned. It may also commence an investigation of its own motion. ①

The Commission publishes a note in the EU's Official Journal when it launches opening an anti-dumping investigation. An investigation must be completed in 15 months and the detailed findings are published in the Official Journal, for example, as a regulation imposing anti-dumping duties or terminating the proceeding without duties being imposed.

During an investigation, the EU must establish that

● there is dumping by the exporting producers in the country/countries concerned;

● material injury has been suffered by the Community industry concerned;

● there is a causal link between the dumping and such material injury;

● the imposition of measures is not against the Community interest.

---

① http://ec. europa. eu/trade/policy/accessing-markets/trade-defence/actions-against-imports-into-the-eu/anti-dumping/.

Where these conditions are met, the Commission may impose anti-dumping measures on imports of the relevant product. Usually, these measures take the form of an *ad valorem* duty, but they could also be specific duties, which must be paid by the importer in the EU and collected by the national customs authorities. Alternatively, exporting producers may offer "price undertakings". Such offers may take the form of offering to sell at a minimum price. If the offer is accepted, then anti-dumping duties are not collected on imports. However, the Commission is not obliged to accept such an offer of an undertaking.

The reasoning behind imposing a duty is to cure the effects of dumping on imports of a particular product. An assessment is also made regarding the level of duty needed to remove the injurious effects of dumping. Measures are imposed at the level of dumping or injury, whichever is lower.

In principle, measures are imposed for five years and may be subject to review. For instance, the circumstances of the exporters may have changed, or new exporting producers may request an accelerated review, if they feel this will help their case. Measures automatically lapse after five years, unless there is an expiry review. ①

Importers may also request a full or partial refund of duties paid, if they feel they have been harmed disproportionately. In particular, importers of products subject to anti-dumping duties can ask for a refund of duties paid when they can demonstrate that the dumping margin, on the basis of which the duties were paid, has been eliminated or reduced to a level which is below the level of the duty in force. For Greece, the importers must address their request to the domestic authorities if they paid the duties in the country. The authorities will then transmit the requests to the European Commission for further investigation.

2. 2   Anti-subsidy rules

The Greek anti-subsidy rules follow the relevant EU regulation (Council Regulation(EC) No. 597/2009), which defines a subsidy as "a financial contribution made by(or on behalf of)a government or a public body which confers a benefit to the recipient".

The EU's anti-subsidy rules are based on a 1994 WTO agreement which allows

---

① http://ec. europa. eu/trade/policy/accessing-markets/trade-defence/actions-against-imports-into-the-eu/anti-dumping/.

remedial action to be taken against subsidies that are considered an unfair trade practice. The rules contain:①

- the definition of a subsidy;
- criteria for determining whether imports of subsidised products are causing injury to the EU industry;
  - procedures for initiating and conducting investigations;
  - rules on the implementation and duration of countervailing measures.

The EU may impose a countervailing duty to offset the benefit of such a subsidy if it is limited to a specific firm, industry or group of firms or industries. Export subsidies and subsidies contingent on the use of domestic over imported goods are deemed to be specific.

Subsidies as a whole can be used to achieve different purposes. For instance, to pursue domestic and social policies, to foster production or exports, to create jobs, to facilitate the creation and expansion of new industries or to support economic activities that might otherwise fail. Yet, they may distort competition by making subsidized goods artificially competitive against non-subsidised goods. This negatively affects competitors since the products become unreasonably cheaper.

For instance, if a non-EU country subsidizes its domestic producers of a certain product, these producers can reduce their export prices to the EU market, artificially increase capacity or improve the quality of their product by investing more on research.

When an EU industry considers that imports of a product from a non-EU country are subsidized and injure the EU industry that produces a like product, they can lodge a complaint with the EU Commission. If the complaint discloses *prima facie* evidence of subsidy and injury, the Commission must open an anti-subsidy investigation. The main questions that the investigation must address are:

- Do the imports benefit from a countervailable subsidy?
- Is any injury suffered by the EU industry?
- Is there a causal link between the injury and the subsidised imports?
- Is the imposition of measures not against the Community interest?

If the investigation establishes subsidy and injury, the Commission may, within

---

① http://ec. europa. eu/trade/policy/accessing-markets/trade-defence/actions-against-imports-into-the-eu/anti-subsidy/.

nine months of launching the investigation, impose provisional countervailing measures, i. e. a temporary security or bond on the imports concerned.

The investigation will substantiate whether definitive measures are warranted. If so, the Commission must impose them within 13 months. Such measures may be effective for a period of five years. See below for further on the effective period. ①

The three basic forms of countervailing duties are:

• *ad valorem* duty: a percentage of the net, free-at-EU frontier (CIF) price. This is the most common duty;

• specific duty: a fixed value for a certain amount of goods, e. g. EUR 1,000 per tone of a product;

• variable duty connected to a minimum import price (MIP): importers in the EU do not pay a countervailing duty if the foreign exporter's export price to the EU is higher than the MIP.

Upon successful application, the authorities could also recognise a company-specific price undertaking. This is a commitment by an exporter to respect minimum import prices. This is not meant to fix prices at specific levels, rather to prevent them from falling below a certain floor price.

Price undertakings are governed by Article 13 of the basic anti-subsidy regulation (which draws on Article 18 of the WTO Agreement on Subsidies and Countervailing Measures). Further, special rules for developing countries are contained in Article 27 of the WTO Agreement on subsidies and countervailing measures.

In terms of monitoring the measures in force, anti-subsidy duties are collected by customs authorities of EU countries. The Commission monitors import volumes and prices of all products subject to measures, to identify and to react to circumvention and other irregularities. In doing so, it collaborates with various bodies, like the customs authorities of EU countries, the Commission tax and customs department, and the European fraud prevention agency (OLAF).

In principle, measures are imposed for five years. However, any interested party (EU countries, importers, exporters, the authorities of the exporting country) may request an interim review if they have *prima facie* evidence that the measures are no longer needed or that they are no longer sufficient to counteract subsidised injurious

---

① http://ec. europa. eu/trade/policy/accessing-markets/trade-defence/actions-against-imports-into-the-eu/anti-subsidy/.

imports.

In the final year of application of the measures, the Community producers may ask the Commission to conduct an expiry review to determine whether the expiry of the measures would be likely to lead to a continuation or recurrence of subsidisation and injury. In such a case, the measures may continue for another five years.

Importers can also request a refund of the duties paid when they think that the a-mount of subsidy has been reduced or eliminated.

2. 3   Market access

International trade is hampered by barriers existing in domestic regulations which inhibit investments. To overcome this hurdle, various tools such as the Services Trade Restrictiveness Index (STRI) provides adequate information and tools that can be used to compare policies among different countries. This information is valuable, *inter alia*, to policy analysts and makers, governmental officials, traders, practitioners and the general public. [1] The STRI provides objective data with regard to trade re-strictiveness and identification of best practices. The index therefore creates a bench-mark for governments and can be used as a tool by trade negotiators to identify bot-tlenecks and warn businesses about the pitfalls that exist when they wish to enter for-eign markets.

The STRI is impartial and thus makes no recommendations to countries, but rather presents the data that can be used should a country wants guidance in prioritiz-ing domestic reform efforts. The STRI does not prescribe solutions, its primary aim being to help governments identify their desired fields of improvement, and suggest paths for this to materialise. One could say that it is a self-detection tool, and every step following the diagnosis rests with the government.

Accessing markets outside the EU is crucial for jobs and growth within the EU. The EU works to keep markets open and to keep trade flowing through a variety of specific trade policies. This is important to the EU since:

 • An open and fair international trading system is one of the foundations of Europe's competitiveness.

 • Market barriers in EU exports in other countries accounts for the bulk of re-

---

[1]   OECD, 2014. Services Trade Restrictiveness Index Regulatory Database, available at: http://qdd. oecd. org/subject. aspx? Subject = 063bee63 − 475f − 427c − 8b50 − c19bffa7392d.

strictiveness. Its leading trading partners are less open than the EU, sometimes significantly so.

- The EU stands to gain from the further opening of markets worldwide.
- Europe's market must be open to supplies of intermediary goods and raw materials for European producers of value-added products. Restricting this flow of goods raises costs for European companies, making them less competitive; the EU needs to import to export.
- The EU has consistently removed these barriers to its own economy and now has one of the most open markets in the world.

Greece does not have a particular policy on market access, but rather follows the relevant EU policy. Since the EU has 15 percent share of world trade for goods and 22.7 percent share of world trade for services, it is a powerhouse that aspires to open markets even more.

The EU wishes to improve the terms of trade around the world through various sectoral policies. In fact, the EU aims to reduce the barriers to the flow of goods and services in the EU's export markets. This strategy targets and removes individual barriers in key export markets. Towards this direction, the EU negotiates the removal of tariff barriers and non-tariff barriers such as technical barriers to trade and sanitary and phytosanitary measures with key partners.

The EU further wants to access government procurement markets around the world on fair terms, and aims to ensure the right balance on intellectual property protection for the EU's innovative output. The EU is developing its rules on investment, which is central to the ability of EU companies to operate effectively in other markets. It defends the functioning of the EU market against unfair distortions, such as dumping or subsidies. When international trade rules are breached the EU takes action through bilateral dispute settlement provisions, WTO-specific dispute settlement procedures or through specific investment dispute provisions.

In terms of steps forward, the EU annually publishes a trade and investment barriers report, which describes the progress achieved in dismantling barriers to the markets of the EU's six strategic economic partners, namely China, India, Japan, Mercosur, Russia and the US. The EU overall perceives that trade barriers greatly resist European businesses that wish to access the markets of these strategic partners.

2.4   The rise of regional trade agreements

A regional trade agreement(RTA)enables its treaty parties to emulate a success-ful path toward trade liberalization and foreign investment. In light of the inertia of the ongoing Doha Round, RTA negotiations are looking better than stalled interna-tional rounds. RTAs can be concluded quickly; they offer significant financial bene-fits; and they are strategic. ①

A free trade agreement(FTA)is an international treaty that removes barriers to trade and facilitates commercial and investment ties. It promotes economic conver-gence between countries and can have a wide reach depending on the participating states. Recently concluded FTAs have five pillars:

(i) elimination of tariff and trade barriers for goods;

(ii) opening up of trade in services;

(iii) legal reform that facilitates greater ties;

(iv) extensive incentives for investment;

(v) establishment of Investor State Dispute Settlement (ISDS) mechanisms to safeguard the effectiveness and implementation of the FTA.

Implementing these principles works. A statistical analysis of several FTAs con-cluded in recent decades found that an FTA between two countries will, on average, increase those countries' trade about 86 percent after 15 years of implementation. ②

Regional trade agreements(RTAs)have been gaining special momentum as more and more nations aspire to conclude them. As of 15 June 2014, 585 notifications of RTAs (counting goods, services and accessions separately) were received by the GATT/WTO, out of which 379 were in force. Several of them are currently under ne-gotiation. For instance, the EU is currently actively pursuing the Transatlantic Trade Investment Partnership(TTIP) with the US, the Comprehensive Economic and Trade Agreement(CETA) with Canada, and the Trade in Services Agreement(TiSA) with 23 WTO members that together account for 70 percent of world trade in services.

---

① https://www. wto. org/english/forums_e/public_forum12_e/art_pf12_e/art19. htm.

② S L Baier and J H Bergstrand, "Do free trade agreements actually increase members' international trade?" (2007) 71 *Journal of International Economics*, pp. 72 – 95.

2. 5   Technical barriers to trade

Technical requirements exist in all sectors of the economy and have an impact on most products. The labelling of the food, the safety of toys, the technical specification of the cars, and the energy efficiency of home appliances, are some examples of standards that need to be met.

Hence, "technical barriers to trade" (TBT) refers to mandatory technical regulations and voluntary standards that define specific characteristics that a product should have, such as its size, shape, design, labelling/marking/packaging, functionality or performance. These procedures are used to test whether a product complies with specific requirements, as provided in the TBT. These "conformity assessment procedures" can include, product testing, inspection and relevant certification activities.

Government authorities introduce TBTs with a legitimate public policy objective. They, for instance, wish to protect human health and safety, animal and plant life and health or the environment, or to safeguard consumers from deceptive practices. TBTs often have an impact on trade and the competitiveness of exporters, particularly small and medium enterprises (SMEs). Adjusting products and production processes to comply with different requirements in export markets increase product costs and time-to-market, and can hurt the competitiveness of EU exporters.

The WTO/TBT Agreement is a preventive instrument that ensures that TBT measures do not result in discrimination or arbitrary restrictions on international trade. The Agreement does not undermine the right of governments to take measures to pursue legitimate public policy objectives. It simply aims to ensure that such measures are prepared, adopted and applied according to basic principles, in order to minimize the negative impact this has on trade. ①

The significance of technical barriers to trade has increased considerably over the years, as tariffs steadily decline and governments worldwide introduce more and more regulatory requirements to address health, safety or environmental concerns. The TBT Agreement is an important tool with which the EU can tackle technical barriers to trade and address requirements of third countries that might pose significant problems to European economic operators.

_____

① http://trade. ec. europa. eu/doclib/docs/2013/april/tradoc_150987. pdf.

In the WTO, the EU has pushed for greater harmonisation through widespread use of international standards. The EU has also tried to adopt a more risk-oriented approach in deciding what conformity assessment procedures should be used for assessing compliance of products. To do so, it must improve the implementation of transparency provisions, ensure that trade partners are systematically consulted on regulatory initiatives that might influence trade and promote the effectiveness of technical assistance to developing countries in the TBT field.

A central EU objective in the TBT is to facilitate exports by EU manufacturers by reducing technical barriers which unnecessarily restrict trade in global markets.

The main principles of the TBT Agreement, that Greece is following under the EU umbrella, that subsequently enforces the WTO principles, are:

• *Transparency*: a WTO member that plans to introduce a measure that can potentially have an important impact on trade should notify the WTO about this, and take into account comments submitted by other countries on the draft legislation;

• *Non-discrimination and national treatment*: a measure must not discriminate among different importing members and should apply in the same way to both imports and similar domestic goods;

• *Proportionality*: a measure should not be more trade restrictive than necessary to achieve the legitimate goal pursued;

• *Use of international standards*: in every possible situation, international standards should be the basis for technical regulations;

• *Equivalence*: WTO members should consider accepting technical regulations of other members as equivalent to their own, provided that these measures are an effective way of addressing the objectives pursued.

2.6 Sanitary and phytosanitary (SPS) measures

Sanitary and phytosanitary (SPS) measures are often necessary to protect human, animal and plant life or health, especially to protect them from risks arising from imported goods. Such measures should be based on the WTO/SPS Agreement, international standards, recommendations or guidelines or be based on scientific principles. However, third countries often impose unjustified SPS measures in a way that the SPS measure negatively affects the EU exports of agriculture and fishery products.

This section outlines relevant food laws applicable to the importation of products into the European Union. The EU implemented a comprehensive legislative framework covering all stages of the production, processing, distribution and placing on the market of food intended for human consumption, which is subject to the supervision of EU and member state authorities. Generally, food products imported into the EU have to comply with general food safety requirements; be produced under hygienic conditions; meet certain composition criteria; be below specific residue limits; and be appropriately labelled and appropriately packaged. ①

First, with respect to food safety, the most relevant laws are:
- Regulation(EC) No. 178/2002(the "General Food Law Regulation"); ②
- Regulation(EC) No. 852/2004(the "General Food Hygiene Regulation"); ③
- Regulation(EC) No. 396/2005(the "Maximum Residue Regulation"); ④and
- Regulation (EC) No. 2703/2005 (the "Microbiological Criteria Regulation"). ⑤

In general, EU law draws a distinction between food of animal origin(carrying a higher risk for public health, and therefore being subject to strict regulations)and food of non-animal origin(for which the regulatory landscape is less strict). In practice, the distinction is not clear. In fact, there are products, which contain components that belong to both categories. These products are categorized as "composite products", which have to comply with legislation regulating food of animal origin and legislation regulating food of non-animal origin.

Second, EU labelling requirements are subject to the following rules and regulations:
- General Food Law Regulation;
- Regulation(EU) No. 1169/2011(the "Food Information Regulation");
- Regulation(EC) No. 1924/2006(the "Nutritional and Health Claims Regula-

① https://www. wto. org/english/tratop_e/sps_e/spsund_e. htm.

② Regulation(EC) No. 178/2002 laying down the general principles and requirements of food law, establishing the European Food Safety Authority and laying down procedures in matters of food safety(the "General Food Law Regulation"), OJ L 31,1. 2. 2002, pp. 1 –24, as amended.

③ Regulation(EC) No. 852/2004 on the hygiene of foodstuffs, OJ L 139,30. 4. 2004, pp. 1 –54, as amended.

④ Regulation(EC) No. 396/2005 on maximum residue levels of pesticides in or on food and feed of plant and animal origin and amending Council Directive 91/414/EEC, OJ L 070 16. 3. 2005, p. 1, as amended.

⑤ Regulation (EC) No. 2703/2005 on microbiological criteria for foodstuffs, OJ L 338 22. 12. 2005, p. 1, as amended.

tion");[1]and

* Regulation(EU) No.432/2012(the "Permitted Health Claims Regulation").

Finally,EU packaging requirements are governed by the following laws:

* General Food Law Regulation;
* Directive 94/62/EC(the "Packaging Directive");
* Regulation(EC) No.1935/2004(the "Framework FCM Regulation");[2]
* Regulation(EU) No.10/2011(the "Plastics FCM Regulation");[3]
* Regulation (EC) No. 282/2008 (the "Recycled Plastics FCM Regulation").[4]

At EU level,the European Food Safety Authority (EFSA), established by the General Food Law Regulation,is the central agency conducting risk assessments regarding food and feed safety. In close collaboration with national authorities,EFSA provides independent scientific advice and communication on existing and emerging risks.

However,the national competent authorities carry out the majority of the control activities to ensure compliance with food safety regulations.[5] Food business operators are required to collaborate with the national competent authorities on action taken to avoid or reduce risks posed by a food which they supply or have supplied.[6]Domestic authorities in Greece therefore ensure that these requirements are met.

---

[1] Regulation(EC) No.1924/2006 on nutrition and health claims made on foods,*OJ L* 404,30.12.2006, pp.9 - 25,as amended,Regulation(EU) No.432/2012 establishing a list of permitted health claims made on foods,other than those referring to the reduction of disease risk and to children's development and health,*OJ L* 136,25.5.2012,as amended,pp.1 - 40,as amended.

[2] Regulation(EC) No.1935/2004 on materials and articles intended to come into contact with food and repealing, Directives 80/590/EEC and 89/109/EEC (the "Framework FCM Regulation"), *OJ L* 338, 13.11.2004,pp.4 - 17,as amended.

[3] Regulation(EU) No.10/2011 on plastic materials and articles intended to come into contact with food (the "Plastic FCM Regulation"),*OJ L* 12,15.1.2011,pp.1 - 89,as amended.

[4] Regulation(EC) 282/2008 on recycled plastic materials and articles intended to come into contact with foods and amending Regulation (EC) No. 2023/2006 (the "Recycled Plastic FCM Regulation"), *OJ L* 86, 28.3.2008,pp.9 - 18,as amended.

[5] See Sections(11)to(16) of the Preamble to Regulation(EC) No.882/2004 on official controls performed to ensure the verification of compliance with feed and food law,animal health and animal welfare rules,*OJ L* 165,30.4.2004,p.1,as amended.

[6] See Article 19(4)of the General Food Law Regulation.

2.6.1　Regulation in Greece

In Greece, several ministries are in charge of food issues, mainly the Ministry of Rural Development & Food, the Ministry of Health & Social Solidarity and the Ministry of Development, Competitiveness & Shipping. However, food safety and consumer protection is the primary responsibility of Food Control Authority (ΕΦΕΤ), which is supervised by the Ministry of Health & Social Solidarity, is the contact point for the European food authorities and the Codex Alimentarius Commission.

Another important authority is the General State Chemical Laboratory (ΓΧΚ), established in 1929 within the Ministry of Finance, with a wide spectrum of activities, such as conducting samplings and laboratory tests on various food including alcohol drinks, granting approvals for new, functional food products and offering technical-scientific support to other authorities. Moreover, the Supreme Chemical Council (ΑΧΣ), an organ of General State Chemical Laboratory, carries out significant legislative work on issues of food composition and food distribution. [1] Worth mentioning is the National Organisation for Medicines (ΕΟΦ), which has exclusive competence in respect of food supplements and dietetic foods.

In Greece, the regulatory framework for food & beverage is based on EU regulations and directives that are implemented through national by-laws, namely ministerial decisions and presidential decrees. Country specific regulations apply in situations where the EU law may be incomplete or absent or allow the member states to make exceptions.

The basic national regulatory law is the Code of Foodstuffs, Beverages and Objects of Common Use (ΚΤΠ, hereafter referred to as the "Food Code"), which was introduced in 1971 and codified by the Ministerial Decision 1100/1987, subject to numerous amendments due to developments in EU and international law, containing general-horizontal und product specific-vertical provisions. Other significant laws are the Market Law Regulation 7/2009, the Ministerial Decision 15523/2006, which is the main act implementing the EU hygiene package, and the Sanitary Regulation Α1β/ 8577/1983.

At national regulatory level, general and specific requirements on food hygiene are stipulated in the Sanitary Regulation Α1β/8577/1983. This law applies to compa-

---

① http://www. greeklawdigest. gr/component/k2/item/108-food-beverage.

nies acting in the sector of retail and wholesale trade of food (supermarkets, cash & carry shops, wholesale centres, bakeries, fast food shops, restaurants, entertainment shops, etc.). It will be soon replaced by a new sanitary regulation that fully complies with the respective EU hygiene standards.

National guides to good practice drawn up for every single food business sector and officially approved by the competent authority (EΦET or the Ministry of Rural Development & Food) in order to comply with the hygiene requirements deserve consideration. This refers especially to food hygiene aspects that are not explicitly or specifically regulated.

In Greece, food labelling regulations are, to a great part, harmonised with EU law. The provisions in Arts. 11 and 11a of Food Code regarding the general labelling requirements comply with the prescriptions of Directive 2000/13/EC, Directive 90/496/EEC, and other related EU Directives. The use of Greek language is obligatory; multi-language labelling is permitted.

Chapter 3   Foreign Direct Investment System and Law

In recent years, some progress has been made towards adopting laws aimed at fostering growth, reducing bureaucratic hurdles and attracting foreign investment. Greece continues to present a challenging climate for investment, both foreign and domestic, even though investment conditions have improved over the years. A number of recent reforms aimed to simplify the investment framework, and the government actively seeks to attract foreign investment to drive the country's long-term economic recovery.

In October 2012, the "Creation of a Business Friendly Environment for Strategic and Private Investments" bill was passed. The bill aimed to attract investors by offering an accelerated and transparent licensing process. Additionally, the bill allowed for "Invest in Greece" to operate as the sole point of contact for investors. Invest in Greece falls under the Ministry of Development and serves as the country's official investment promotion agency, acting as a source of information for investors, reviewing business proposals, and interfacing with other agencies of the Greek government on behalf of investors.

Screening of FDI Law 4146, passed in April 2013 and implemented in early 2014, established the General Directorate of Strategic Investments under the Ministry of Economy, Infrastructure, Maritime, and Tourism as a one-stop shop for investors. Its goal is to be the competent authority for accelerating licence procedures for strategic investments. The Directorate also oversees Enterprise Greece, which evaluates business plan applications from investors and makes recommendations to an Inter-Ministerial Committee on Strategic Investments(ICSI). Currently, Enterprise Greece has 10 affiliated fast track projects, whereas another five are in the pipeline, including in renewable energy, tourism and mining.

3.1   The one-stop shop law

Law 3853/2010 provides for a "one-stop shop" approach to establishing new businesses. The one-stop shop is operated by Enterprise Greece. Key to the new programme is that the time needed to start a business is reduced from 19 days to one day, costs are reduced by 50 – 62 percent, and the government hopes Greece's ranking on the World Bank's "Starting a Business" list will improve dramatically. In addition, the Prime Minister said the move would improve transparency, reduce bureaucracy, and unleash the pent up potential to create new businesses in Greece, to the benefit of the national economy and employment (see Tables 1 and 2).

The programme aspires to make Greece more attractive to investment, and have enterprises operate more responsibly, with chambers playing a much larger role in facilitating entrepreneurship.

Table 1. Benefits of "One-Stop Shop" Law

	BEFORE	NOW	BENEFIT
Steps required to set up a business	11 steps	1 step	With one visit to a chamber, public notary or Citizen Information Centers (KEP). The procedures required now are drastically reduced
Days required to set up a business	From 5 to 38, average 19 days	1 day	Given there are no pending issues with public services and all necessary documentation is ready
Cost required to set up a business	Depending on the legal entity, the relevant chamber and the capital required	Fees for name preapproval and publication in Government Gazette are abolished and administrative costs drastically cut	Example: for a LTD company the cost is reduced by 61.7 percent
General Commercial Records	Legislated in 2005 without being implemented before 2011	Operational	Operation for the first time of unified records for all Greek businesses
Information systems and one-stop service	Systems and records without interoperability	Achievement of interoperability between 5 Ministries and 60 record archives	For the first time the TAX-IS services of taxation offices, information systems of insurance funds(IKA, OAEE)Chambers, Government Gazette achieve interface ①

---

① Table available at: http://www. enterprisegreece. gov. gr/en/about-us-/media-center/newsletter-view? nwsllD = 17&sec = 2.

Table 2. Cost Savings for New Companies

Cost Estimate (EUR)	O. E (Partnership)		E. E (Partnership)		E. P. E (LTD)		S. A	
	Before	Now	Before	Now	Before	Now	Before	Now
Administrative costs	1099	385	1099	385	1752	568	2362	968
Fees, Taxes & other charges	246	231	246	231	624. 8	341. 8	1490	951
Total	1345	616	1345	616	2376. 8	909. 8	3852	1919
Reduction	54. 2%		54. 2%		61. 7%		50. 2%	

3. 2   The fast track law

Law 3894/2010 (known as "fast track" law) allows Invest in Greece to expedite licensing procedures for qualifying investments in the following sectors: industry, energy, tourism, transportation, telecommunications, health services, waste management or high-end technology/innovation. The law has been amended with Law 4072/2012, Law 4146/2013, Law 4242/2014 and Law 4262/2014. To qualify, investments must meet one of the following conditions:

• The investment's total cost exceeds the amount of EUR 100,000,000; or

• The investment's total cost exceeds the amount of EUR 15,000,000 for investments in the field of manufacturing within already organised receptors, and the amount of EUR 3,000,000 for investments in approved projects within the framework of the JESSICA (Joint European Support for Sustainable Investment in City Areas) portfolio fund; or

• The investment's total cost exceeds the amount of EUR 40,000,000 and at the same time the investment creates at least 120 new employment contracts; or

• The investment creates, in a viable and sustainable manner, at least 150 new jobs or at least 600 jobs are maintained in a viable and sustainable manner; or

• The investment's total cost exceeds EUR 5,000,000 for investments regarding the development of Business Parks provided for in the 2nd part of Law 3982/2011.

A qualifying fast track investor must submit a business plan along with a non-refundable evaluation management fee to Invest in Greece. Invest in Greece has 15 days to evaluate the plan and submit its recommendation to an Inter-Ministerial Committee of Strategic Investments(ICSI). ① If the ICSI approves the business plan, the investor pays Invest in Greece the Forwarding Management Fee(0. 2 percent of the investment amount) and submits a Guarantee Letter of Participation as well as all supporting doc-umentation to complete the licensing process. As of 2013, Invest in Greece has 11 fast track projects in the pipeline ranging from renewable energy and tourism to gold min-ing. ②

Fast Track works as an accelerating and transparency enhancement mechanism for the procedures③ relating to the implementation of strategic investments in Greece, whether these consist of private-private ventures (a private investment on a private asset, such as a hotel or tourist development, an industry, etc.) or public-private part-nerships (a private investment in a state asset/property such as the development of the old airport of Athens site, the development of Greek state-owned tourism real es-tate, development of an airport, etc.). Fast Track accelerates the licensing procedure by (a) creating a legally-binding timeframe for the issuance of licences with significantly reduced deadlines, (b) immediately activating the investment process, and (c) enhan-cing the speed and efficiency of public bodies' relevant actions.

The law considers as a strategic investment any investment that has quantitative characteristics (e. g. large budget) and/or qualitative characteristics (e. g. promotes innovation). These investments are expected to deliver high-impact, positive results to the Greek economy and create added value for the country as a whole and its citi-zens. Fast track applies to major investments with significant multiplier effects on Greece's GDP. It is designed to attract investments that utilise and capitalise on the geopolitical strategic advantage of Greece, both as a domestic investment destination and within the broad context of the global investment map.

The implementation of a strategic investment under Fast Track provisions is voluntary, since a private investment is included in this procedure only if (a) the prospective investor desires this inclusion, (b) the investment fulfils the law's re-quirements and (c) the investment is approved by the Interministerial Committee for Strategic Investments. If the ICSI does not approve the investment as a Fast Track qualifying venture or if the investor never applied to Invest in Greece, the in-

---

① *Greece Tax Guide, Volume* 1, *Strategic, Practical Information and Regulations.* International Business Publications, USA, 2002.

② More information on the 2010 fast track law can be found at http://www. investingreece. gov. gr.

③ http://www. greeklawdigest. gr/topics/banking-system-finance-investmentitem42-fast-track-law.

vestor can still forward his plan within the existing procedures(non-Fast Track)defined for the type of investment envisioned.

The ultimate objective is for all investments in Greece to be implemented in a swift and transparent way and to benefit Greece's economy and society. ① Greece, first and foremost, aims at capitalising on its strategic advantages so that investment becomes the main driver of economic growth and development. Fast Track, in practice, will lead to beneficial and advantageous results, consolidating the investment procedure in Greece. The Fast Track procedure will initially operate as a pilot application, resulting in the simplification and the acceleration of licensing procedures and, ultimately, to be implemented in the entire gamut of business activities in Greece.

The main objective of the Fast Track Law is to promote investments that create added value for the country and preserve the existing national wealth, of which the environment is a vital part. The Law makes clear the need to accelerate the implementation of Strategic Investments in full accordance with the need to protect the environment. The task of the Law is not the abolishment of the existing environmental legislation, but to create a regime of fast processes. Wherever a specific processing time line is provided, the deadline is shortened. This acceleration has also been deemed as essential in the past and has been accordingly applied, in cases of major national priority.

The Fast Track framework does not interfere or overlap with any other existing framework or agency. It has been designed to minimise delays and overlapping risks. Fast Track is not a "financial incentive provision mechanism". Fast Track does not give money, capital grants, subsidies, etc. Fast Track gives speed, transparency and legal contractual certainty to investors who have a solid, sound and tangible investment and who until today have fallen prey to bureaucracy or corruption.

3. 3   The Investment Incentives Law

Law 3908/2011 is the primary investment incentive law currently in force. Incentives are provided in the form of cash grants, lease payment subsidies and tax exemptions. The aim of the law is to harness private investment to promote economic development in Greece by encouraging investments that improve business operations,

---

①   http://startupgreece. gov. gr/sites/default/files/FAQs_en. pdf.

technological development, competitiveness and regional cohesion. The incentives apply to investments in all economic sectors, with some exemptions, and the type of incentive depends on the sector in which the investment project falls. ①

The law builds on previous investment incentives by extending tax breaks to small and medium investment projects (foreign and Greek) for up to six years for investments in existing companies and eight years for start-up companies. Investors seeking capital grants must submit a business plan to the Ministry of Development, which ranks the plan based on several criteria, including the viability of the planned investment. The limited capital grants are awarded to the highest ranked projects. Preference is given to projects in renewable energy, tourism, innovative technologies and "green" projects.

The Investment Incentives Law (IIL) contains a defined annual budget and an aid ceiling. It addresses all sectors of the economy, except those expressly articulated in Article 2 of the Law. It is mindful of scarce public funds by providing incentives through tax exemptions, subsidies, leasing and soft loans. In fact, for every one euro of subsidy provided, three euro of tax exemptions are provided. The law provides for both the electronic submission of every investment plan and the submission in hard copy to the Investor Service Offices.

The law contains specified and fixed application deadlines (April and October) except for Major Investment Plans (more than EUR 50 million), which are submitted throughout the year. It introduces a new evaluation process by establishing the National Register of Evaluators and Auditors. It focuses on sustainable investment projects that are environmentally friendly, promote innovation, regional cohesion, youth entrepreneurship and create jobs. Finally, it provides for aid rates from 15 percent to 55 percent dependent on the region that the investment is realised and the size of the company. ②

3.3.1   Which investment categories fall within the scope of the IIL?

Investment plans are divided into the following categories:

(a) General Entrepreneurship

Target Group: all enterprises irrespective of sector.

---

① http://www.state.gov/e/eb/rls/othr/ics/2013/204649.htm.

② http://www.greeklawdigest.gr/topics/banking-system-finance-investment/item/41-investment- incentives-law.

Provides: tax breaks of up to 100 percent of the maximum allowable amount of aid.

(b) Technological Development

Target Group: enterprises that invest in technological and operational innovation and want to upgrade their technology infrastructure. For further details, see Article 1 of Ministerial Decision 173/2011 of the Minister of Development, Competitiveness and Shipping.

Provides: all forms of aid. The rate of subsidy and leasing subsidy may reach up to 80 percent of the maximum allowable amount of aid. For new enterprises this percentage is increased by 10 percent.

(c) Regional Cohesion

Target Group: investors with projects that address local needs or capitalise on local competitive advantages. For further details, see Article 2 of Ministerial Decision 173/2011 of the Minister of Development, Competitiveness and Shipping.

Provides: all forms of aid. The subsidy rate and leasing subsidy may reach up to 70 percent of the maximum allowable amount of aid. For new enterprises this percentage is increased by 10 percent.

(d) Youth Entrepreneurship

Target Group: investors from 20 to 40 years old.

Provides: aid for virtually all costs (including operational) for five years from the start of the business. Total aid may reach up to EUR 1,000,000.

(e) Large Investment Plans

Target Group: investments with a budget of at least EUR 50,000,000.

Provides: all forms of aid, either in one form or a combination of forms. The level of aid decreases as the amount of investment increases. The percentage of the subsidy may not exceed 60 percent of total aid.

(f) Integrated, Multi-Annual Business Plans

Target Group: companies legally formed at least five years previous to application, to implement integrated multi-annual (two to five years) business plans with a budget of at least EUR 2,000,000 in total.

Provides: technological, administrative, organisational and business modernisation. 100 percent of the maximum regional aid applicable shall be granted.

(g) Partnerships and Networking

Target Group: partnerships and networking configurations or clusters. These clusters shall be comprised of at least 10 enterprises in the Regions of Attica and Thessaloniki and of at least five enterprises in other regions, operating in the form of a consortium.

Provides: for any form of aid.

3.3.2　What sectors are excluded from the aid scheme ?

Sectors excluded from the General Block Exemption Regulation (Regulation No. 800/2008 of 6 August 2008, OJ L 214 of 9.8.2008, p.3) are:

(a) the steel sector, as defined in Article 2(29) of the Regulation;

(b) the synthetic fibres sector, as defined in Article 2(30) of the Regulation;

(c) the coal sector, as defined in Regulation No 1407/2002 (OJ L 205 of 2.8.2002, p.1) on State aid to the coal industry;

(d) the shipbuilding sector, as defined in the framework on State aid to shipbuilding (2003/C 317/06 of 30.12.2003, p.11).

Further, the aid scheme does not apply to the following:

(a) investment plans of public corporations and organisations or their subsidiaries in which they hold over 49 percent of the share capital and investment plans of companies in which the State or a public legal person or a first- or second-level local authority holds over 49 percent of the share capital or which are regularly or occasionally subsidised by them, where the subsidized accounts for over 50 percent of their annual revenue;

(b) undertakings which operate in the form of a society, civil partnership or consortium, subject to the provisions of Article 13(1)(d) of the IIL;

(c) firms in difficulty, as defined in the Community guidelines, from time to time in force, on State aid for rescuing and restructuring firms in difficulty (2004/C 244/02 of 1.10.2004, p.2) and the General Block Exemption Regulation for small and medium-sized enterprises;

(d) investment plans implemented at the initiative and on behalf of the State by a private individual on the basis of a works, franchise or service contract;

(e) investment plans of bodies against which an aid recovery order is pending further to a previous decision by the Commission declaring the aid illegal and incompatible with the Internal Market;

(f) certain industries and branches of economic activity (e.g. production of electricity from photovoltaic systems, construction of buildings, and civil engineering), as defined on the basis of the National Nomenclature of Economic Activities-Activity

Code Number 2008, as amended by POL 1086/2009.

Finally, the aid scheme does not apply to investments to:

(a) establish, extend or modernise hotel facilities. This does not include investments to establish, extend or modernise an integrated form of hotel facility belonging to or being upgraded to at least the three-star category, or investments in health tourism. Also excluded are investments to convert traditional or listed buildings into hotel facilities of at least the three-star category, and investments to modernise hotel facilities that operate in traditional or listed buildings belonging to or being upgraded to at least the three-star category;

(b) modernise an integrated form of hotel facility within six years of the date on which the facility opened or the date on which the decision was issued to complete an investment to modernise the facility. The six-year period from when the facility referred to in this subparagraph opened shall also include the period during which the facility operated as rented rooms or apartments, when it is about hotel facilities that resulted from the obligatory conversion of a rented rooms or apartments facility;

(c) erect, extend or modernise self-catering accommodation, rented rooms and rented furnished apartments, regardless of category. Types of investment plans in the fishing and aquaculture industry and in the agricultural sector, may be declared eligible by joint decision of the Minister for the Economy, Competitiveness and Shipping and the Minister for Rural Development and Food.

3.3.3   The types of aid provided

(a) Tax relief: tax relief comprising the exemption from payment of income tax on pre-tax profits which result, according to tax law, from any and all of the enterprise's activities.

(b) Subsidy: gratis payment by the State of a sum of money to cover part of the subsidized expenditure of the investment.

(c) Leasing subsidy: includes payment by the State of a portion of the instalments paid under a leasing agreement executed to acquire new machinery and/or other equipment.

(d) Soft loans by the Credit Guarantee Fund for Small and Micro Enterprises (TEMPME S. A.): the amount to be covered by a bank loan may be funded by soft loans from credit institutions that cooperate with enterprises.

The aid referred to above shall be aggregated for the purpose of determining the total amount of aid allocated to the investment project. In this case the benefit of the funding above is included in total aid, which may not exceed the limits delineated on the Regional State Aid Map.

3.4   Other relevant legislation

- Law 3919/2011 is a comprehensive reform law, which aims to liberalize more than 150 regulated or "closed-shop" professions.
- Law 3982/2011 reduces the complexity of the licensing system for manufacturing activities and technical professions, and modernises qualification and certification requirements.
- Law 4014/2011 simplifies the environmental licensing process.
- Law 2246/94 and supporting amendments opened Greece's telecommunications market to foreign investment.
- Law 2289/95, which amended Law 468/76, allows private(both foreign and domestic) participation in oil exploration and development.
- Law 2364/95 and supporting amendments govern investment in the natural gas market.
- Legislative Decree 2687 of 1953, in conjunction with Article 112 of the Constitution, gives approved foreign "productive investments" (primarily manufacturing and tourism enterprises) property rights, preferential tax treatment, and work permits for foreign managerial and technical staff. The Decree also provides a constitutional guarantee against unilateral changes in the terms of a foreign investor's agreement with the government, but the guarantee does not cover changes in the tax regime.
- Law 2773/99 initially opened up 34 percent of the Greek energy market, in compliance with EU Directive 96/92 concerning regulation of the internal electricity market.
- Law 3175/2003 harmonises Greek legislation with the requirements of EU Directive 2003/54/EC on common rules for the internal electricity market.
- Law 3389/2005 introduces PPPs, creating a market-friendly regulatory environment for PPPs in the service and construction sectors.
- Law 3426/2005 completes Greece's harmonisation with EU Directive 2003/54/EC and provides for the gradual deregulation of the electricity market.
- Law 3427/2005, which amended Law 89/67, provides special tax treatment for offshore operations of foreign companies established in Greece.

Chapter 4　Monetary and Banking System and Law

4. 1　The banking system in Greece

Banks in Greece are one of the most significant pillars of the economy. They have consistently funded all major investment activities and the modernisation of the infrastructure of the country along with consumers and SMEs. The Greek State controlled a substantial number of banks in the past. Over the last years, a number of banks has been privatised and is no longer owned or controlled by the state. Currently, only the National Bank of Greece, and that to a certain extent, is the main representative of state influence in the economy.

Private banks include Alpha Bank, EFG Eurobank Ergasias and Piraeus Bank. Further, the French banks have a strong presence in the Greek market with Societe Generale acquiring Geniki Bank and Credit Agricole acquiring the Commercial Bank of Greece. Certain foreign banks have established themselves in Greece either through a branch or a representative office.

The Bank of Greece is the regulatory authority in the country. It is a member of the Eurosystem since Greece is a member of the Eurozone and its Director sits in the Board of the European Central Bank.

The Greek banks are suffering from the severe financial situation of the country. Although the financial crisis in Greece was mainly a crisis of the Greek State, the banks where indirectly affected as they lost access to the market and had to find refuge to the European Central Bank and the Bank of Greece for liquidity in a number of occasions. It is expected that further mergers and acquisitions will take place in the banking sector. [1]

---

[1]　http://www. greeklawdigest. gr/topics/banking-system-finance-investment.

4. 2   Capital controls currently imposed

The capital controls originally imposed by the Greek Government on 18 July 2015①(the "Act") were further relaxed pursuant to a ministerial decision② issued by the Greek Minister of Finance on 25 September 2015③(the"Decision"). In particular, the Act restricts cash payments and fund transfers as follows:

• Up to EUR 500 per depositor(Customer ID) or payor per month can now be transferred abroad from credit and payment institutions supervised by the Bank of Greece(including their agents) as well as from payment institutions of other EU member states which lawfully provide money remittance services in Greece either through their agents or through Hellenic Post SA.

• New accounts(current or deposit accounts) can now be opened for the following purposes:

—to make payroll payments to employees and workers, including the issue and redemption of social security vouchers for self-employed workers (in Greek "ergosimo");

—to serve newly-established legal entities set up after May 2015, as well as personal undertakings and freelancers who have started working after this date;

—for students commencing their studies within the academic year 2015/2016 (including students participating in the Erasmus programme), provided that they are studying in a different place to their permanent residence and there is no other account in their name, whether as a sole or joint beneficiary. Students may also be added as joint-holders to existing accounts;

—for persons who are called up for military service after the imposition of the Act, provided that they do not have other available accounts in their names; and

—for charity fundraising.

• Accounts can now be opened to serve loans granted prior to, or after, 18 July 2015 with the same credit institution that granted the loan, even if the beneficiary

① Act No. 84/18. 07. 2015 as amended and in force, (the "Act").
② Ministerial decision No. Γ. Δ. O. Π. 0001258EΞ2015/X. Π. 2672.
③ Published in the Greek Government Gazette Volume B, No. 2100/25. 09. 2015.

holds accounts with other credit institutions. However, no cash withdrawals are permitted from the new account;

• Fixed-term deposits can be terminated entirely or in part in order to pay suppliers by transfer to the supplier's account in Greece against invoices or other equivalent documents. The depositor must make a solemn declaration that it has no other available funds in an existing savings or current account at any credit institution.

• The early partial termination of a fixed-term deposit account is permitted to cover living expenses of up to EUR 1,800 per calendar month, provided that the applicant declares that he/she has no other available funds in the same or any other credit institution.

• Fixed-term deposit accounts can also be terminated early for the purchase of real property, only in an amount up to the purchase price set out in the sale contract, plus notarial fees, taxes and other expenses. The amount must be transferred directly to the account of the seller, notary or lawyer.

• The following transactions, which were prohibited until 28 September 2015, are now permitted:

—Cash withdrawals of up to 10 percent of amounts transferred from foreign bank accounts to existing Greek bank accounts(via credit transfer), in accordance with procedures to be determined by the Committee of Approval of Banking Transactions;

—Cash withdrawals of up to EUR 1,800 per client/beneficiary per calendar month from foreign remittances made to Greek or EU member-state financial institutions which lawfully provide money remittance services in Greece, either through their agents or through Hellenic Post SA, provided that (a) at least an equal amount has been received by the institution from abroad after 18 July 2015 and it has been declared to the Bank of Greece, or(b) the institution has collected the same amount in cash from clients in Greece making remittances abroad;

—Payments abroad of up to EUR 5,000 each in respect of commercial transactions can be made by legal entities and businesses on submission of supporting documentation to the bank. These transactions will be handled through the banks' branch networks and will be included in the monthly maximum amount that each bank is permitted to transfer abroad in accordance with the relevant decision of the Committee of Approval of Banking Transactions;

—Individuals can make payments abroad or withdraw cash of up to EUR 2,000 per person per month for expenses relating to serious health conditions or exceptional personal reasons. Supporting documentation will need to be submitted through the banks' branch networks;

—Monthly cash withdrawals of up to EUR 10,000 per diocesan authority ("Metropolis" in Greek) and up to EUR 20,000 by the Archbishopric of Athens, but in each case only from one account at a single credit institution per month.

Furthermore, the Decision provides that the activities of the Black Sea Trade and Development Bank, the European Bank for Reconstruction and Development and the European Investment Bank do not fall under the scope and restrictions imposed by the Act.

Finally, by virtue of the Joint Ministerial Decision of the Ministers of Justice and Finance No. 70905 of 29 September 2015 (Greek Government Gazette No. 2110/2015 issue B), the suspension of any enforcement measure (and in particular the conduction of auctions, seizures, evictions and detentions) which was initially imposed by virtue of the Joint Ministerial Decision of the Ministers of Justice and Finance No. 49214 of 21 July 2015 and then extended by virtue of the Joint Ministerial Decision of the Ministers of Justice and Finance No. 57384 of 31 August 2015 is now further extended.

4.3 The legal framework governing the provision of banking services in Greece

Law No. 3601/2007 (as modified by laws 3693/2008 and 3746/2009) on Credit Institutions implemented Directive 2006/48/EC of the European Parliament and Council into the domestic legal system. Greek law regulates the establishment and operation as well as the supervisory status of credit institutions. The Greek supervisory framework draws heavily on the relevant Community legislation, which is in turn consistent with the Basel principles.

Specifically, Law 3601/2007 and Bank of Greece Governor's Acts 2587/2007, 2588/2007, 2589/2007, 2590/2007, 2591/2007, 2592/2007, 2593/2007, 2594/2007, 2595/2007 and 2596/2007 make up the new supervisory framework, while Bank of Greece Governor's Acts 2577/06, 2595/2007 and 2597/2007 deal with the issue of the Internal Control Systems(ICS), including auditing, compliance and risk management functions, as well as with Pillar 2 (ICAAP and SRP) and other matters.

Similarly, Banking and Credit Committee decisions, 281/5/26. 3. 2009, 285/6/ 2009 and 290/12/2009 constitute the institutional framework for the prevention of the use of the financial system for money laundering and the financing of terrorism. More specifically, Law 3601/2007 (hereinafter the "Law") provides for (a) the establishment and operation of the business of credit institutionsl, (b) the activities of the credit institutions and (c) the supervision on credit institutions and their activities.

4. 4   Activities that are considered banking activities under Greek law

According to Article 2 of Law No. 3601/2007 , credit institutions are undertakings whose business is to receive deposits or other repayable funds from the public and to grant loans or other credit for their own account.

Furthermore, Article 11 of the Law, stipulates the activities of the credit institutions as follows:

- acceptance of deposits and other repayable funds;
- lending including, *inter alia* , consumer credit, mortgage credit, factoring with or without recourse, financing of commercial transactions(including forfeiting) ;
- financial leasing;
- money transfer services;
- issuing and administering means of payment (e. g. credit cards, travellers' cheques and bankers' drafts) ;
- guarantees and commitments;
- trading for own account or for account of customers in:
    —money market instruments (cheques, bills, certificates of deposit, etc.) ;
    —foreign exchange;
    —financial futures and options;
    —exchange and interest rate instruments; or
    —transferable securities.
- participation in securities issues and the provision of services related to such issues;
- advice to undertakings on capital structure, industrial strategy and related

questions and advice on mergers and purchase of undertakings;

- money broking;
- portfolio management and advice;
- safekeeping and administration of securities;
- credit reference services;
- safe custody services.

All the activities mentioned above, also included in Annex 1 of Directive 2006/48 of the EC, can be freely exercised by credit institutions of any member state, either by the establishment of a branch, or by way of provision of services without establishment(cross border), and provided of course that they are regulated in their home member state.

4.5 How Greek law implements the freedom to provide services under EU Law

According to Articles 49 – 55 of the EU Treaty, the citizens of a member state can provide services to other member states freely. Greek Law 3106/2007 in implementation of the Directive 2006/48, regulates the freedom to provide services in Greece by entities established in other member states. According to Article 15, any credit institution of another member state wishing to exercise the freedom to provide services by carrying on its activities within the Greek territory for the first time, should meet the following requirements:

- It must have received a licence to operate in another member state and must be supervised by the competent authority of the other member state.

- The activities that the credit institution intends to carry on in the Greek territory, should be included in its operation licence.

- The credit institution of another member state must notify the competent authorities of the home member state of the activities on the above list, which it intends to carry on. The competent authorities of the home member state shall, within one month of receipt of the above notification send that notification to the competent authority of Greece, i. e. the Bank of Greece. This is a direct consequence of the "Single licence system".

- The credit institutions should comply with the rules of the Greek territory in connection with banking legislation as well as legal rules that have been adopted in the interests of the general interest.

• The credit institutions advertising their services through all available means of communication in the Greek territory are subject to any rules governing the form and the content of such advertising adopted in the interests of the general interest.

More specifically, the competent authority of the home member state must only notify to the Bank of Greece its intention to provide cross border mutually accepted services in Greece. Such activities should be provided in the same manner as they are provided in their home country, and they should not violate the provisions of the legislation on credit institutions, capital market and consumer protection that aim at protecting investors and consumers of banking products and services or other provisions of public interest.

4.6   Regulation of EU member states banks providing their services in Greece

The Bank of Greece, pursuant to Article 55A of Law 3424/7 December 1927, exercises prudential supervision over credit institutions. The object of such supervision is to ensure the stability and efficiency of the banking system and, more generally, the smooth operation and stability of the Greek financial system.

The Department for the Supervision of Credit and Financial Institutions of the Bank of Greece is responsible for the prudential supervision of credit and financial institutions. The provisions of Article 25 of Law 3106/2007 regulate the supervision of credit institutions and their activities. The Bank of Greece supervises the credit institutions with the registered seat in Greece and their branch offices abroad, as well as the branch offices in Greece of credit institutions of third countries. [1]

In contrast, branch offices of credit institutions of other member states are supervised by the competent authority of the home member state, except that: (a) the supervision of their cash flow is also supervised by the Bank of Greece in cooperation with the authority of the home member state, and (b) the supervision of their activities will be in the same manner as they are supervised in their home country, so long as such supervision is in conformity with the provisions of the Greek legislation. The provision of cross border services in Greece by credit institutions authorised in another member state is only supervised by the competent authority of the

[1]   http://www.bankofgreece.gr/Pages/en/Bank/LegalF/statute.aspx.

home member state. According to Art. 16 of Law 3106/2007, credit institutions authorised in other member states, which are pursuing activities listed in Art. 11 of Law 3106/07 as above, through provision of services without an establishment in Greece, may pursue these activities in the same manner as in their home country, provided they do not violate the provisions of the legislation on credit institutions, capital market and consumer protection or other provisions of public interest.

4.7　Potential measures and penalties if credit institutions breach their obligations

Article 65 of Law 3106/07 provides that in case a credit institution that is authorized in another member state, and which provides services in Greece, does not comply with the legal provisions, the Bank of Greece may require the credit institution to comply with these provisions. In case the credit institution fails to comply, the Bank of Greece may inform the competent authorities of the credit institution's home member state, which can subsequently take all the appropriate measures to ensure compliance.

If, despite the above actions, or in case such measures prove inadequate or are not available in the member state, the credit institution persists in violating the related provisions, the Bank of Greece shall, after informing the competent authorities, take all the appropriate measures to prevent or condemn further irregularities or impose penalties according to the provisions of Law 3106/07. In doing so, it may prevent the credit institution from initiating further transactions in Greece.

The Bank of Greece, prior to initiating this procedure, can also take precautionary judicial or extrajudicial measures that it deems necessary to protect the interests of depositors, investors or other persons to whom services are provided. It shall inform the Commission of the European Union and the authorities of the home member state of such measures.

In case of withdrawal of the authorisation of a credit institution by the competent authority of the member state, the Bank of Greece has the right to prevent such institution from initiating further transactions in Greece, and shall take necessary measures to secure the interest of depositors, investors or other persons to whom services are provided.

Governor's Acts 336/29 of February 1984, 2593/24 of February 2004 and 2612/13 of November 2008, established the Banking and Credit Committee (BCC), a body composed of members of the Administration and Heads of specific Departments of the Bank of Greece, with a main duty to impose fines and penalties for violations of the above provisions on credit institutions.

4. 8   Consumer protection provisions pertinent to the banking sector

Credit institutions, as every service provider, must abide by Greek consumer protection and advertising legislation. The provisions that are pertinent to the banking sector are, initially, the general provisions of the Greek Civil Code (in particular Articles 57, 281 and 288). Law 2251/1994 on Consumers' Protection establish a regulatory framework shelter for consumers against creditors' abusive and unfair behaviour.

Law 2251/1994 stipulates that contracts, including contracts within the financial services market, must not contain unfair terms. This law is purposed to protect the economic interests of consumers regarding a potential abuse of power by the suppliers of financial services. The law protects consumers from standard contracts prepared by financial institutions that sometimes exclude essential rights of consumers. These general transaction terms (GOS) (i. e. terms that have been made in advance for an indefinite number of future contracts) are prohibited and void, if they result in excessive imbalance of rights and obligations of the parties to the detriment of consumers.

Greek courts have provided such examples of important decisions on unfair terms that credit institutions use. For instance, terms that give the financial supplier the right to alter unilaterally basic terms of a contract are considered illegal. Further, terms that limit the liability of the banks only for fraud or gross negligence of their employee and exclude responsibility for strict liability are disproportionate. ①

4. 9   Other relevant legislation

Banking Law:

• Law 1266/1982—Authorities responsible for the conduct of monetary, credit and exchange rate policies, and other provisions;

---

① http://eur-lex. europa. eu/legal-content/EN/ALL/? uri = CELEX%3A52000DC0248.

- Law 2331/1995—Prevention and combating of the legalisation of income from criminal activities;
- Law 2515/1997—Article 16: Mergers of credit institutions;
- Law 2832/2000—Deposit Guarantee Scheme;
- Law 3016/2002—On corporate governance, board remuneration and other issues;
- Law 3148/2003—Accounting Standardisation and Audit Committee, replacement and supplementation of the provisions on electronic money institutions, and other provisions;
- Law 3601/2007—Taking up and pursuit of the business of credit institutions, capital adequacy of credit institutions and investment firms, and other provision;
- Law 5076/1931—on Sociétés Anonymes and Banks.

Insurance Law:

- Law 489/1976 "Compulsory Insurance of Civil Liability Arising from Motor Accidents";
- Law Decree 400/1970 "Regarding Private Insurance Undertakings".

Chapter 5   Laws Relating to Construction of Infrastructure

Legislation relevant to construction of infrastructure in Greece is well documented in the OECD Services Trade Restrictiveness Index (STRI) construction for buildings (residential and non-residential) as well as construction work for civil engineering. Construction services have historically played an important role in the functioning of economies, providing the infrastructure for other industries. These services account for a significant share of GDP and employment in most countries. Public works, such as roads and public buildings, account for about half of the market for construction services. Therefore, the STRI for construction services entails detailed information on public procurement procedures.

According to the Index, in 2014 Greece exported services worth USD 41 billion and its services import value was USD 15 billion. Transport services, particularly maritime transport, are the largest services exporting and importing sector. The overall score for all the sectors is seen in Figure 1 below.

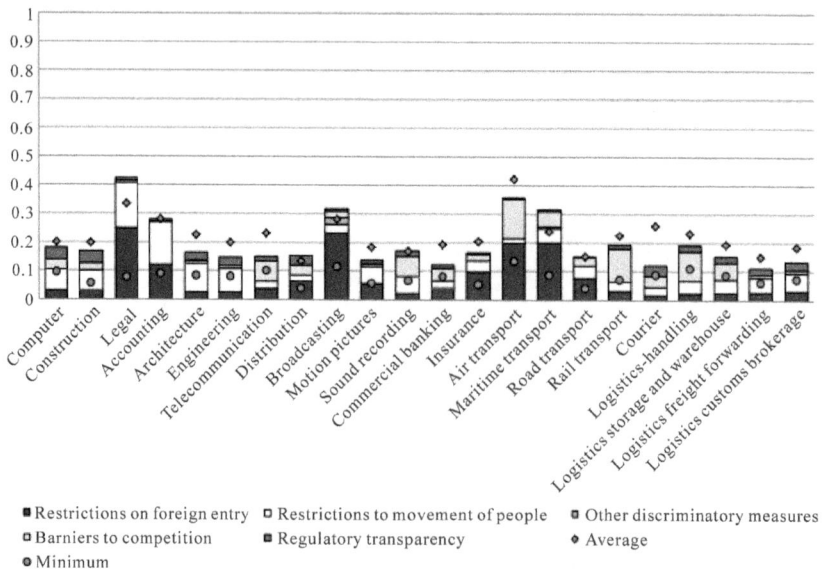

Figure 1. STRI Score by Sectors

The construction sector appears to be moderately restrictive, with the main barriers being in competition. Overall, Greece imposes restrictions on ownership of land and real estate by foreigners. A minimum amount of capital must be deposited in a bank or with a notary in order to register a business. Greece does not apply labour market tests for workers seeking to provide services in the country on a temporary basis as intra-corporate transferees, contractual services suppliers or independent services suppliers. However, the duration of stay for these categories is limited to six months for contractual service suppliers and 12 months for the other two categories on their first entry permit. There is at least one major state-owned enterprise in computer, construction, maritime, rail, banking and insurance services. [1]

Services represent 54 percent of Greece's gross exports, but 71 percent in value added terms. Services also account for over two-thirds of GDP and 70 percent of employment in Greece, which implies that earnings and aggregate demand depend significantly on productivity in services sectors. Greece could further increase the efficiency of its economy by prioritising reforms that enhance competition in services markets. The STRI suggests that this may be particularly the case for business and transport services, both of which are essential inputs in downstream industries.

5. 1   Restrictions on foreign entry

Greece is generally not restrictive in foreign entry with regard to construction. A total of 100 percent of maximum foreign equity share is allowed, as provided by Articles 2,8, Presidential Decree (ΠΔ) 96/1993 on the Liberalisation of Movement of Capital (Implementation of Directive 88/361/EC and 92/122/EC) and Articles 10 § 1 of the Legislative Decree 2687/1953 on the investment and protection of foreign capital. [2]

There are no limits to the proportion of shares that foreign investors can acquire in publicly-controlled firms, as per Articles 2, Law 4092/2012 on the Urgent Measures for the Implementation of Medium-Term Strategic Plan for Fiscal Adjustments for 2012 – 2015 and on the elimination of Article 11 on the transfer of control of public firms. [3] Yet, the upper limit of 20 percent above which government ap-

---

[1] https://www. oecd. org/tad/services-trade/STRI_GRC. pdf.

[2] http://www. et. gr/index. php/2013 – 01 – 28 – 14 – 06 – 23/search-laws.

[3] Http://www. hfsf. gr/files/legal/13. L4092_am10. pdf.

proval is needed for the acquisition of shares of firms that have (or had) been under government control, and own network infrastructure has been eliminated.

Joint ventures are not required for a construction work, as per Arts. 11 (4) ,15 Law 3844/2010 on Services (Implementation of Directive 2006/123/EC) , Art. 80 Law 3669/2008 on Public Works and Law 3316/2005 on studies of public works. ① Foreign branches are allowed, according to Arts. 11 (4) , 15 Law 3844/2010 on Services (Implementation of Directive 2006/123/EC) and Art. 80 Law 3669/2008 on Public Works-Law 3316/2005 on studies of public works, and generally no other legal restrictions exist.

Further, there is no requirement for the majority of the board of directors to be Greek nationals (as per Art. 15, Law 3844/2010 on Services (Implementation of Directive 2006/123/EC) and Art. 7, Legislative Decree 2687/1953 on the investment and protection of foreign capital) , ② or residents (as per Art. 15, Law 3844/2010 on Services (Implementation of Directive 2006/123/EC) , Art. 7, Legislative Decree 2687/1953 on the investment and protection of foreign capital). ③ The same laws provide that not even one in the board of directors or the manager need be a national or resident.

As discussed above, according to Law 4146/2013, there is a two-speed investment process that allows fast-track investments considered to be of " strategic importance" upon the fulfilment of certain criteria, such as net economic benefits, labour market contribution, improvement of the competitiveness of the national economy and business environment, exports intensification. There is a requirement that foreign investors must obtain prior approval; such approval is not automatic. Moreover, the law provides for the right to condition the provision of the service on a licence (Art. 10) , to restrict provision in certain regions of the country (Art. 11) or limit the duration of the licence (Art. 12) wherever this is justified in terms of national interest. Relevant legislation includes Law 3427/2005 on the establishment of foreign enterprises into Greece as amending the Obligatory Legislative Decree 89/1967 (A. N. 89/1967) , Art. 1, Law 4146/2013 on the creation of an environment conducive to strategic and private investments, and Ministerial Decision YA 4487/466/2006 re-

---

① http://www. et. gr/index. php/2013 – 01 – 28 – 14 – 06 – 23/search-laws http://websdit. ypes. gr/fileadmin/documents/N_3669_2008. pdf http://www. dsanet. gr/Epikairothta/Nomothesia/n3316_05. htm.

② http://www. et. gr/index. php/2013 – 01 – 28 – 14 – 06 – 23/search-laws.

③ http://www. et. gr/index. php/2013 – 01 – 28 – 14 – 06 – 23/search-laws.

garding the criteria for the establishment of foreign enterprises into Greece, Art. 15 (5), Law 3844/2010 on Services (Implementation of Directive 2006/123/EC).

Despite the abovementioned openness, acquisition of land and real estate by foreigners is restricted. Pursuant to the Royal Decrees of 1927, 1928 and 1932, aliens were not allowed to conclude juridical acts in the frontier areas. Nevertheless, Law 1892/1990 introduced some modifications and now determines the conditions for conclusion of juridical acts in such areas. According to the provisions of this law, any *inter vivos* juridical act which constitutes real rights or contractual claims in favour of natural or legal persons on the frontier areas is prohibited. Furthermore, the assignment of shares or parts of any type of company, which owns real estate in this area, as well as any change in partners of such companies, is prohibited. Legal and natural persons with Greek nationality, ethnic Greeks, including Cypriots, as well as EU nationals, may apply for an exemption. Legal or natural persons originating from third countries can also, upon request, obtain the above-mentioned rights after decision of the Ministry of Defence. ①

5. 2   Restrictions to movement of people

Greece is generally not restrictive regarding movement of people engaged in construction. There are no quotas for intra-corporate transferees, as per Art. 17, Law 3386/2005 on the entry, residence and social integration of third-country nationals on Greek territory, as amended by Laws 3448/2006, 3536/2007, 3613/2007, 3731/2008, 3772/2009 and 3801/2009. Yet, according to Art. 17. 1. bb. , the number of employees cannot exceed five percent of national employees. Similarly, there are no quotas for contractual service suppliers, nor for independent service suppliers.

Further, there are no requirements for labour market tests for intra-corporate transferees, contractual service suppliers, or independent service suppliers as per Art. 17, Law 3386/2005 on the entry, residence and social integration of third-country nationals on Greek territory, as amended by Laws 3448/2006 (GG A 57), 3536/2007 (GG A 42), 3613/2007 (GG A 263), 3731/2008 (GG A 263), 3772/2009 (GG A 112) and 3801/2009 (GG A 163). ②

There is, however, a limitation on stay for intra-corporate transferees (between

① http://www. helleniccomserve. com/greekproperty. html.
② http://www. mfa. gr/images/docs/ethnikes_theoriseis/codification_of_legislation_en. pdf.

12 and 36 months), contractual service suppliers (less than 12 months) and independent service suppliers (between 12 and 36 months). The legal basis is Art. 17, Law 3386/2005 on the entry, residence and social integration of third-country nationals on Greek territory, as amended by Laws 3448/2006, 3536/2007, 3613/2007, 3731/2008, 3772/2009 and 3801/2009.

For intra-corporate transferees, according to Art. 17. 1. bb, the residence permit shall be initially issued for a period of one year and may be renewed for two more years (Added by Art. 8. 3. of Law 3536/2007). Subject to the relevant special regulations, the residence permit shall be renewed every two years provided that third countries' citizens shall provide supportive documents evidencing special conditions. For contractual services the residence permit may be renewed for six more months in exceptional cases, if justified by the need to fulfil the contractual commitment of the undertaking. For independent services suppliers, it may be extended every two years.

Some restrictions however exist, mostly relating to qualifications. For instance, foreign professionals are required to take a local examination in engineering. The examination is oral and written, in Greek, on topics outlined in Art. 5 of the EΔ 5/4/3399. This practice has been debated yet it still stands, according to the opinion 34/23. 1. 2014 of the Competition Authority on the amendment of the Law 4663/1930 regarding the Practice of Construction Engineers and Architects and the joint Ministerial Decision EΔ 5/4/3399 dated 14/09/1984 on the procedures for the recognition qualifications of Architects and Engineers, as well as Law 1225/1981 on the Recognition of qualifications of Architects and Engineers.

Further, at least one engineer must be licensed for the issuance of construction permits. Law 4030/2011 in its Article 8 (1) clearly stipulates as a precondition for issuing a construction permit to an engineer the need to be licensed and officially be part of the Special Registry for Construction Engineers. The following laws are also relevant for this measure: Ministerial Decision 2759/15 (148/B/15) on Creating a Register for Design Consultants and Supervising Engineers; Subsection IΓ-12, Law 4254/14 on Measures for the support and development of the Greek economy within the framework of implementing Law 4046/12, and other provisions. ① Law 4030/

---

① http://energy_inspectors. et. teiath. gr/ee/images/stories/energy/4030_2011. pdf http://www. et. gr/index. php/2013 −01 −28 −14 −06 −23/search-laws.

2011 in its Article 8(1) also clearly stipulates as a precondition for issuing a construction permit to an engineer the need to be licensed and officially be part of the Special Registry for Construction Engineers.

5.3   Barriers to competition

Decisions by the regulatory body can be appealed since the law states that appeal procedures are open to an "affected party". Article 3 refers to the identity of the interested party, referring to Greek citizens, aliens or legal entities. Law 2690/1999 on Ratification of the Administrative Procedure Code and Article 30 of the Competition Act(Law 3959/2011, amended to Law 703/1977) are the relevant documents.

Firms can also have redress when business practices restrict competition in a given market, according to Art. 36, New Competition Act(Law 3959/2011). The government also controls two major firms in the sector, based on Art. 5(6), Law 2229/1994 and Law 2190/1920 on Corporations. It controls Attiko Metro AE and Egnatia Odos AE.

Minimum capital requirements also exist for corporations, namely EUR 60,000. Since 2014, a simplified form of LLCs have been enforced and capital requirements for these companies have been eliminated. There is no capital requirement for partnerships or personal firms. The requirements are not discriminatory. These rules are found in Art. 8, Law 2190/1920 on Corporations, Art. 16 of Law 3661/2008 amending Art. 4 Law 3190/1955 on Limited Liability Corporations with multiple members or a single member and Arts. 741 – 784 of the Civil Code(Presidential Decree ΠΔ 456/1984) on General Partnerships and Personal Enterprises.

5.4   Regulatory transparency

There is a legal obligation to communicate regulations to the public prior to entry into force, according to the transparency portal. [1] Second, the country is part of the UN initiative of Open Government Partnership(OGP). There is a public comment procedure open to interested parties, including foreign suppliers.

---

[1]   You may refer to http://diavgeia. gov. gr/en regarding the purpose of the programme and http:// www. opengov. gr/en/ to gain access where almost every piece of draft legislation prior submission to the Parliament.

Otherwise, certain bias like processing time, cost to obtain a business license, and time and cost required to acquire a construction permit do not appear to hamper construction activity.

5.5 Other discriminatory measures

Overall, foreign suppliers are not treated less favourably regarding taxes and eligibility to subsidies according to Art. 2 of the New Tax Code and Law 4172/2013. There is no explicit preference for local suppliers during the public procurement stage according to Art. 22 and Part 2 (New Public Procurement Law), Law 4281/2014 on Measures to Support the Growth of the Greek Economy and other matters including and transposing EC Directives 18/2004, 17/2004, 51/2005, 75/2005, 66/2007 and EEC Directives 665/89, 13/92 on public works. Importantly, procurement regulation explicitly prohibits discrimination against foreign suppliers.

Procurement laws, regulations and procedures are considered transparent as per Arts. 29, 30, Presidential Decree 60/2007 (Implementation of EC Directive 18/2004 on the coordination of procedures for the award of public works and Part 2 (New Public procurement Law), Law 4281/2014 on Measures to Support the Growth of the Greek Economy and other matters including and transposing EC Directives 18/2004, 17/2004, 51/2005, 75/2005, 66/2007 and EEC Directives 665/89, 13/92 on public works.

Laws and regulations do not impose national standards that deviate from the international standards on building design or construction product, as per Art. 135, Law 4070/ 2012 on Telecommunications, Transportations and Public Works amending Law 3669/2008 on Public Works Construction-Circular 98 (1989), Ministry of Public Works, Planning and the Environment.

Chapter 6   Laws Relating to Labour Management and Treatment

6.1   Individual employment contract

Employment contracts are generally open-ended. Fixed-term employment contracts are only permitted exceptionally, for instance when there is a specific task, or time required to undertake. In lack of such ground, the contract is considered open-ended, even if the agreement is fixed-term. When there is an exceptional ground, the renewal of a fixed-term contract without limit is permitted. When this ground is no longer relevant, the employment contract is automatically considered open-ended.

Fixed-term contracts terminate after their term expires or they can be rescinded where there is a serious reason for so doing. Open-ended contracts are terminated by rescinding them. When a fixed-term contract expires no compensation is owed, but where an open-ended contract is rescinded the compensation specified by law is as follows:[1]

Table 3. Termination of Open-End Employment Contracts

Duration of Employment	A. Termination without a term of notice		B. Termination with a term of notice		
	Compensation in monthly earnings	Extra compensation (if a total of 17 years with same employer reached on 12.11.2012)	Term of Notice	Compensation in monthly earnings	Extra compensation (if a total of 17 years with same employer reached on 12 Nov. 2012)
Over 1 year + up to 2 years	2 Months		1 Month	1 Month	

(**continued**)

From 2 up to 4 years	2 Months		2 Months	1 Month	
From 4 up to 5 years	3 Months		2 Months	1 ½ Months	
From 5 up to 6 years	3 Months		3 Months	1 ½ Months	
From 6 up to 8 years	4 Months		3 Months	2 Months	
From 8 up to 10 years	5 Months		3 Months	2 ½ Months	
10 years completed	6 Months		4 Months	3 Months	
11 years completed	7 Months		4 Months	3 ½ Months	
12 years completed	8 Months		4 Months	4 Months	
13 years completed	9 Months		4 Months	4 ½ Months	
14 years completed	10 Months		4 Months	5 Months	
15 years completed	11 Months		4 Months	5 ½ Months	
16 years completed	12 Months		4 Months	6 Months	
17 years completed	12 Months	1 Month(up to a max. of EUR 2,000)	4 Months	6 Months	½ Month
18 years completed	12 Months	2 Months	4 Months	6 Months	1 Month

(**continued**)

19 years completed	12 Months	3 Months	4 Months	6 Months	1 ½ Months
20 years completed	12 Months	4 Months	4 Months	6 Months	2 Months
21 years completed	12 Months	5 Months	4 Months	6 Months	2 ½ Months
22 years completed	12 Months	6 Months	4 Months	6 Months	3 Months
23 years completed	12 Months	7 Months	4 Months	6 Months	3 ½ Months
24 years completed	12 Months	8 Months	4 Months	6 Months	4 Months
25 years completed	12 Months	9 Months	4 Months	6 Months	4 ½ Months
26 years completed	12 Months	10 Months	4 Months	6 Months	5 Months
27 years completed	12 Months	11 Months	4 Months	6 Months	5 ½ Months
28 years completed + more	12 Months	12 Months	4 Months	6 Months	6 Months

The first year of an open-ended contract is a probationary period, during which the contract can be rescinded without compensation being payable. However, the compensation to be paid cannot exceed a certain amount (30 times the lowest daily wage for unskilled workers or 8 times the number of months of compensation; see Table 4).

Table 4. Compensation to Employees

Length of service	Compensation equal to pay for
up to 1 year	–
1 year – 2 years	7 wages
2 – 5 years	15 wages
5 – 10 years	30 wages
10 – 15 years	60 wages
15 – 20 years	100 wages
20 – 25 years	120 wages
25 – 30 years	145 wages
30 years or more	165 wages

When rescinding an open-ended employment contract, the employer does not have a statutory requirement to state the reason for terminating the contract. However, the court can examine whether the rescission was abusive. The employer must prove by means of counter-evidence, that the rescission did not take place for the abusive reason alleged by the former employee.

6. 1. 1   When is rescission of an open-ended employment contract invalid in law ?

Rescission of an open-ended employment contract is invalid in the following situations:

● Where the notice is not given in writing and the compensation specified by law is not paid simultaneously.

● Where a trade union official is dismissed without approval (for specific reasons only) from the special committee for this purpose.

● Where the dismissal takes place during the course of annual leave.

● Where the dismissal takes place during pregnancy or 18 months after childbirth, unless there is a serious ground for dismissal.

● Where the dismissal is for reasons of gender or marital status, as revenge for not giving into harassment by the employer or as a reaction to a complaint related to unequal treatment of men and women.

● Where the employer does not participate in the cost of self-insurance for the dismissed person aged between 55 and 64 years old, who has at least 4,500 days or

15 years of insurance for social security purposes.

● Where group redundancies exceed the limit set by law.

● Where, in the case of group redundancies, the number of persons aged 55 to 64 dismissed exceed more than 10 percent of the total number of persons dismissed each month.

6. 1. 2   Rules on the pay, work and leave of employees

Pay can be freely negotiated, but is subject to the minimum amount specified in the applicable Collective Labour Agreement(CLA). If the employee falls within the scope of some sectoral, cross-sectoral or other CLA because of his area of special-isation, the most favourable CLA overall for him will apply, i. e. it is not possible to select and put together individual provisions from various CLAs. ①

As for working hours, the rule is eight hours of work, five days a week. In gen-eral, it is not permissible to "offset" working time, not even with the employee's consent. The only exceptions are as follows:

● a nine-hour working day is permitted, where the total working time for the week does not exceed 40 hours.

● over the course of a six-month period, work can be increased by two hours a day(i. e. up to 10 hours) with a corresponding reduction in the working time each day by two hours during the next six-month period(i. e. up to six hours). Instead of reduced employment, it is possible for rest days to be given.

● It is also possible to increase the rate of work by up to 256 hours within a period of eight calendar months, with a corresponding period of reduced employ-ment during the other months of the same calendar year.

With regard to night work, there is a 25 percent augment to the statutory hourly wage. An agreement concerning the salary paid to cover night work, where it ex-ceeds the minimum statutory limits, is lawful.

Work between 41 and 45 hours a week is called "extra work" and is not taken into account in the limits specified for permissible overtime. Work exceeding nine hours a day and/or 45 hours a week is called overtime.

Overtime within the limits specified by law is lawful overtime, but the limit de-pends on the sector of employment(industry, retail outlets, offices, etc.). A notice

---

① http://www. greeklawdigest. gr/topics/employment/item/114-individual-labour-law.

of overtime work must be sent to the authority either before or after the overtime takes place, depending on whether it is urgent or not, and must be entered in the O-vertime Register. Overtime exceeding the lawful limit or for which the aforementioned procedures are not complied with is unlawful overtime.

Extra work is paid at the rate of 20 percent on top of the hourly wage paid. Lawful overtime is paid as follows: up to 120 hours a year by augmenting the hourly wage paid by 40 percent, while for overtime above the 120 hour limit, the augment is 60 percent. Unlawful overtime is paid with an 80 percent augment. Contrary to the situation with extra work, the agreement that the salary paid will also cover an undefined number of overtime hours, is invalid.

Employees are entitled to a minimum of 20 working days of leave(in the case of a five-day working week) or a part thereof for *pro rata temporis* of employment. For each additional year of work, employees are entitled to an additional day of leave up to a total of 22 days. Where the employee works for 10 years with the same employer or 12 years with any employer, he is entitled to 25 days leave. After completing 25 years of work, employees are entitled to 26 days leave. Full pay is owed for the days employees are on leave. In addition they are also entitled to an annual leave bonus equal to the pay for leave, maximum half a salary.

Where the employee is insured for social security purposes with the IKA Fund, the employer is exempted from the obligation to make restitution of the material harm suffered by the employee. The employer is, however, obliged to make restitution of the moral harm suffered where the accident was due to the employer's fault.

6. 1. 3   Rules for managerial staff

Managerial staff and employees, who hold positions of trust, are those who perform general management-related duties which affect the work of the business which employs them, as well as those employees who hold positions of special trust which could substantively affect the taking of decisions. The criterion for determining whether an employee falls into this category include high pay, the power to represent the company, the ability to hire or dismiss staff etc.

This category of employees is excluded from the application of the favourable provisions relating to overtime, work on official holidays, night work, work away from normal place of work and leave.

6. 1. 4   Rules for non-EU foreigners

Non-EU foreigners can be employed after the receipt of the relevant entry visa from the consular authority at their place of residence, which is provided after an invitation is sent by the Greek employer. A residence and work permit for this type of case is provided in numbers that are regulated by the public administration, is for one year, and must be renewed every two years.

The following persons are exempted from this procedure:

- Senior executives of Greek branches and subsidiaries of foreign companies;
- Persons seeking to make an investment of EUR 300,000 or over;
- Technicians performing emergency repairs for a period of up to three months;
- Persons employed by an undertaking established in the EU or EEA, who are sent to Greece to be employed by a Greek undertaking;
- Technicians from non-EU companies sent to Greece to install or maintain machinery.

6.2　The content and scope of a Collective Employment Agreement(CEA)

A CEA is the agreement reached at as a result of collective bargaining between the employer(s) and trade unions of the employees. CEA provisions apply to employees engaged under employment agreements of a private nature, to people engaged in agricultural and related activities as well as to domestic employees. A CEA may regulate issues arising from the exercise of the trade union rights, social insurance issues except for pension issues, issues relating to the business policy as far as it affects employment relations, the interpretation of regulatory terms of CEA, rights and obligations of the contracting parties, the terms and conditions applicable to the individual employment agreements, as well as the mediation and arbitration procedures.

There are different kinds of CEAs, depending on their scope of application. In particular, there are: (a) General National CEAs, whose regulatory terms, except for the salary, apply to the employees of all the country, (b) Branch CEAs, that relate to employees that are engaged in the same branch of business activity of a certain area or of all the country, (c) Professional(national and local) CEAs, that relate to employees that are engaged in the same profession in national or local level, and(d) Business CEAs, that relate to employees engaged in the same undertaking.

6. 2. 1   Competency to conclude CEAs

Any employer is competent to enter into a CEA as regards all employees engaged in its undertaking, regardless of the number of the employees. On the part of the employees, competent are the trade unions of all grades that are most representative within the scope of application of the specific CEA. The most representative trade union is determined by the number of employees who have voted at the last elections for the election of the members of union's Board of Directors. For instance, the General National CEA is concluded by third grade trade unions and employers' organisations of broad representation. Certain trade unions are not authorised to conclude CEA (local branches, labour centres, legal entities). By way of exception, in case of absence of a competent first grade trade union to conclude CEA, legal entities are entitled to proceed to the conclusion of CEA, provided that they have been established by at least 3/5 of the employees of the undertaking, irrespective of the total number of the undertaking's employees and that their duration is limited.

As a general principle of labour law, the provision that is most favourable for the particular employment relation, initially as regards remuneration and then as regards other issues, is applicable. Based on the above, the following conclusions can be made:

(a) The regulatory provisions of CEAs are directly enforceable in the sense that they prevail over any law provisions that contain less favourable provisions for the employee unless they are of mandatory nature for both parties.

(b) The provisions of the individual employment agreement prevail over those in the CEA if the first is more favourable for the employee.

(c) The provisions included in the Branch and the Business CEA prevail over those contained in the Professional CEA, even if they are less favourable for the employee.

(d) The General National CEA contains the minimum regulatory, namely, non salary provisions for the employees of the country, apart from the basic salary terms, which are determined by virtue of law provisions (ministerial decisions). Any deviation from the terms thereof to the detriment of the employees is absolutely prohibited.

(e) As long as the application of the newly enacted Medium-Term Legal Framework of Financial Strategy (provisional law) is in force, in case of concurrence between Branch and Business CEA, the Business prevails, but it cannot contain regulatory provisions less favourable for the employees than those provided under the National General CEA and basic salary provisions less favourable for the employees than those provided in the law provisions(ministerial decisions).

(f) In any case, in case of succession of CEA, the above general principle is not applicable.

6. 2. 2 Binding force and termination of the CEA

The National General CEA binds all the employees of the country, as well as those engaged in the public sector under an agreement of private nature, in legal entities of public law and in local authorities only in relation to regulatory, namely non-salary provisions. The other CEAs bind the members of the contracting parties thereof. The Business CEA bind all the employees engaged in the employer's undertaking. Accession to the CEA is allowed if made by a trade union that is not bound by any other CEA and in relation to CEAs within its competence and binds the employer.

CEA can be stipulated for a time period from one year(minimum duration) to three years(maximum duration). The CEA is effective from the date of its registration in the book kept at the Labour Inspection Authority of the competent Prefecture and the competent Central Service of the Ministry of Employment and terminates after the lapse of the time period stipulated or by a termination notice. It should be noted that either party could legally terminate the agreement for any reason, on condition that it is already in force for more than one year(minimum time limit provided under the law for terminating a Collective Labour Agreement freely). Before this period, the CEA can be terminated if the working conditions have significantly been altered.

6. 2. 3 What was the impact of new legislation as regards the CEAs and which terms thereof did it affect?

The regulatory terms of the agreements(namely those regulating the employer-employee relation) are also effective for a time period of three (instead of six) months, starting from its expiration or termination(automatic extension of validity). After the lapse of the three-month extension of validity period, the terms of the CEA are not obligatory but they remain valid as terms of contractual nature of each individual employment agreement. Under the former legislative regime at that point the terms of each individual employment agreement could not be amended unilaterally but only following the employee's prior consent(mutual amendment agreement).

Pursuant to the newly enacted legislation, in particular Law 4046/2012 and the legislative documents issued for its implementation(Act of Ministerial Council with No. 6/2012 and Interpretative Circular issued by the Ministry of Labour and Social Insurance dated March 2003), the only terms that still remain in force automatically, namely, unilaterally by the employer without the employees' consent are: (A) the basic salary/ daily wage-earnings, and (B) as regards the allowances of pecuniary nature only the (i)allowance of seniority/work experience(however only at the level that this allowance will have reached for each employee until 14 February 2012), (ii)children's allowance, (iii)studies' allowance, (iv)dangerous work, provided that the aforementioned allowances are provided under the applicable Collective Labour Agreement. This means that any other allowance provided by the CEA is automatically invalid. What is more, from 14 February 2012 onwards, any term included in Collective Labour Law Agreements that provides for any increase in salaries which is connected to the completion of a specific time period of work with the same or not employee(i. e. seniority allowance) are not applicable. In particular, their validity is suspended until the unemployment rate in Greece reaches a lower percentage than 10 percent. In addition, the new law also provides that, from 14 February 2012 onwards, any term included in Collective Labour Law Agreements that sets or implies permanence of the employees in the service is automatically abolished.

6. 3   Strikes / Lockouts

The right to strike is recognized and guaranteed by the Constitution and by virtue of Law 1264/1982 as a means for the safeguard and promotion of the rights of the employees of financial, insurance and employment nature in general. The Constitution further provides for exemptions, for instance regarding judges, and restrictions on the right to strike, for instance for professionals working for the public sector or in public utility services.

Trade unions exercise the right to strike, following a resolution by the body of the most representative trade union in the company which is competent to call a strike, namely the Board of Directors of the second and third grade trade unions and the General Assembly of the first grade unions. The employers must be given notice 24 hours in advance, as well as care for the maintenance of essential minimum service during the strike period to guarantee the safety and prevent accidents and destructions in the workplace. The security staff during a strike is determined through a special agreement between the employer and the employees. If this process is not followed, the strike is illegal.

Any employee who is a member of the union that called the strike can join it, as well as any employee of the service/branch or the undertaking that is not a member of the union that called in the strike, as well as any employee that is not member of any union but the strike was called in by the most representative union in relation to their employment rights.

To mitigate the impact of a strike going on for an extended period of time, the employer can resort to court by a petition and request that the strike is declared abusive. During the strike period, the employer cannot replace the existing employees who are on strike by hiring temporary or permanent personnel or strike-breakers.

The employer cannot prevent employees from working as a means against strike since lock-out is forbidden by the law.

6. 4　Trade/ Labour unions

The aim of trade unions is to negotiate with the employers in order to conclude a CEA. Their aim is to continuously safeguard and promote the labour, financial, social, insurance and union interests of the employees.

The trade unions are ranked as first, second and third grade trade unions. A first grade trade union may acquire the status of labour associations, local branches of trade unions of a broader area/region and legal entities. The eligibility criteria relate either to the profession or the undertaking itself or the branch of the undertaking's business activity, where the employee provides its services. The legal entity constitutes a special form of trade union, aiming at the facilitation of trade unionism in the absence of an association which has as members half of the employees and the constitution thereof is provided under specific conditions.

In fact, the requirements are that they do not have legal personality, that their founding members must be at least 10, they must deposit their founding act in the court, only one entity can be established for each undertaking, its duration cannot exceed six months, and it should expressly refer in its objectives to dealing with any problem arising out of the relation between employer and employees.

The second grade unions consist of (a) Federations, which consist of at least two labour associations and (b) Labour Centres, which consist of at least two labour associations or local branches and organise employees with the same profession.

The third grade unions consist of (a) Union of Federations and (b) Union of Labour Centres. The organisational structure of the trade unions is linked to the kind of CEA that each union can conclude, and binds respectively its members.

Chapter 7   Environmental Law

The legal framework for the protection of the natural environment is stricter compared to that of the majority of the European countries. *Inter alia*, this is attributable to the fact that Greece's territory includes extensive coastline, a large number of islands and mountainous landscape. In fact, almost 30 percent of the territory is included in the European ecological network NATURA 2000.

Naturally, the rules for the protection of the environment, the severity of which is compounded by the jurisprudence of the Supreme Administrative Court (Council of State) can affect the potential for development of investment projects. Yet, compliance with those rules facilitates the preservation of the unique natural environment and the particular landscape of the country. Hence, the development of significant investments, particularly in the areas of tourism and holiday housing, is feasible.

7. 1   The main legal framework

The core rules of the environmental protection are grouped in Article 24 of the Greek Constitution, which entrenches the environmental protection in its three aspects: the natural, the residential and the cultural.

Article 24 reads: "The protection of the natural and cultural environment constitutes a duty of the State and a right to every person. The State is bound to adopt special preventive or repressive measures for the preservation of the environment in the context of the principle of sustainable development. "[1] These principles also touch upon aspects of sustainable development, in conjunction with Article 106 of the Constitution, the prevention principle, the precautionary principle and the polluter pays principle.

Two basic pieces of legislation specifically address these constitutional rules:

---

[1] http://www. hri. org/docs/syntagma/.

the Law 1650/1986 on the protection of the natural environment and the Law 998/ 1979 on the protection of forests and forest expanses. These laws, which constitute the backbone of the legislation on the protection of the natural environment, have been consecutively modified until the present day.

During 2011 a series of laws was enacted regarding the environmental protection which aim to illustrate the legal framework and, hence, facilitate possible investments. In fact, these laws are the Law 3937/2011 on the protection of biodiversity and NATURA 2000 network areas, the Law 3982/2011 on the establishment and development of Business Parks, the Law 3983/2011 on the protection and management of the marine environment, the Law 3986/2011 on the management of public property and the Law 4014/2011 on the environmental licensing of projects and activities. ①

All these laws were connected to the Law 3894/2010 on the acceleration and transparency regarding the realisation of "Strategic Investments".

Lastly, the approval of the general and certain specific regional planning frameworks has significantly increased legal certainty in this area. In particular the "General Context of Regional Planning and Sustainable Development" (Gov. 128/A/ 03. 07. 08), the "Specific Context of Regional Planning and Sustainable Development for Renewable Energy Resources" (Gov. 246/B/03. 12. 08), the "Specific Context of Regional Planning and Sustainable Development for the Industry" (Gov. 151/AAP/13. 04. 09) as well as the "Specific Context of Regional Planning and Sustainable Development for Tourism" (Gov. 1138/B/2009).

7. 2   How the legal framework on natural environment interacts with the development of investment projects

The legal framework for the protection of the natural environment in Greece is considered stricter compared to the rest of the European countries. There is a specific process that needs to be followed to license environmental projects and activities. In fact, the settings of the Law 1650/1986 (Articles 3 and 4) on the procedure for environmental licensing were replaced by the Law 4014/2011. These provisions aim to simplify and rationalise related procedures since the previous framework was less

---

① http://investingingreece. blogspot. be/2012_02_01_archive. html? view = classic.

flexible.

The law provides that projects and activities of both public and private sector, the construction or operation of which may have an impact on the environment, are classifies in two categories(I and Ⅱ) depending on the effects on the environment. The first category (I) includes projects and activities likely to cause significant effects on the environment and which require an Environmental Impact Study(EIS) in order to impose specific conditions and restrictions for the protection of the environment on a specific project.

The second category (Ⅱ) includes projects and activities entailing local and non-significant effects on the environment which are subject to general standards, conditions and restrictions placed on environmental protection. For the new projects to fall under category I , the environmental licensing procedure must be established through holding an EIS and issuing a Decision Approving the Environmental Conditions(DAEC).

The operator of the project or activity in category I may request the opinion of the competent environmental authority with the submission of a dossier of Preliminary Determination of Environmental Requirements(PDER) , before submitting the EIS. For each new project, the Ministry of Culture and Tourism must provide an opinion on whether the region, the project or the activity is of archaeological interest, with the exception of projects or activities regulated receptors of productive activities.

An opinion of the forest service is only required for projects located in forests, groves, parks, and generally in areas outside the approved urban projects, outside the limits of settlements and outside organized receptors. The DAEC imposes conditions, terms, limitations and variations for carrying out the project or activity, in particular as regards the location, size, type, the applied technology and general technical characteristics.

Projects or activities in category Ⅱ do now follow the procedure of elaborating an EIS : yet, they are subject to Standard Environmental Commitments(SEC). These projects or activities are automatically subject to SEC with the responsibility of the competent authority, which has granted the operating permit.

7. 3   The development of investment activities in NATURA 2000 network areas

In the NATURA 2000 network areas the environmental licensing process is stricter. Nonetheless, neither the Directive 92/43/EEC on natural habitats and wild fauna and flora, nor the national legislative framework prohibits such development projects and activities, provided that they do not cause significant deterioration of the natural environment. ①

For example, the integrated touristic developments are, in principle, permissible provided that it is comprehensively deduced by the EIS that their construction and operation will not lead to a serious risk or damage to the natural environment of the region. In any case, the environmental conditions are expected to ensure sustainable development.

The Law 3937/2011, and Article 9 thereof, prohibits "especially disturbing and dangerous industrial installations covered by Directive 96/82/EC" as well as "nuisance high industrial installations". In that regard, the minimum integrity and fragmentation limit of the land in these areas is 10,000 square meters. Land areas of at least 4,000 square meters are exceptionally considered buildable in case the petitioners were already beneficiaries of these characteristics according to the existing urban planning regulations when the Law 3937/2011 was published.

Further, the Law 3937/2011, in Articles 5 and 6, provides for the adoption of presidential decrees concerning the designation of special areas with fragile ecosystems as well as the delimitation and definition of land use within their boundaries. Namely, there are three types:

(a) "Strict Nature Reserves" that include extremely sensitive ecosystems and also rare and endangered species of flora and fauna. In these areas, no activity is permitted;

(b) "Nature Reserves" include areas of high ecological or biological value. In these areas, any activity which may alter or affect their natural status is prohibited;

(c) "Nature Parks" include areas with particular environmental value due to the quality and the diversity of natural and cultural characteristics. In these parks, it

---

① http://eur-lex. europa. eu/legal-content/EN/ALL/? uri = CELEX%3A62010CJ0002.

is allowed exclusively to exercise cautious agenda and activities.

7. 4   Environmental licensing of "Strategic Investments"

According to the Law 3894/2011, Article 1, "Strategic Investments" are defined as "the productive investments which have quantitative and qualitative results of significant tension in the overall national economy and promote the country's exit from the financial crisis". The provisions of the aforementioned law seek to simplify and expedite procedures for environmental licensing of these investments. In such case, the approval of the environmental conditions must take the form of common ministerial decisions, whilst the opinions of the Services of Ministries, which approve the environmental conditions, are not required. ①

Deviations from the applicable urban planning regulations and the conditions and building restrictions that are permitted for these investments are related to the main contractor who is granted the right to use foreshore, beaches, contiguous or adjoining sea space or bottom soil. It is also provided for a special procedure that concerns the expropriation of land as well as the concession of public land for the construction, extension and modernisation of Investment Strategies. ②

7. 5   Relevant case law on environmental protection and its impact on the promotion of investments

The Supreme Administrative Court's case law has been decisive in defining the scope and particulars of environmental protection connected with investments. A key feature is the acknowledgment of priority to the protection of the environment. The control of legality on the approval acts of environmental conditions and, broadly, of environmental licensing, is strict.

The rigid application of the theory of the "environmental acquis", as well as of the "residential acquis", in a way that leaves no room for a substantial rehabilitation of a more equitable balance between environmental protection and the protection of property rights and promotion of financial development. The principle of sustainable development is indicative of the aforementioned strictness.

---

① http://media. assets. eco. on. ca/web/2016/04/The-Environmental-Bill-of-Rights-Your-Environment-Your-Rights. pdf.

② http://ec. europa. eu/environment/nature/conservation/species/guidance/pdf/guidance_en. pdf.

Settled case law of the Court provides that the natural environment is a separately protected good in order for the ecological balance and preservation of natural resources to be ensured in favour of subsequent generations. When taking measures of environmental protection, the various executive power bodies, with respect to the principle of sustainable development, ought to consider more factors regarding the wider national and public interest. For instance, this includes those relating to the purposes of financial development, management of national wealth, aid for regional development and ensuring labour to citizens.

Nonetheless, the pursuit of these purposes and the weighting of the relevant legal goods must be combined with the obligation that the State has to ensure the protection of the environment in a way as to ensure the constituent and, at the same time, community-legislator intended sustainable development. Towards this direction, the competent state instruments must take into account the existence of any special risk for the natural environment, emerging from the construction and operation of a particular project or the development of a specific activity.

In any case, and towards the evaluation of the situation to be consistent with the need to protect each conflicting legitimate goods, one must expose the way and method of construction and operation of the establishment, as well as the particular nature of public interest. Since the above-imposed evaluation reflects the type and extent of the imminent harm, this will relate to the nature of the project that needs to be justified.

It is expected that the Court of State will be more lenient in the years to come, particularly since the country is committed to a more intense developmental trajectory compared to the past, which necessitates more licences to be awarded.

Chapter 8   Laws Relating to Dispute Resolution Concerning Foreign Entities

8.1   Dispute resolution in courts of law

8.1.1   The process in domestic courts

Private law disputes fall under the jurisdiction of the civil courts, meaning that all legal relations under private law that have been disturbed and require judicial protection are governed by private law and they are tried exclusively at the civil courts. The case is introduced to the court by the plaintiff filing an action with the competent court of first instance.

For cases which fall under the jurisdiction of civil courts of first instance the competent courts are:

- The Court of the Peace(for claims up to EUR 20,000);
- The Single-Member Court of First Instance (for claims up to EUR 250,000);
- The Multi-Member Court of First Instance(for claims worth more than EUR 250,000).

The territorial competence is decided by the location of the residence of the defender, as well as, by other criteria, such as the location where has been contracted the disputed legal act, the location of the disputed immovable property etc. Disputes under private law are tried according to their type following two basic procedures:

- The Ordinary Procedure;
- The Special Proceedings.

The difference between the Special Proceedings and the Ordinary Procedure is the completion of the hearing of the case in one only oral discussion without the strictly typical system of written pretrial preparatory work, which is obligatory in the case of the Ordinary Procedure. Eventually in the Special Proceedings besides the filling and servicing of the action, all other procedures take place during the trial where the defenders submit their rebuttals presenting the appropriate evidence. Within three working days after the trial, the parties may submit their rebuttals to the other party's claims.

All disputes under private law fall to be considered under the Ordinary Procedure with the exemption of those disputes that explicitly fall to be considered under Special Proceedings.

The basic stages of the Ordinary Procedure are:

• Filing an action with the material and territorially competent Court.

• Within 30 days from the submission of the action, a copy of this action should be served to the defendant. Should the defendant resides abroad or is of an unknown address the serving deadline is 60 days.

• Within a period of 100 days from the submission of the action, the pleadings of the parties, as well as, any documents and supporting evidence must be filed with the competent secretariat. Should the defendant resides abroad or is of an unknown address the deadline is 130 days.

• Within 15 days from the completion of the file, the composition of the court is defined and, after 30 days from defining the composition a trial day is set. If pleadings are not submitted by the parties, the trial is postponed and, within a period of 60 days from its postponement the trial date may be set again and the new trial date is served to the parties. Otherwise, the action is considered to be unfounded.

• Issue of a final judgment.

8.1.2   Appeal before the courts of first instance

With the exception of the Courts of the Peace judgments on minor disputes (e. g. disputes for claims and rights on movable property with a value non exceeding the EUR 5,000) which are irrevocable, an appeal may be filed for the judgments of the Courts of the Peace, the Single-Member and Multi-Member Courts of First Instance in case that they are final and conclude the first degree trial.

The party which lost the case has a right to appeal. The party who won the first degree trial may file for an appeal only if it has a legitimate interest. The appeal is filed within a period of 30 days from the serving of the contested decision to the other party (a period of 60 days if the respondent is a foreign resident or its residency is unknown).

The deadline for filing for an appeal, in case that the first degree decision is not served, shall be two years, and starts from the day of its publication aiming to a timely and binding *res judicata* in order to speed up the administration of justice in its entirety.

The deadline for filing an appeal, as well as, the right to appeal, assuming that is taking place legally and on time, prevent the execution of the contested judgment, except in case that the first degree judgment has been declared by the court of first instance as provisionally enforceable.

The Court of the Peace judgments are contested in the Single-Member Court of First Instance. Respectively, the judgments of the Single-Member Court of First Instance are contested in the Single-Member Court of Appeals and the judgments of the Single-Member Court of Appeals are contested in the Three-Member Court of Appeals.

8. 1. 3 Appeal before the Supreme Court

The judgments of the Courts of the Peace, Courts of First Instance and Courts of Appeal are challenged before the Supreme Court by the appeal of cassation. Cassation is an appeal which disputes the court judgment on substance for legal defects.

Cassation is permitted only against *res judicata*, meaning judgments against which an appeal is prohibited either because the law does not foresee such possibility or because a judgment on the appeal has been issued or because the appellee waived its right to appeal.

If the appellee is a Greek resident, the deadline for a cassation is 30 days from the date of serving the contested judgment, while if it is a foreign resident the deadline is 60 days. If the judgment is not served, the deadline is two years and starts on the date of the publication of the judgment which terminates the trial.

However, with the exclusion of matrimonial 60 cases, the deadline for cassation, as well as, its effect do not inhibit the execution of the judgment subject to cassation.

8. 1. 4 Enforcement of foreign judgments

Foreign judgments are enforceable in Greece irrespective of the country where they have been issued. This can be done by virtue of EU law instruments for the judgments emanating from other member states, by virtue of bilateral conventions and by virtue of the Greek Code of Civil Procedure for the rest of the world. Under Greek law, enforcement is different to recognition, which takes place automatically without any particular procedure, provided that the relevant reasons of non-recognition of Greek law are observed.

Greece is party to all EU regulations in the field of judicial cooperation in civil matters. A large number of these regulations are integral to international business transactions. For instance, Regulation 44/2001 of the Council on jurisdiction and the recognition and enforcement of judgments in civil and commercial matters (Brussels I),① Regulation (EC) No. 1896/2006 of the European Parliament and of the Council of 12 December 2006 creating a European Order for payment procedure (we refer to this regulation as well even though the "payment order" is not a "judgment" as such), Regulation (EC) No. 805/2004 of the European Parliament and of the Council creating a European Enforcement Order for uncontested claims and Regulation 861/2007 of the European Parliament and of the Council of 11 July 2007 establishing a European small claims procedure.

Practically, judgments as well as payment orders issued in other member states will be enforced in Greece under the provisions of these regulations and provided that they fall in their field of application. Greek courts are very careful with the application of the provisions for non-enforcement of foreign judgments under Brussels I Regulation. Very rarely are judgments denied enforceability in Greece, and when this is the case it is limited to the ones of Art. 34 of Brussels I Regulation. ②

8. 2   Alternative dispute resolution (ADR)

8. 2. 1   Scope and application of domestic Arbitration according to CCP

In principle, the Code of Civil Procedure (CCP) regulates the so-called domestic arbitration, where no extraneous elements are present. On the other hand, Statute No. 2735/1999, under which Greece adopted UNCITRAL's Model Law on international commercial arbitration, governs international commercial arbitration. The CCP is applicable for international arbitrations usually on an ancillary basis, if an issue is not directly regulated by Statute No. 2735/1999.

Both existing and future private disputes that result from a legal relationship can be referred to arbitration. Yet, disputes arising from public-law relationships and administrative claims cannot, in principle, be referred to arbitration. Law also prohibits resulting to arbitration in employment disputes, disputes relating to public order or in

①   http://eur-lex. europa. eu/legal-content/EN/TXT/? uri = URISERV%3Al33054.

②   http://www. loble. co. uk/enforcement_of_foreign_judgments. html.

cases inextricably linked to the protection of human personality. As for public-private contracts for public works, the law stipulates that arbitration may be agreed upon in disputes arising from the performance of such contracts. However, if stipulated by law, tax-related disputes may be resolved by arbitration. Arbitration is, finally, not a valid dispute resolution method in cases that concern voluntary jurisdiction, such as child adoption.

Both natural and legal persons may enter into arbitration agreements. All persons agreeing to arbitration must have the legal capacity and the right to dispose of the object of arbitration. In principle, the arbitration agreement must be in writing, either in a separate contract or in the main contract. The arbitration clause does not have to form part of an official document(e. g. private contract). [1] Simply exchanging signed letters, telegrams, faxes etc. is sufficient to establish an arbitration agreement. The law does not stipulate a minimum content for the arbitration clause. A simple statement referring disputes to arbitration shall suffice. Any unspecified condition is usually accounted for by the Code. However, because one of arbitration's greatest advantages is precisely the freedom for the parties involved to use their own initiative, it is often preferable to provide at least for the main details of the process.

8.2.2   Appointment

Any natural person with legal capacity who has not been deprived of his/her civic rights can be appointed arbitrator. There may be one or more arbitrators. Sole-arbitrator tribunals offer higher speed in issuing an award and are less costly. However, multiple-member arbitral tribunals offer greater assurance as to the impartiality of the award issued. In multiple-member tribunals, both parties appoint an equal number of arbitrators.

As a rule, there is also an umpire, who is either provided by the parties in the arbitration clause, or otherwise appointed by the arbitrators. As to magistrates and prosecutors, they are selected from a list by the President of the Court of First Instance and must have at least five years of experience. They can either be the sole member of an arbitral tribunal or umpires. It is forbidden by law to directly name or indirectly suggest a particular judge in the agreement. There are three appointment methods for arbitrators and umpires:

---

[1]   http://eur-lex. europa. eu/legal-content/EN/TXT/? uri = CELEX%3A52010PC0748.

(a) By agreement of the parties. This constitutes one of arbitration's major attractions since the parties can expressly name the arbitrators(given that these are not magistrates). If no appointment method is provided in the agreement,each party has the right to call the other to appoint arbitrators within a period of eight days,while at the same time notifying their own arbitrator(s) of their appointment.

(b) Directly by law. If there is no agreement as to the number of arbitrators, each party shall choose one arbitrator and call the other party to choose an arbitrator too,as above.

(c) By court order,in cases where it is impossible to appoint arbitrators by mutual agreement or by law. The Single-Member Court of First Instance of the arbitration's seat,or otherwise of the applicant's address, or otherwise of the state's capital issues a decision,on application filed by any one party,or by the arbitrators if it concerns the umpire's appointment.

The CCP provides for the possibility of establishing,by decrees,arbitration organisations called permanent arbitration boards in chambers,stock and commodity exchanges or professional associations. After special agreement of the parties within the arbitration clause,such organisations may conduct the arbitration. While arbitration organisations are governed by the CCP,decrees may provide for different types of disputes subject to each organisation's jurisdiction,the seat of arbitration etc. Thus,to this day,arbitration organisations have been established in Bar Associations across the country,the Technical Chamber of Greece,in Professional,Commercial and Industrial Chambers as well as the Stock Exchange etc.

8.2.3   Arbitration particulars

Contrary to international arbitration,there is no single rule that governs the commencement of arbitral proceedings in domestic arbitration. Ways to initiate such proceedings vary depending on whether the parties decide to use an arbitration organisation or not.

Remuneration is determined by the arbitral tribunal according to what appears fair and reasonable. The party that initiates the hearing advances half of the remuneration. In exceptional cases, a 50 percent cut on the remuneration and the advance payment may be granted. 20 percent of the remuneration is paid to the financial fund for the court premises,though this percentage and related deductions shall differ in case a magistrate is appointed arbitrator. The law provides for the possibility of making a claim against the arbitral provision which stipulates remuneration and expenses.

The period for issuing the arbitral award may be fixed by the agreement of the parties and may be either indicative or peremptory. This agreement is independent of the agreement referring disputes to arbitration, unless the parties decide that the agreement's termination shall coincide with the expiration of the deadline for issuing an award. If there is no agreement for a peremptory period, the competent Court of First Instance shall set a reasonable and fair time-limit for this purpose.

The arbitration agreement may provide the time and way of its termination. If not, in principle, the agreement terminates by agreement of the parties in writing. Termination may also occur for reasons concerning the arbitrators (death, refusal to accept appointment, absence of replacement or method to appoint one, impossibility to provide the arbitral services). Furthermore, termination may occur in case of a delay in conducting the arbitration or issuing the award, or if the agreed deadline for issuing an award has expired, if no extension has been made. If there is no such agreement, the arbitration agreement terminates with the expiration of the deadline set, upon request, by the competent Court of First Instance.

Further, the arbitration agreement may also terminate for general reasons for which substantive law contracts terminate (e. g. change of circumstances, repudiation of agreement, right abuse, annulment because of error, fraud or threat etc.). Finally, the agreement terminates when the arbitral award is issued, having served its purpose. However, an arbitration clause remains in force since it extends to future disputes.

8. 2. 4   The arbitral procedure

The arbitral procedure is set out by agreement of the parties. The agreement in question is independent of the arbitration agreement, and is not required in written form. The CCP provides for some mandatory judicial prerequisites, namely compliance with the principle of equality and the right to be heard. If there is no agreement as to the procedure to be followed, this is determined by the arbitrators, who have the right to use any rules (including foreign rules). The parties appear in person or are represented by a lawyer. ①

If a party is called to participate and fails to do so, the arbitration will take place in their absence. Arbitrators shall determine their jurisdiction. Arbitrators cannot impose penalties or order compulsory measures for the submission of evidence, except if

---

① http://www.iclg.co.uk/practice-areas/international-arbitration-/international-arbitration-2015/france.

the arbitrator is a state court. Arbitrators can refer the taking of evidence to the Court of the Peace. The arbitrators cannot order, reform or revoke interim measures. If, after an interim measure is taken, the law or the court requires that the action be brought within a specific time-limit, the claimant must cause arbitral proceedings to start within the given time-limit, or the interim measure is withdrawn.

The agreement of the parties determines the applicable law. It can be a foreign law or the common practices of a particular field. In the absence of an agreement thereof, the dispute resolution obeys the enforced substantive law. The parties have the right to relieve the arbitrators from the obligation to apply the substantive law, allowing them to judge according to what is fair and just.

8. 2. 5   Issuing, appealing and annulling an award

An arbitration panel decides on the award by a majority vote. In case it cannot be reached, the umpire's decision prevails. The award is considered complete after the arbitrators sign it. The original document must be submitted to the Court of First Instance, and all interested parties must receive a copy.

The award is binding to the parties. Unless there is a pending action or claim on its deficiency, it has the same effects as a final court judgment. In particular, (a) primary effects, namely *res judicata* status and enforceability and (b) secondary effects between the parties, e. g. the arbitral award can serve as a title to raise a mortgage. ①

The arbitral award is not subject to any ordinary appeal process, or exceptional review procedure. A special agreement can provide for the possibility of recourse to other arbitrators against the arbitral award, with the aim of re-arbitrating the dispute rather than conducing a second-level review of the arbitral award. The time-limit, conditions and hearing method of the appeal must be agreed, no later than the award issuance date.

The right of annulment is provided exclusively for reasons regulated by the CCP. These are:

(a) for reasons concerning the arbitration agreement (agreement nullity and termination);

(b) for reasons concerning the arbitral tribunal (illegal composition or constitu-

---

① www. ila-hq. org/download. cfm/docid/446043C4 – 9770 – 434D-AD7DD42F7E8E81C6.

tion and excess of power);

(c) for reasons concerning the arbitration procedure (breach of the principle of equality or the right to a fair hearing or procedural defects, namely infringements in the method of issuing, drafting and signing the award, unintelligibility or inclusion of contradictory provisions);

(d) if the award is contrary to Greek public order or moral values;

(e) for all the reasons of review provided under Article 544 of the CCP, as interpreted through the flexible scope of arbitration.

In practice, the claim for annulment is brought before the Court of Appeal of the region where the court judgment was issued, within three months of the notification, and is heard according to the special proceedings for labour disputes. When brought for the reasons laid down in Article 544 of the CCP, there is a 60-day delay if the claimant is Greek resident and a 120-day delay if the claimant resides in foreign territory or his/her residence is unknown. The delay period starts running varyingly according to the reason triggering the review, as laid down in Article 545 of the CCP. Three remedies are applicable against the Court of Appeal's decision: setting aside default judgment, review and appeal. Because bringing an annulment action does not suspend the enforcement of the arbitral judgment, it is possible to request suspension to the competent court, according to injunction proceedings.

The award can also be declared inexistent, either by objection or by independent action, exclusively for the reasons provided in the CCP, namely:

(i) there was no arbitration agreement;

(ii) the arbitral award was issued in relation to a matter that could not be subject to arbitration proceedings;

(iii) the arbitral award was issued against a non-existent natural or legal person.

The action is brought before the Court of Appeal of the region where the judgment was issued. Bringing the action does not suspend the enforcement of the arbitral award.

8. 2. 6   International arbitration

Arbitration is a form of alternative dispute resolution that differs from ordinary civil courts, excluding their jurisdiction. It is very flexible since it gives parties the freedom to decide all aspects of the arbitration process like the seat, arbitrators and award issuing method, with the sole limitation being to observe public policy rules. The award is generally issued by experienced professionals who are familiar with the particularities of the dispute. Arbitration can also offer confidentiality and is usually quicker compared to court proceedings. Yet, arbitration has received criticism over the past years for its non-binding nature for third parties, as well as the expenses associated with it, which can be substantially higher than normal court proceedings. ①

International Commercial Arbitration is regulated by Law No. 2735/1999. In this law, Greece transposed the UNCITRAL Model Law on International Commercial Arbitration of 21 June 1985, save for minor amendments. According to applicable law, arbitration proceedings are foreign if:

　• one or both of the litigant parties is established outside Greek territory;

　• the place of arbitration or execution of a commercial agreement is located outside Greek territory; or

　• the subject matter of the arbitration agreement is more closely connected with one or more countries.

Essentially, the UNCITRAL Model Law was transposed onto the Greek legal system by Law 2735/1999. The main differences between Law 2735/1999 and the UNCITRAL Model Law are summarised as follows:

　• Law 2735/1999 does not allow requests to set aside a partial award on the arbitral tribunal's jurisdiction. Only requests for setting aside final awards are allowed under Law 2735/1999.

　• According to Law 2735/1999, arbitral awards ordering interim measures or provisional relief are not enforceable upon issuance by the arbitral tribunal. Their enforceability is proclaimed by the court.

　• Unlike the provisions of the UNCITRAL Model Law, Law 2735/1999 states that arbitral awards constitute *res judicata* and are enforceable as of the date they are issued without any requirement for filing with the local court.

　• A Greek court may set aside an award because it deals with a dispute not contemplated by or not falling within the terms of the arbitration agreement, whereas the UNCITRAL Model Law provides as reason for setting aside an arbitral award the fact that it deals with a dispute not contemplated by or not falling within the terms of the submission to arbitration.

Greece is also a contracting party to the New York Convention (NYC) on the Recognition and Enforcement of Foreign Arbitral Awards, ratified pursuant to Law

---

　① http://www. mediate. com/articles/grant. cfm.

No. 4220/1961, without any declarations or reservations and in force since 14 October 1962. For states who are not part to NYC, Greece had been a contracting party to the Geneva Protocol of 24 September 1923, pursuant to Legislative Decree No. 4/1926 and, later, to the Geneva Convention of 1927 for the Enforcement of Foreign Arbitral Awards, pursuant to Law No. 5013/1931.

As for Investment Arbitration, Greece is a contracting party to the Washington Convention of 1968 on the settlement of investment disputes between states and nationals of other State(the ICSID Convention), ratified by the Law No. 608/1968, and in force since 1969. [1]

In connection with that, Greece has signed 44 Bilateral Investment Treaties that regulate investment disputes arising between Greece and investing nationals or legal entities of the other contracting State.

In order to settle the dispute, and apart from the *ad hoc* Arbitral Tribunals, the most prominent Permanent Arbitral Tribunals in Greece are:

- The Arbitral Tribunal of the Athens Chamber of Commerce and Industry (www. acci. gr);
- The Greek Centre of Mediation and Arbitration(www. sae-epe. gr);
- The Hellenic Chamber of Shipping(www. nee. gr);
- The Piraeus Association for Maritime Arbitration(www. pama. gr);
- The Organisation of Mediation and Arbitration to support collective bargaining between social partners;
- Panels organized by respective Bar Associations(as www. dsa. gr);
- Panel organized by the Technical Chamber of Greece(www. tcg. gr);
- Panel organized by the Stock Exchange of Athens(www. sea. gr).

8. 2. 7 Mediation

Mediation is a structured process, regardless of how it is named or referred to, whereby two or more parties to a dispute attempt to reach a voluntary settlement agreement with a mediator's assistance. This definition excludes any attempts to settle the dispute made by a Magistrate Judge or a Judge, pursuant to Articles 208 *et seq* and 233 of CCP, in the context of judicial proceedings and is conducted out of the Court's premises and at a private provider. Mediation in Greece is regulated by Law

---

[1] http://www. gregorioulaw. gr/index. php? option = com_content&view = article&id = 97&Itemid = 283&lang = en.

3898/2010 under the title "Mediation in Civil and Commercial Matters", published in the *Official Gazette of the Hellenic Republic*, Volume A, No. 211 on 16 December 2010.

Disputes under private law can be submitted to mediation provided that the parties involved are entitled to freely dispose the object of the dispute and settle by any means of a compromise. Furthermore, the Greek Law on Mediation implements the EU Directive 2008/52/EC "on certain aspects of mediation in Civil and Commercial Matters in cross-border disputes" of the European Parliament and the Council and its scope also explicitly covers all civil and commercial cases in cross-border disputes within the EU except from rights and obligations which are not at the parties disposal under the relevant applicable law. Mediation Law shall not extend, in particular, to revenue, customs or administrative matters or to the liability of the state for acts and omissions in the exercise of State authority (*acta iure imperii*).

The Greek authorities have recently amended the Code of Civil Procedure to optimise access to justice and introduce judicial mediation in the Court-connected scheme. Specific provisions regulate several ADR processes, such as Conciliation, Judicial/ Court-Settlement, Judicial Mediation and Mediation for resolving disputes in an amicable, cost-effective and time-effective way.

According to Law 4055/2012 and Law 4139/2013, parties can recourse to Judicial Mediation both prior to litigation and after the occurrence of *lis pendens* for cases applicable both before the Court of First Instance and the Court of Appeal. [1] The multi-door scheme has therefore been enriched and gives from now on access to resolution through many procedures within the Courts. As per the provisions of the CCP (Article 214A of CCP), after the occurrence of *lis pendens* and until a final decision, litigants may attempt to reconcile through negotiation efforts regardless of the standing stage of the trial and by acting out of its proceedings with or without the engagement of a third person.

Disputes of private law nature are heard with all parties present through a Judicial/Court-Settlement. This is a Court-based Settlement procedure that is initiated and facilitated by the sitting Judge/s and is regulated and provided for all Court hearings under the provisions of the CCP (Article 233). This procedure can be initiated after the commencement of the hearing of the case and at every stage of the trial until a fi-

---

[1] http://www.hiifl.gr/wp-content/uploads/10_Diamantopoulos-Koumpli.pdf.

nal decision is reached. Attempt for a settlement can be continued at a subsequent day and at another place within the Court's premises or it can be adjourned restrictively. ①

According to another provision of the CCP(Article 208), Magistrates Judges at all Courts of Peace have the duty to attempt settlement before the first hearing of every case. They are also entitled to refer the case to another Magistrate, even from another prefecture, if they believe this would be appropriate for the likelihood of a successful resolution.

Recourse to Mediation suspends temporarily and until the end of the mediation process any judicial proceeding. It is determined by Mediation Law that limitation or prescription periods for a claim subject to mediation shall cease to run during mediation proceedings initiated by recourse to mediation. In the event of the mediation being terminated without a settlement agreement, the limitation and prescription periods shall continue to run from the moment the mediation proceedings are terminated. To that respect the Mediation shall be terminated as follows: by a written statement from the mediator to the parties stating that the mediation has ended unsuccessfully, by a written statement from either party to the other party and to the mediator stating that it withdraws from the mediation or by any other way of abolition of the mediation (Article 3 par. 1 & Article 11).

8. 2. 8　The mediator

The mediator is a neutral third body that meets the specific qualifications required by the relevant legislation (Mediation Law, Presidential Decree and specific Ministerial Decisions of the Greek Ministry of Justice, Transparency and Human Rights(MoJ)) and who is asked to conduct Mediation in an effective, impartial and competent way, regardless of the way in which it has been appointed or requested to conduct the mediation(Article 4c).

Mediations in domestic disputes can only be conducted by lawyers that have been trained adequately, assessed accordingly and have been accredited as mediators by the Administration Directorate General of the Greek Ministry of Justice, Transparency and Human Rights. The MoJ forms a panel with a list of the names and short bios of all registered and licensed Mediators that can conduct mediations in Greece.

---

①　http://www.diamesolavisi.net/kiosk/pdf/Greek%20Law%20Digest.pdf.

This panel is distributed to all courts and is also posted at the Ministry of Justice website. Mediations in cross-border disputes can be conducted by accredited mediators who come from various professions and are not exclusively lawyers (Articles 4c & 7).

8. 2. 9 Structure of mediation procedure

The Law on Mediation draws the general lines of a very open framework where the parties, along with the mediator, can work together in consultation, on the basis of voluntariness, making an effort to resolve their issue and reserving their right to put an end to the mediation at any time. There are strict provisions only with regard to confidentiality, the prohibition of keeping records and the restrictions in communicating each party's information during his/her meetings with them without their consent. Procedure is structured in a customary way depending on the parties and the needs of the issues to be resolved (Article 8). ①

On the acceptance of his/her instruction the mediator draws up a mediation agreement with specific rules regarding breach of confidentiality and the range of the confidentiality issues that are covered, unless otherwise agreed by the parties. Confidentiality can be agreed even on the content of the agreement of settlement if ever reached, unless its disclosure is necessary for the enforcement of the agreement. Mediation agreement determines the whole process and after been signed up before the beginning of the mediation initiates the procedure (Article 10 par. 1).

Finally, it is mandatory and hence mediation cannot take place unless parties or their legal representatives (for legal entities) proceed to mediation with their lawyers throughout the duration of the procedure (Article 8 par. 1).

8. 2. 10 Successful-Unsuccessful outcome

The minutes of the agreement should be recorded in writing and undersigned. A litigant can unilaterally submit the original undersigned minutes to be ratified by the judge or presiding judge before whom the case is pending. Ratification is given provided that the judge ascertains that: (a) the dispute qualifies for settlement by means of a compromise, (b) minutes have been lawfully undersigned and (c) the nature of the right which was acknowledged, as well as the amount of the consideration due and the terms of its fulfilment clearly arise out of submitted minutes. Following the

---

① http://www. wipo. int/export/sites/www/about-ip/en/iprm/pdf/ch2. pdf.

ratification process and depending on the nature of the claim minutes accordingly constitute an enforceable title or merely evidence of entitlement and result in abolition of proceedings.

If the attempt is unsuccessful, CCP provisions dictate that this event has no effect to the trial's outcome and all judicial remarks and proposals, as well as parties' positions and recessions expressed for the sake of the attempt, are disregarded by the court while reaching its decision. ①

In the event of a mediation successfully leading to a settlement, the mediator draws up a mediation agreement record, which should contain the following: the mediator's full name; the location and time of the mediation meeting; the full names of the participants; the agreement to mediate upon which the mediation session was based; the agreement reached . At the end of the mediation session, the mediation a-greement record is signed by the mediator, the parties and their lawyers. The Mediator can submit the original agreement unilaterally, upon the request of one of the parties, to the Secretariat of the Court of First Instance of the local jurisdiction where the mediation took place. Once submitted in this manner, the mediation agreement becomes enforceable(Article 9).

8. 2. 11   Cost and advantages of mediation

A mediator cannot charge an hourly fee for more than 24 hours of work. The 24-hours fee ceiling also includes time spent for preliminary mediation preparation. The parties and the Mediator can agree on a different structure of charging. The hourly rate of a Mediator is defined by a decision of the minister of Justice, Transparency and Human Rights. The current hourly fee that is set by latest Ministerial Decision 85485/2012(Off. Gaz. B 3417/21-12-2012)is at the amount of EUR 100. Unless the parties agree otherwise, each party is obliged to pay half of the mediator's fee, and each party pays his or her own attorney's fee(Article 12). ②

Greek law provisions are mainly focused on ensuring high protection for parties' interests in mediation in five main directions:In terms of wide range of confidentiali-ty, limitation and prescription periods, taking measures to ensure mediator's quality and professional competence, rapid and unilaterally submitted enforcement of settle-ment agreements and reasonable cost.

---

① http://www. potamitisvekris. com/wp-content/uploads/2015/06/fil_publications271696711. pdf.

② http://www. lcia. org/Dispute_Resolution_Services/LCIA_Mediation_Costs. aspx.

Further incentives include that mediated agreements are not subject to judicial stamp costs in order to become enforceable. According to Greek Law 4111/2013 such specific costs for filed cases are fixed at eight percent of the value of the claim surcharged by 37. 4 percent. For the mediated cases this does not apply and there is only a procedural fee of EUR 100 applicable(Ministerial Decision 85485/2012).

Hungary

Writing Group led by Professor József Hajdú

About the Authors

Dr József Hajdú is a Professor of Labour Law and Social Security Law at the U-niversity of Szeged, Faculty of Law and Political Sciences in Hungary and elected member of the European Committee of Social Rights at the Council of Europe, Strasbourg, France.

Dr Erika Farkas Csamangó is a senior lecturer PhD at the Universiy of Szeged Faculty of Law and Political Sciences Institute of Business Law.

Dr Klára Gellén is an associate professor (PhD habil.) at the University of Szeged, Faculty of Law and Political Science, head of the Institute of Business Law.

Dr Peter Hegyes is a senior lecturer PhD at the Universiy of Szeged Faculty of Law and Political Sciences Institute of Business Law.

Dr Orsolya Johanna Sziebig (lawyer) is currently working as an assistant lecturer at the University of Szeged Faculty of Law and Political Sciences, International and European Law Department and she is undertaking PhD studies at the same university. She is the Hungarian assistant coordinator of Regional Academy on the United Nations.

Dr Benedek Tóth is lecturer at the University of Szeged and individual attorney at law in the fields of international business law, international commercional law and private international law.

Introduction

József Hajdú

Hungary is a landlocked Central European country, the 16th largest in Europe ($93,030 \text{ km}^2$). It is a member of the European Union since 1 May 2004 and a member of the Schengen area since 2007. Its neighbours are: Slovakia, to the north; Ukraine, to the north-east; Romania, to the east; Serbia, Croatia and Slovenia to the south; and Austria to the west. Hungary's climate is temperate, being influenced by three important climate zones: oceanic, continental and Mediterranean. [1]

The population of Hungary totals 9,909,000 (January 2013). [2] The population is projected to fall to 9.2 million by 2060 (European Commission, 2015). [3] With a population of 1.7 million inhabitants, Budapest has the role of economic and political centre of the country. [4] Hungary's main ethnic group is Hungarian (92.3 percent). Its most numerous minorities include: Romany (five percent), Germans, Romanians, Slovakians, Serbians and Ukrainians. [5] English is widely spoken in Hungary, particularly among the younger generation.

Located in the heart of Europe, Hungary offers ideal access to European common market of more than 500 million people. But getting started and running business operations in the country can be a difficult endeavour without having local help on board. [6]

---

[1]   It can experience dramatic weather changes. The weather in winter is rather cold, cloudy and damp, or windy, while summers are warm to hot and dry.

[2]   Population ageing is more advanced in Hungary than in other countries; indeed, the population peaked in 1981 at nearly 11 million and the fertility rate is one of the lowest in Europe.

[3]   http://www. oecd. org/eco/surveys/hungary-2016-OECD-economic-survey-overview. pdf (accessed on 12 May 2016)

[4]   The largest Hungarian cities, beside Budapest, are: Debrecen (205,000), Miskolc (178,000), Szeged (164,000), Pécs (159,000) and Györ (126,000).

[5]   http://businessculture. org/eastern-europe/hungary/(accessed on 3 May 2016).

[6]   http://www. tmf-group. com/en/media-centre/resources/top-challengesemeahungary (accessed on 13 May 2016).

Hungary has capitalised on its ideal geographical position to become a manufacturing, services and logistics powerbase. Excellent infrastructure, ready-made industrial sites, offices and science parks combined with a good balance of labour costs and quality make it an ideal location for expanding firms to build a presence within Europe's consumer market.

Governmental incentives—from cash subsidies to tax allowances—are available for foreign firms looking to grow in Hungary, making up an investment friendly economic policy. A competitive tax system and strong, modern economy have also proved to be big pull factors for international firms looking to grow.

But despite the attractiveness of the Hungarian business environment, there are several areas of business operations which can be difficult to navigate for foreign companies. The World Bank and International Finance Corporation(IFC)rank Hungary outside the top 100 nations in the world for ease of getting electricity, investor protection and paying taxes, which is why having local expertise to help navigate these difficult areas is crucial. Hence, starting a business, company must be represented by a lawyer when setting up a corporate entity in Hungary who will represent the company, create the company deeds and prepare all other legal documents.

In their business dealings, Hungarians tend to be formal, adhering to hierarchical organizational structures, and yet expressive, with typical negotiations taking place through open dialogue. Hungarians are also generally outspoken and for this reason some foreigners may perceive them as abrupt, rude or even cruel. However, they always provide evidence in support of their words and when they cannot reach an agreement they tend to explain why and may propose new talks.

In business and in private life, the right relationships are important and common sense and discernment are much. The Hungarians' tendency towards distrust and suspicion can be attributed to historical reasons, so unpleasant points are discussed to mitigate future business problems as much as possible. The first meeting is always characterized by a reserved attitude but, once the ice is broken, Hungarians are rather passionate and their verbal exchanges can be very intense and spirited.

A Hungarian business partner can easily turn into a friend. Nevertheless, building a trusting relationship usually takes a long time. A good sociable atmosphere at work plays a bigger role than other factors(business results, financial statements). When they feel part of an inspiring project, Hungarians show passion, originality, generosity and industry. Important decisions are usually made by the top management, which may sometimes slow down the talks.

Young people are enthusiastic about trying their chances abroad or in different areas in Hungary, but the older generation is generally reluctant to move around, being attached to the places and the people they are used to.

Some of the major industries are: mining, metallurgy, textiles, chemicals, construction, processed food, motor vehicle manufacturing and agriculture. Among the areas of recent growth, one can find the domains of retail, services, telecommunications, finance, machinery and the pharmaceutical industry. ①

A key driver behind faster growth is more rapid business capital accumulation. Inward FDI and EU structural funds are strong investment drivers. On the other hand, domestic business investment, particularly by SMEs, is held back by a frequently changing regulatory environment and entry barriers in network industries. Reforms on these fronts could increase the integration of domestic firms, which are overwhelmingly SMEs, into global value chains. ②

Hungary's participation in the global value chains is among the highest in the OECD. This success is linked to the large presence of foreign firms in the (intertwined) electrical and transport equipment producing sectors, which are characterised by high inflows of inward FDI and intensive links with manufacturing in other countries, especially Germany. The multinational companies behind this inward FDI typically use a high share of foreign produced intermediates in their production or rely on inputs from foreign-owned producers in Hungary. In contrast, domestically-owned producers of intermediate inputs have been less successful than in other countries in integrating themselves into the production chain of the large foreign-owned exporters, which means that the value added in exports is relatively low. In addition, producers of intermediate inputs have a relatively low contribution to the production of other countries' exports (known as low "forward participation" in global value chains). Moreover, services contribute less to manufacturing exports than in any other European country. As a consequence, Hungary has missed out on direct services provision, such as communication, but also indirect services that help to differentiate and up-

---

① http://businessculture. org/eastern-europe/hungary/(accessed on 13 May 2016).

② http://www. oecd. org/eco/surveys/hungary-2016-OECD-economic-survey-overview. pdf(accessed on 12 May 2016).

grade products (such as design, development, and marketing). ①

As for educational standards, just as in other European countries, the educational standards are similar for all levels of education. This offers the advantage of compatible education with other countries. During undergraduate studies, certain specializations require the students to go through a practical work experience. ②

One of the competitive advantages Hungary has compared to other countries in the region is the government's strong commitment to streamlining business processes and to increasing the competitiveness of both SMEs and large enterprises in Hungary through a wide range of available incentives.

Hungary work culture is mainly based on seriousness, good quality and respect of the customers. The working program is according with the international labour regulation of 40 hours per week, but it could be extended since the employees are interested in additional income. Second jobs are also an option for the once interested, the general behaviour is in favour of work.

Punctual and dedicated to their jobs, Hungarians are efficient at their working position no matter the field of activity. In business they are hard negotiators, but once their obligations are settled the results are on the way.

Both refundable and non-refundable incentives are available to investors going to or expanding in Hungary. The main types of incentives related to investments are cash subsidies (either from the Hungarian Government or from EU Funds), tax incentives, low-interest loans, or land available for free or at reduced prices. The regulations on incentive opportunities are in accordance with EU rules. ③

The central location of Hungary makes the country optimal for manufacturing, services and logistics. Hungary is the ideal base for investors who are planning cross-border business developments. Foreign capital is, in a large part, attracted by the highly skilled and highly educated labour force, particularly in the engineering, IT, pharmaceutical, economics, mathematics, physics and professional services sectors. Around two-thirds of the workforce in Hungary has completed a secondary, technical or vocational education.

The average wages in Hungary are 60 percent less than the average of the EU

---

① http://www. oecd. org/eco/surveys/hungary-2016-OECD-economic-survey-overview. pdf (accessed on 12 May 2016).

② http://businessculture. org/eastern-europe/hungary/ (accessed on 13 May 2016).

③ http://businessculture. org/eastern-europe/hungary/ (accessed on 13 May 2016).

27, which makes the Hungarian workforce highly competitive.

In sum, beside the favourable business climate and availability of various incentives, there are many other reasons making Hungary an ideal place for doing business, such as: (a) ideal geographical position in the centre of Europe for manufacturing, services and logistics; (b) excellent infrastructure, ready-made industrial sites, offices and science parks; (c) good balance of labour costs and quality; (d) governmental and municipal incentives (cash subsidy, tax allowance); (e) investment friendly economic policy; (f) competitive tax system; (g) financial and fiscal stability, and (h) success in reducing public debt. ①

---

① http://eugo.gov.hu/doing-business-hungary (accessed on 13 May 2016).

Chapter 1   Customs System and Law

József Hajdú

The customs union is one of the earliest achievements of the EU. In 1957 the Treaty of Rome which created the European Economic Community (EEC) established the customs union as one of the two principal means of bringing about European economic integration, the other being the creation of the common market. Since the end of the 1960s, there is freedom to import and export goods within the EEC[1] without paying any customs duties. Furthermore, any goods or services imported from a third country[2] can be re-exported to any other member state without having to pay additional duties. Import duties are paid only once, to the Commission, at rates determined by it, when goods are imported into a member state of the EU. Thereafter no custom duty is payable when such goods are moved around the EU.[3] Excise duty is levied on items such as alcoholic beverages, petrol and tobacco products.[4]

Since its accession to the EU on 1 May 2004 Hungary has conducted trade with other member states within the framework of the EU's internal market, the main principle of which is the free movement of goods, services capital and persons.

Trade between the EU and third countries is regulated by EU legislations, within the framework of the EU's common commercial policy. Council Regulation (EC) No. 3285/94 of December 1994 on the common rules for imports (hereinafter "Im-

---

[1]   Renamed European Union (EU) since the entry into force of the Maastricht Treaty in 1993.

[2]   A country that is not a member of the EU or a non-EU country that has a customs union agreement with the EU.

[3]   The characteristics of a custom union are the use of common external customs tariffs and the abrogation of customs regarding the internal commerce between the member states.

[4]   The member states of the EU use the TARIC system (TARIC = "Tarif Intégré de la Communauté"), which includes the Combined Nomenclature (All goods imported into or exported from the EU must be classified for Customs purposes. Each separate product is assigned a particular classification code. The Combined Nomenclature sets out the general rules for the classification of goods to an eight-digit level and is updated on a yearly basis), the applicable tariffs and custom, and the commercial and agricultural measures regarding each tariff. Due to its structure, the TARIC enables the national customs administrations in the EU to act in a uniform way.

port Regulation") applies to import of products originating in third countries, except for textile products, which are covered by special common rules, and products originating in certain third countries, which are listed in Council Regulation (EC) No. 519/94 of March 1994. ①

Neither the EU rules on the internal market nor the Import Regulation preclude the adoption or application by member states of measures to control imports and exports on grounds of public order, public morality, public security, the protection of health and life of humans, animals and plants, the protection of national treasures, the protection of industrial and commercial property, and special formalities concerning foreign exchange.

Act CXXVI of 2003 on the Enforcement of the Community Custom Rules② provides the basis for the use of the community customs system in Hungary. This is supplemented by Decree No. 15/2004 (Ⅳ.5) of Minister of Financial Affairs on the Detailed Enforcement of Community Customs Rules.

Hungary's tax authorities are the State Tax Authority and the Customs Authority (NAV)③ and the notaries of the municipal governments (local tax authority). ④ The tax authorities' responsibilities include maintaining taxpayer records, assessing taxes, collecting and enforcing taxes and other public dues enforced as taxes, controlling and supervising compliance with tax obligations, disbursing central subsidies, and effecting payment of tax refunds.

The Hungarian Government Decree No. 52/2012 (Ⅲ. 28) on the Trade of Goods, Services and Rights of Material Value Traversing the State and Customs Frontier (Trade Decree) provides for certain exceptions from the EU free trade rules set out above. According to this decree, export or import transactions of certain products

---

① http://www. mkik. hu/en/magyar-kereskedelmi-es-iparkamara/foreign-trade-and-customs-regulations-2654.

② This Act and the provisions of international agreements to which Hungary is a party pertaining to export and import procedure apply to issues not regulated under Community law with regard to transactions conducted in the territories governed in this Act with respect to international trade, if it is conferred under the jurisdiction of the customs authority under other specific legislation.

③ Act CXXII of 2010 on the National Tax and Customs Administration contains the determination of competence and jurisdiction, organisation, and several other issues.

④ See detailes in Act CXXII of 2010 on the National Tax and Customs Administration.

require a licence from the Hungarian Trade Licensing Office. ①

The issuance of export and import licences falls within the scope of authority of the Hungarian Trade Licensing Office. ② While the EU licensing rules apply to Hungary, special Hungarian legislation too applies in relation to some special products so long as they do not contravene any applicable EU regulations. ③

1. 1   Procedural rules

1. 1. 1   Customs and excise duties

No customs duties apply in relation to movement of goods among EU member states. Rates determined by the Community Customs Code apply in respect of goods imported from outside the EU. ④

In order for this system to work efficiently, and especially to counteract smuggling and tax evasion, the EU decided in 1997 to place all relevant information concerning customs into one central database. ⑤

The Customs Files Identification Database(FIDE) was added to the Customs Information System(CIS) to facilitate investigations carried out by the Commission and

---

① http://www. mkeh. hu. For example, transactions involving armaments, radioactive materials, recyclable or harmful waste, parts or derivatives of endangered animal and plant species, devices used in surveillance, and military engineering defence technology.

② The main activity of the Hungarian Trade Licensing Office is to implement authoritative-administrative tasks in the field of(a)state administration of foreign trade, (b)surveillance of production and service in armament industry, certain tasks in(c)trade, (d)market-surveillance, (e)surveillance of public warehouses, (f)assaying and hallmarking of precious metals and(g)metrology and(h)technical safety. See http://mkeh. gov. hu/.

③ These special Hungarian statutes are:

(1)Governmental Decree No. 52/2012(Ⅲ. 28)on the Cross-Border or Cross-Customs Commerce of Goods, Services and Valuable Rights. This decree applies to export import and re-export between EU and non-EU countries as well. It provides that the export, import and re-export of goods listed in the Schedules of the Decree may be undertaken only upon receiving a licence granted by the Hungarian Trade Licensing Office;

(2)Governmental Decree No. 160/2011 (Ⅷ. 18)on the Export, Import, Transfer and Transit Licensing of Military Equipment and Services and on the Certification of Enterprises also provides separate rules on licensing; and

(3)Governmental Decree No. 13/2011(Ⅱ. 22)on the licensing of the international commerce of dual-use items.

④ https://www2. deloitte. com/content/dam/Deloitte/global/Documents/Tax/dttl-tax-hungaryguide-2015. pdf.

⑤ See Council Regulation(EC) No. 515/97 of 13 March 1997 on mutual assistance between the administrative authorities of the member states and cooperation between them and the Commission to ensure the correct application of the law on customs or agricultural matters.

the national competent authorities. It brings together files relating to persons and businesses that have been suspected or found guilty of offences.

A. Customs control

The provisions pertaining to customs control also apply where the customs authority is required to carry out controls relating to goods by virtue of some specific legislation. The customs authority has the power to make sound and video recordings in connection with customs proceedings of the person affected, the scene and any circumstance and/or articles closely connected to the case in question. The sound and video recordings taken by the customs authority, as well as the personal data contained therein, may be used in criminal or misdemeanor proceedings conducted for infringements committed on the scene, or in the administrative proceedings conducted by the customs authority or with a view to enforcing the rights of the person affected. [1]

B. Identification markings and customs seals

The identification of goods must be ensured by affixing customs seal or other appropriate markings so as to render the inscription, symbol or serial number clearly visible and legible. Use of a customs seal or identification marking must not result in any damage to the goods and must not jeopardise its authorised use. Seals and markings prevent the packages, containers or means of transport containing the goods from being opened, compromised or exchanged. A seal affixed by a foreign customs authority, approved consignor/consignee or by a railway carrier may also be accepted as means of identification. [2]

C. Objective of post-clearance inspections

In order to ensure that the risks provided for in Community customs legislation are managed appropriately, in particular to prevent cases of fraud relating to customs duties and non-Community taxes and dues, the customs authority exercises some monitoring powers. The customs authority frequently monitors economic operators engaged in external trade activities with non-Community goods and Community goods subject to customs controls and other persons linked to such economic operators (hereinafter: post-clearance inspection). This power is exercised after the economic event, namely after the goods are released and after the authorisation or certificate is

---

[1]   Act CXXVI of 2003 on the Implementation of Community Customs Law, Article 6.

[2]   Ibid. , Article 7.

issued.

The objective of post-clearance inspections is to enforce the provisions of customs regulations and other relevant legislation and detect any violation or infringement of these regulations. In post-clearance inspections the customs authority must gather data and information, determine the legality of actions, and investigate the facts and circumstances of any alleged infringement to support such allegations in the ensuing proceedings. Post-clearance inspection may be conducted at clients, and also at any indirect customs representative involved in taking actions and handling formalities before the customs authority by authorisation, and on behalf, of a client. ①

D. Prescribed itineraries and secondary itineraries

All goods moving across the customs frontier must be transported via prescribed itineraries, with the exception of goods carried by way of a secondary itinerary under special permit and the transport of goods within the framework of cross-border trading. ② The opening or termination of prescribed itineraries will be decreed by the Government. ③

E. Authorisation of deferred payment and payment by instalment

Deferred payment and instalment payment(hereinafter referred to collectively as "payment facilities") may be granted upon the debtor's request relating to customs duties, non-Community taxes and dues owed to the customs authority, and to the compensatory interest provided for in Article 519 of the EC Implementation Regulation. Payment facilities may be granted if the payment difficulty:

a. cannot be attributed to the applicant or if he/she has taken reasonable measures to prevent it as is expected in the given situation; and

b. is of a temporary nature, that is to say that payment of the debt at a later time

---

① Act CXXVI of 2003 on the Implementation of Community Customs Law, Article 6.

② Prescribed itineraries mean tracks of public railway lines crossing the customs frontier, international waterways, border ports, public roads crossing the customs frontier, commercial airports handling international traffic and interstate pipelines and power lines designated as prescribed itineraries by the Government. Secondary itineraries means all roads other than prescribed itineraries which cross the frontier. Public airports opened to international traffic on a temporary or occasional basis are also regarded as secondary itineraries. The following goods may be transported by way of a secondary itinerary without a special permit: (a) the goods exempt from export or import duties and permitted within the framework of cross-border trading, and (b) fire brigades and fire extinguishing equpment, ambulance and other emergency response units if crossing the frontier for the purpose of providing aid under an international convention in case of a natural disaster or other emergency situation.

③ Act CXXVI of 2003 on the Implementation of Community Customs Law, Article 8.

appears evident.

Payment facilities may be granted to a private individual also if the applicant is able to verify that payment of the customs duties, non-Community taxes and dues, and the compensatory interest provided for in Article 519 of the EC Implementation Regulation at that particular time or in its entirety would constitute unreasonable hardship on his family, given his income, financial and social circumstances.

When submitting an application for, and in respect of the granting of, payment facilities, the applicant must provide security for the customs duties and non-Community taxes and dues to which it pertains, plus any accrued interest over and above the amounts so payable.

If the client fails to comply with the requirements for payment facilities, or fails to pay any instalment, the payment facilities will be withdrawn, and the debt becomes due and payable in full. [1]

F. Appeals[2]

The customs authority may amend an unlawful decision it has made on any number of occasions, or withdraw it any time before it is declared unlawful by the 2nd instance customs office decision or court decision.

If any part of a resolution that has been appealed is found unlawful, the authority empowered to hear the appeal case shall annul the resolution only with respect to the said unlawful sections, and shall sustain or overturn the remaining sections, where it is suitable for the case in question.

If there are any changes in terms of persons, physical evidence or in the issues of facts in connection with a decision of the customs authority, it will not be considered an amendment, but rather as a new decision.

G. Assistance between EU member states

The provisions of Council Regulation(EC) No. 515/97 on mutual assistance between the administrative authorities of the Member States and cooperation between them and the Commission to ensure the correct application of the law on customs and agricultural matters apply in connection with assistance pertaining to:

(a) the collection of export and import duties;

(b) refunds or repayment of export duties and other export charges; and

---

① Ibid. , Article 54/A.

② Ibid. , Article 60.

(c) trade embargoes and restrictions. ①

Cooperation between the customs authority and the competent authorities of EU member states in discharging their official duties are governed by the Convention on the mutual assistance and cooperation between customs administrations created on the basis of Article K. 3 of the Treaty on EU. ②

H. Assistance for third countries

The customs authority may provide assistance to the customs authorities of third countries and may request assistance from them for the implementation of its duties relating to customs and agricultural matters. ③

Assistance from the customs authorities of third countries may be requested only if it is relevant to ensuring the effectiveness of Community measures. However, international agreements with non-member countries on mutual assistance and cooperation may not contain any restrictions in terms of the rights and obligations stemming from Community membership.

The customs authorities of non-member countries may be notified without prior request of the following: (a) any new or particularly harmful methods of circumventing customs regulations; (b) goods hidden in the transport vehicle or in containers; (c) any known cases of falsifying or forging documents, stamps or identification marking used in customs procedure; , and (d) any cases considered harmful to the State's interests in view of their economic, humanitarian, social or political importance, such as any criminal conduct or infringement involving drugs, firearms, ammunition, explosives, or cultural assets under protection. ④

1. 1. 2   Import procedures

As part of the "SAFE standards" advocated by the World Customs Organisation (WCO), the EU has set up a new system of import controls, the "Import Control System" (ICS), which aims to secure the flow of goods at the time of their entry into the customs territory of the EU. This control system—a part of the Community Program "e-Customer"—has been in operation since 1 January 2011. Since then, opera-

---

① The administrative assistance of customs authorities may not involve the provision of any legal assistance in criminal matters.

② Act CXXVI of 2003 on the Implementation of Community Customs Law, Article 69.

③ However, the administrative assistance of customs authorities may not involve the provision of any legal assistance in criminal matters.

④ Act CXXVI of 2003 on the Implementation of Community Customs Law, Article 70.

tors are required to pass an Entry Summary Declaration(ENS) to the customs of the country of entry, prior to the introduction of goods into the customs territory of the EU.

For goods that are less than 1,000 kg or worth less than EUR 1,000 it is sufficient to make a verbal declaration at customs upon presentation of the invoice. For values that are superior the applicant must produce a summarizing declaration(air or sea transport) in order to register the goods and a legal declaration(unique administration document, commonly known as UAD) with all the necessary documents. ①

1.1.2.1   EU regulations requirements

The Integrated Tariff of the Community, referred to as TARIC(Tarif Intégré de la Communauté), is designed to show the various rules which apply to specific products that are imported into the customs territory of the EU or, in some cases, exported from it. Many EU member states maintain their own list of goods subject to import licensing.

The TARIC contains information on what products require a licence and can be searched by country of origin, Harmonised System(HS) Code, and product description on the interactive website of the Directorate-General for Taxation and the Customs Union. The online TARIC is updated daily. ②

1.1.2.2   Import documentation

A. The Single Administrative Document(SAD)

The Single Administrative Document(SAD) is the official model for written declarations to customs. Goods brought into the EU customs territory③ are, from the time of their entry, subject to customs supervision until customs formalities are completed. Goods must be covered by a Summary Declaration which is filed once the items have been presented to customs officials. The customs authorities may allow a period for filing the Declaration which cannot be extended beyond the first working day following the day on which the goods are presented to customs.

The Summary Declaration must be filed by the person bringing the goods into

---

① The UAD documents can be obtained at the chamber of commerce.

② See http://ec. europa. eu/taxation_customs/customs/customs_duties/tariff_aspects/customs_tariff/index_en. htm.

③ However, European Free Trade Association(EFTA) countries including Norway, Iceland, Switzerland and Liechtenstein also use the SAD.

the customs territory of the Community or by any person who assumes responsibility for carriage of the goods following such entry; or by the person on whose behalf such person acted.

The Summary Declaration can be made on a form provided by the customs authorities. Customs authorities may also allow the use of any commercial or official document that contains the specific information required to identify the goods. The SAD serves as the EU importer's declaration. It encompasses both customs duties and VAT and is valid in all EU Member States. The declaration is made by whoever is clearing the goods, normally the importer of record or his/her agent.

B. Union Customs Code (UCC)

Information on import/export forms is contained in Council Regulation (EEC) No. 2454/93, which lays down provisions for the implementation of the Community Customs Code. ①

Regulation (EC) No. 450/2008 laying down the Community Customs Code or the so-called "Modernised Customs Code" (MCC) is aimed at the adaptation of customs legislation and at introducing the electronic environment for customs and trade. This Regulation entered into force on 24 June 2008 and was due to be applicable once its implementing provisions were in force by June 2013. However, the Modernized Customs Code was recast as the Union Customs Code before it became applicable. The Union Customs Code Regulation, which repealed the MCC Regulation, entered into force in October 2013, but its substantive provisions will be applicable only from 1 May 2016, until when the MCC and its implementing provisions continue to apply.

The UCC recasts the Community Customs Code (the current customs legislation) and the MCC. The purpose of the recast is to simplify and ensure the transparency of customs rules, taking into account the legal changes which have occurred in recent years. Important changes introduced by the UCC include the following:

• Reducing the number of customs procedure types. The number was reduced from eight to three. The new three types are: release for free circulation, special procedures, and export. This does not mean that five procedures will disappear, as the category of "special procedures" will include external and internal transit, Union transit, storage (customs warehousing and free zones), specific use (temporary admis-

---

① UCC's Articles 205 through 221. In addition, Articles 222 through 224 provide for computerised customs declarations and Articles 225 through 229 provide for oral declarations.

sion and end use), and processing (inward and outward processing). ①

• Single-window administration and one-stop-shop checks. To simplify administrative matters for economic operators, the UCC introduces single-window administration and one-stop-shop checks for cases in which data must be supplied to other authorities. This means that the customs authorities will make such data available to those other authorities, and have other controls performed, wherever possible, at the same time and place as customs controls.

• A paperless environment for customs and trade. The aim of UCC is to establish a legal framework which ensures that all customs and trade transactions are handled electronically and that information and communication systems offer, in each member state, the same facilities to economic operators.

• Simplified system of guarantees. The UCC also allows for the use of a single guarantee for all categories of special procedures.

• The VAT Directive and the Excise Duty Directive. Simplifications will also be introduced to the customs formalities to be applied to trade between parts of the customs territory to which the provisions of Council Directive 2006/112/EC on the common system of value added tax or Council Directive 2008/118/EC concerning the general arrangements for excise duty apply and parts of that territory where those provisions do not apply.

C. The Economic Operator Registration and Identification (EORI) number

Since 2 July 2009 all companies established outside of the EU are required to have an Economic Operator Registration and Identification (EORI) number if they wish to lodge a customs declaration or an Entry/Exit Summary declaration. Foreign companies must use this number for customs clearance. If a foreign company wishes to apply for Authorised Economic Operator (AEO) status② or apply for simplifications in customs procedures within the EU, it must first obtain an EORI number.

---

① The inward processing drawback procedure will be discontinued, and the inward processing suspension procedure will be merged with processing under customs control.

② One of the main elements of the security amendment of the Community Customs Code (Regulation (EC) No. 648/2005) is the creation of the AEO concept. On the basis of Article 5a of the security amendments, member states can grant the AEO status to any economic operator meeting the following common criteria: customs compliance, appropriate record-keeping, financial solvency and, where relevant, appropriate security and safety standards. The status of authorised economic operator granted by one member state is recognised by the other member states. This does not automatically allow AEO to benefit from simplifications provided for in the customs rules in the other member states.

Companies should request an EORI number from the authorities of the first EU member state to which they export. Once a company has received an EORI number, it can use it for exports to any of the 28 EU member states. There is no single format for the EORI number.

D. Waste Electrical and Electronic Equipment(WEEE) Directive

EU rules on WEEE do not require specific customs or import paperwork, but may impose a financial obligation on exporters. The Directive requires exporters to register relevant products with a national WEEE authority or arrange for this to be done by a local partner. The WEEE Directive was revised on 4 July 2012 and the scope of products covered was expanded to include all electrical and electronic equipment. This revised scope will apply from 14 August 2018 with a phase-in period that has already begun.

E. Agricultural documentation

Goods imported into the EU must meet the EU sanitary and phytosanitary requirements in order to protect human and animal health. ① They are: Phytosanitary Certificates for most fresh fruits, vegetables, and other plant materials; and Sanitary Certificates for commodities composed of animal products or by-products. EU countries require that a shipment carrying relevant goods is accompanied by the appropriate certificate issued by the competent authority of the exporting country. This requirement applies regardless of whether the product is for human consumption, for pharmaceutical use, or strictly for non-human use (e. g. veterinary biologicals, animal feeds, fertilizers, research).

The vast majority of these certificates are uniform throughout the EU, but the harmonization process is not complete. In addition to the legally required EU health certificates, a number of other certificates are used in international trade. These certificates, which may also be harmonized in EU legislation, certify origin for customs purposes and certain quality attributes.

F. Temporary entry(ATA Carnet)

---

① Regulation(EC) No. 882/2004 of the European Parliament and of the Council of 29 April 2004 on official controls performed to ensure the verification of compliance with feed and food law, animal health and animal welfare rules, and Regulation(EC) No. 854/2004 of the European Parliament and of the Council of 29 April 2004 laying down specific rules for the organisation of official controls on products of animal origin intended for human consumption.

For temporary entry of goods, Hungary accepts an ATA Carnet, ① an international customs document that simplifies customs procedures for the temporary importation of commercial samples, professional equipment, and goods for exhibitions and fairs. The ATA Carnet facilitates international business by minimising extensive customs procedures and by eliminating payment of duties and VAT.

Goods temporarily imported into Hungary must be kept in a bonded warehouse until re-export. Customs authorities determine the period within which these goods must be re-exported or assigned a new customs-approved treatment or use. The maximum period the goods may remain in the status of temporary importation is 24 months, although customs authorities may shorten or extend this period. A temporary import shipment does not have to be re-exported in whole. Any portion of the shipment destined for the domestic or EU market is subject to duties and VAT at the time of importation.

G. Prohibited and restricted imports

An estimated 95 percent of products imported into Hungary no longer require an import licence; however, licences are still required for some goods like arms/military equipment, explosives & pyrotechnic products, security paper, uranium, radioactive isotopes. ②

The TARIC is designed to show various rules applying to specific products imported into the customs territory of the EU or, in some cases, when exported from it. The TARIC sets out what products are prohibited or subject to restriction.

1. 2. Additional important issues

1. 2. 1 Anti-dumping regulations

Since Hungary's EU accession, EU anti-dumping regulations have been applicable, the main source of which is Council Regulation(EC) No. 384/96 of 22 De-

---

① The ATA Carnet is an international customs document that permits the tax-free and duty-free temporary export and import of goods for up to one year. It is jointly administered by the World Customs Organisation and the International Chamber of Commerce through its World Chambers Federation. The Carnet eliminates the need to purchase temporary import bonds. So long as the goods are re-exported within the allotted time frame, no duties or taxes are due. Failure to re-export all or some of the goods listed on the Carnet results in the payment of applicable duties and taxes. Failure to remit those duties results in a claim from the foreign customs service to the importer's home country.

② The link to the Hungarian Trade Licensing Office is: http://mkeh. gov. hu.

cember 1995. The intention of the Anti-Dumping Regulation is to protect the EU a-gainst imports dumped from third countries, and its application is based on two conditions: the existence of dumping and the proof of injury to the Community industry, be it injury caused to an industry established in the Community, the threat of injury, or substantial retardation of the establishment of such an industry.

1.2.2   Quotas and other non-tariff barriers

Council Regulation(EC) No. 520/94 of 7 March 1994(Quota Regulation) established a Community procedure for administering quantitative quotas. The Quota Regulation applies to import and export quotas established by the Community, be they autonomous or conventional.

The Quota Regulation does not apply to agricultural products listed in Annex II of the Treaty of Rome, to textile products, or to products covered by special import rules which set out specific provisions for the administration of quotas.

The Commission will publish a notice in the Official Journal of the EU which will announce the opening of quotas, set the allocation method, the conditions to be met by licence applications, time limits for submitting them, and a list of the competent national authorities to which they must be sent. Quotas are allocated among applicants as soon as possible after they have been opened.

Quotas may be administered by one of the three methods set out in the Quota Regulation: (a) the method based on traditional trade flows; (b) the method based on the order in which applications are submitted; and (c) the method of allocating quotas in proportion to the quantities requested. They may be administered by a combination of these methods, or by any other appropriate method.

1.2.3   Foreign exchange

Hungary's foreign exchange authority is the National Bank of Hungary(www. mnb. hu). Many of the restrictions on foreign exchange transactions and foreign currency were repealed with the enactment of a series of laws, the latest being Act XCIII of 2001 on Foreign Exchange Liberalisation. The 2001 Act provides that transactions and acts of foreign residents and foreign non-residents performed with foreign currency, Hungarian currency and claims in Hungarian currency may be freely pursued. It provides however that payment obligations in respect of tax, contributions and other fees to the Hungarian state must be fulfilled in Hungarian currency, the Forints. Certain other laws continue with obligations affecting foreign exchange transactions, such as regulations on money laundering, supplying data for statistical purposes to the National Bank of Hungary.

Companies doing business in Hungary are required to open a bank account at a Hungarian bank. Companies engaged in foreign-trading activities may also open foreign-currency accounts in Hungary. Foreign-currency receipts, such as receipts derived from the export of goods and loan proceeds, may be deposited in such accounts.

Hungarian legislation allows dividend remittances and, as applicable, capital repatriation to the foreign investor. The Hungarian Forint is converted at the foreign-exchange rate set by commercial banks.

Chapter 2   Foreign Trade System and Law

Benedek Tóth

2.1   Framework of Hungary's foreign trade system

Hungary's foreign trade is carried out fundamentally in the context of its membership in the World Trade Organisation and in the European Union.

One of the original goals of the World Trade Organisation was to dismantle altogether legal barriers to international trade of goods, services, intellectual property rights, investment measures and in subject matters of the optional agreements. However, WTO agreements have so far succeeded only in reaching the goal of massive reduction of duties.

The EU established a single market and customs union covering the territory of all the member states. The EU constitutes an autonomous entity from the point of view of international trade. The common trade policy and customs policy are within exclusive competence of the EU.

All the EU member states and the EU(in its capacity as an international organisation) are members of the World Trade Organisation. Due to its exclusive competence on common trade policy and customs union, the EU is able to represent all of its member states in WTO bodies. [1]

Considering that legal regime of foreign trade can exist only within the framework of the WTO multilateral system, and the exclusive competence of the EU to legislate on foreign trade and customs, Hungary has very little regulatory power over foreign trade.

2.2   The economy of the EU and global trade

Operating as a single market with 28 countries, the EU is a major world trading

---

[1]   https://www. wto. org/english/thewto_e/countries_e/european_communities_e. htm.

power. The EU economic policy seeks to sustain growth by investing in transport, energy and research while minimising the impact of further economic development on the environment. The EU's economy, measured in terms of the goods and services it produces(GDP), is now bigger than the US economy: EU GDP in 2014 was EUR 13,920,541 million. With just seven percent of the world's population, the EU's trade with the rest of the world accounts for around 20 percent of global exports and imports.

The EU is followed by the United States with 15.5 percent of all imports, and China with 11.9 percent. The EU was also the biggest exporter, accounting for 15.4 percent of all exports—compared with 13.4 percent for China and the 10.5 percent for the United States. ① Around two-thirds of the EU countries' total trade is done with other EU countries.

The above data clearly establishes that the EU is the largest economy and market in the world. The EU's economic interests are spread all over the world, and almost all the countries are interested in furthering their business presence in the EU.

2.3   The economy of Hungary and world trade

Hungary has a medium-sized, structurally, politically and institutionally open economy in Eastern-Central Europe and is part of the EU's single market. Like most Eastern-Central European economies, Hungary experienced market liberalisation in the early 90s transiting from a socialist economy to a market economy.

Hungary is a contracting party of the General Agreement on Tariffs and Trade (GATT) since 1973, ② a founding member of the WTO since 1995, ③ a member of the Organisation for Economic Cooperation and Development(OECD) since 1996④ and a member of the EU since 2004.

Hungary has over 31,000 km of roads, of which almost 1,200 km are motorways. The total length of motorways has doubled in the last ten years with the most of it built and completed in 2006. The capital, Budapest is directly connected to the

---

① http://europa. eu/about-eu/facts-figures/economy/index_en. htm. See also http://ec. europa. eu/economy_finance/international/index_en. htm.

② The accession was promulgated in Hungary by the 23/1973. (IX.9)MT regulation.

③ Promulgated in Hungary by Act IX of 1998.

④ The accession was promulgated in Hungary by Act XV of 1998.

Austrian, Slovenian, Croatian and Serbian borders via motorways. Due to its location and geographical features, several transport corridors cross Hungary. Three Pan-European corridors and five European routes lead through Hungary. As a result of its radial road system, all of these routes connect to Budapest. There are five international, four domestic, four military and several non-public airports in Hungary. The largest airport is the Budapest Liszt Ferenc International Airport(BUD) located at the south-eastern border of Budapest. The Hungarian railroad system covers 8,000 km, nearly 3,000 km of which is electrified.

Along with related businesses, agriculture contributes about 13 percent of the GDP. Hungarian agriculture is virtually self-sufficient and export-oriented due to traditional reasons: exports related to agriculture make up 20 – 25 percent of the total. About half of Hungary's total land area is agricultural area under cultivation. This ratio is high when compared to other EU members. This is due to the country's favourable conditions including its continental climate and the plains that make up about half of Hungary's landscape. Hungary also has several wine regions producing, among others, the internationally famed white dessert wine Tokaji and the red Bull's Blood.

The main sectors of the Hungarian industry are heavy industry, energy production, mechanical engineering, chemicals, food industry and automobile production. Manufacturing leans mainly on processing industry and(including construction) accounted for about 30 percent of GDP. Following Hungary's transition to a market economy, Hungarian industry underwent restructuring and remarkable modernisation. The leading industry is machinery, followed by chemical industry(plastic production, pharmaceuticals). Although it has decreased in the last decade, food industry is still accounts for up to 14 percent of total industrial production and for 7 – 8 percent of the country's exports.

The service sector accounts for over 60 percent of GDP and its role in the Hungarian economy is growing steadily because of constant investments into transport and other services in the last 15 years. Located in the heart of Central Europe, Hungary's geostrategic location plays a significant role in the rise of the service sector.

Tourism industry employs nearly 150,000 people. One of Hungary's top tourist destinations is Lake Balaton, the largest warm freshwater lake in Central Europe, attracting more than a million visitors annually. The most visited region is Budapest, the Hungarian capital, which attracted over three million visitors in each of the recent five years. The world-famous Hungarian spa culture is rich with thermal baths of all sorts and over 50 spa hotels located in many towns. Each of them offers the opportunity of a pleasant, relaxing holiday and a wide range of quality medical and beauty treatments. ①

The economy of Hungary is highly open and export-import oriented. Apart from historical reasons, this is because of foreign investments, including from Western European countries, accounting for a large proportion the national production. Foreign investment is the engine of the economy and development.

Strong international economic integration of the country is mainly directed towards other EU member states, but in recent years Hungary has made great efforts to make closer relations with countries outside the EU as well.

2. 4   Regulatory instruments on foreign trade

The economy of the EU and of Hungary being a market economy, in principle, trade—including foreign trade—is completely free.

Because of the membership of the EU and the WTO multilateral system, a member state or the EU may unilaterally restrict international trade only in exceptional circumstances and within strict limits. Basically, the legal instruments affecting foreign trade can be divided into three groups:

• Legal tools on foreign trade regulated and allowed in the WTO multilateral system, in particular those covered by the GATT;

• Legal instruments on fields of subject matters that are not covered by the WTO multilateral system and particularly by the GATT;

• Those legal tools that cannot be applied directly to foreign trade, but affect international trade.

Each of these will be discussed in the following pages in 2. 4. 1, 2. 4. 2 and 2. 4. 3.

2. 4. 1   Legal tools on foreign trade regulated and allowed in the WTO multilateral system, in particular those covered by the GATT

Legal trade instruments covered by the WTO multilateral system, in particular

---

① Webpage of the Embassy of Hungary in China, Beijing: http://www. mfa. gov. hu/kulkepviselet/CN/en/en_Bilateralis/economy. htm.

by the GATT, belong to the exclusive competences of common trade policy or common customs policy of the EU.

2. 4. 1. 1 Customs and other tariff barriers

In the absence of exceptional circumstances, the only permitted legal tools that affect or restrict foreign trade are customs and other tariffal barriers(taxes, fees) under Article XI of the GATT with the temporary exceptions specified therein.

The customs tariffs are the results of tariff negotiations within GATT 1947 (later the WTO) and are annexes of the GATT in form of protocol. They are therefore obligations under international law. The tariff levels applied by the EU are among the lowest around the world, the average level of import tariffs is around five percent.

As the territory of the member states of the EU make up a customs union area and as common customs policy is within the exclusive competence of the EU, the EU has created a uniform Customs Code on procedures in customs. Customs procedures are conducted by the member states' customs authorities by using the unified EU law. In Hungary the national customs authority is the National Tax and Customs Administration. ①

The modernised Customs Code covers the following issues:

• general provisions on the scope of customs legislation, the mission of customs and the rights and obligations of persons with regard to customs legislation;

• factors on the basis of which import and export duties and other measures in respect of trade in goods are applied(common customs tariff, origin of goods, value for customs purposes);

• customs debt and guarantees of this debt;

• customs treatment of goods brought into the customs territory of the Community;

• rules on customs status, placing goods under a customs procedure, as well as verification, release and disposal of goods;

• release for free circulation on the EU's single market and relief from export duties; special customs procedures organised into four economic functions(transit, storage, specific use, processing);

• customs treatment of goods leaving the customs territory of the Community

---

① http://en. nav. gov. hu/.

(goods leaving the territory, export and re-export, relief from export duties) ;

　　• the Customs Code Committee and procedures enabling the Commission to a-dopt the measures implementing the Code. ①

One of the most important issues of the Customs Code is the release for free circulation on the EU's single market. That means that any good passed through the common customs procedure and released for free circulation can move freely in the single market made up of all the member states.

The EU and its member states are at the forefront not only in the elimination of non-tariff trade barriers, but also in the reduction of customs duties prescribed by the GATT. In order to reach these targets, the EU established a number of free-trade areas with many countries or group of countries, within these areas the resident enterprises in contracting states can trade free of duty.

2.4.1.2　Market protection devices: safeguards, anti-dumping and anti-subsidy measures

According to the WTO Agreement on Safeguards, ② Council Regulation (EC) No. 260/2009 of 26 February 2009 on the common rules for imports③ regulates the definition and the conditions for application of safeguards and the community investigation procedure.

Unlike subsidies and dumping, safeguards are not meant to address unfair trade practices. Rather they are concerned with imports of a certain product that increase so suddenly and sharply that EU producers cannot reasonably be expected to adapt immediately to the changed trade situation.

In such cases, WTO and EU rules allow for short-term measures to regulate the imports, giving EU companies temporary relief and time to adapt to this unforeseeable surge in import. Such measures usually apply to imports of the product from all non-EU countries. In return, the affected EU industry is required to restructure. Provisional safeguard measures may last up to 200 days and definitive measures up to four years. Where they exceed three years, they must be reviewed at mid-term and can be extended for up to eight years in total. ④

①　http://eur-lex. europa. eu/legal-content/EN/TXTHTML? uri = URISERV: do0001 &from = HU.
②　https://www. wto. org/english/docs_e/legal_e/25-safeg. pdf.
③　http://trade. ec. europa. eu/doclibdocs2009/april/tradoc_142728. Reg-260. en. L84-2009. pdf.
④　http://trade. ec. europa. eu/doclibdocs2013/april/tradoc_151014. pdf.

The anti-dumping procedure: This is the oldest type in the protection practices in international trade. It is known since the 1930s. The rules of procedure are made up of the Agreement on Implementation of Article VI of the General Agreement on Tariffs and Trade 1994① and the so-called Anti-Dumping Code. Additionally, the EU is governed by Council Regulation(EC) No. 384/96 of 22 December 1995. ②

A product is dumped which is to be sold in the importing country at a price below it is sold on the market of the exporting country. If a suspicion of dumping occurs, the Agreement and also the EU Regulation prescribe that the competent authority should examine "the fact of dumping", i. e. the volume of dumped imports, the impact on the prices of like products on the domestic market and the impact on the producers of the like products in the import country.

If there is deemd to be dumping, anti-dumping duty can be applied to dumped products. The application of anti-dumping duty is intended to compensate for the difference between the healthy market value and the dumping price in the import market, i. e. to raise the price to the appropriate value. This can prevent the harm or disadvantage caused by unrealistically low prices of the exporter for the domestic economy, traders and producers in the import country.

The rate of anti-dumping duty can be up to the full extent of the dumping price difference but a lower rate can also be applied. The anti-dumping duty can remain in force for the time and to the extent necessary for the elimination of the harm caused on the domestic market.

The anti-subsidy procedure: This aims to filter distorted prices caused by governmental subsidies. Not all the subsidies are prohibited; what are prohibited subsidies? They are set out in the relevant WTO agreement, the Agreement on Subsidies and Countervailing Measures, the so-called Subsidy Code, ③ and Council Regulation (EC) No. 2026/97 of 6 October 1997 on protection against subsidised imports from countries not members of the European Community. ④ According to Regulation 2026/97/EC, a subsidy is considered a prohibited subsidy if the government or oth-

---

① https://www. wto. org/english/docs_e/legal_e/19-adp. pdf.

② http://eur-lex. europa. eu/legal-content/EN/TXT/PDF/? uri = CELEX : 31996R0384&qid = 1458637286508&from = HU.

③ https://www. wto. org/english/docs_e/legal_e/24-scm. pdf.

④ http://eur-lex. europa. eu/legal-content/EN/TXT/PDF/? uri = CELEX : 31997R2026&qid = 1458639941247&from = HU.

er public authority in any form provides financial support for the production, export or transport of the product imported to the domestic market, and as a result, it enjoys price-advantage on the market. There is no prohibited subsidy if the export product is exempted from taxes on export as compared to like products for domestic consumption.

If the fact of application of prohibited subsidy is deemed, countervailing duty may be imposed. Countervailing duty can be applied for the time required for the elimination of the harm caused on the domestic market not exceeding five years.

Countervailing duty has the same function as anti-dumping duty. By prohibited subsidies the exporter can use lower prices for the same profit on foreign markets, countervailing duty raises the price to the normal healthy level, and thereby eliminates the distortion of competition between the exporter and domestic players.

The anti-subsidy procedure can be applied only if prohibited subsidies are given to a specific company or a specific group of companies.

The common feature of the anti-dumping and the anti-subsidy procedure is that both are administrative proceedings by nature conducted by the EU Commission. These trade defence measures can be reviewed by the European Court of Justice and the WTO Dispute Settlement Body.

2. 4. 1. 3   Preferential treatment for developing counties

The EU actively encourages developing countries to exploit the opportunities offered by trade in order to build their own economy and improve their living standards. Trade expansion can increase their export income and promote diversification of their economies moving away from producing raw materials. In order to boost the export of developing countries, in 1971 the EU introduced the Generalised System of Preferences(GSP) as the first in such measures. The GSP is a system of preferential import tariffs for each developing country and provides very important help for their goods to enter the European market.

However, during the last four decades the global economic and trade balance has shifted significantly. Many developing countries have successfully integrated into the world trade system, but the number of poor countries which are increasingly lagging behind the others has increased. In the current fierce competition, tariff preferences should be given to those countries that are most in need of help.

With regard to these new circumstances, in 2014 a reformed general tariff preference system came into force, which aims specifically to help the least developed countries which do not receive any other type of market entry benefit. Currently, 88 countries compose this group.

A special incentive initiative is the GSP + system, which provides additional tariff preferences to the most vulnerable countries if they sign 27 international agreements on human and labour rights, environmental protection and good governance.

The "Everything but Arms" EU initiative provides duty and quota exemption for imports from the least developed 49 countries to Europe except weapons and ammunition.

2.4.2   Legal tools on areas which the WTO treaty system does not cover

This category includes legal tools used in areas that are exempt from the WTO multilateral system, or originally do not compose a subject matter of global trade regulation.

Article XX of the GATT includes the matters that are exceptions from the GATT (and the GATS) rules:

Article XX. General Exceptions

Subject to the requirement that such measures are not applied in a manner which would constitute a means of arbitrary or unjustifiable discrimination between countries where the same conditions prevail, or a disguised restriction on international trade, nothing in this Agreement shall be construed to prevent the adoption or enforcement by any contracting party of measures:

(a) necessary to protect public morals;

(b) necessary to protect human, animal or plant life or health;

(c) relating to the importations or exportations of gold or silver;

(d) necessary to secure compliance with laws or regulations which are not inconsistent with the provisions of this Agreement, including those relating to customs enforcement, the enforcement of monopolies operated under paragraph 4 of Article II and Article XVII, the protection of patents, trade marks and copyrights, and the prevention of deceptive practices;

(e) relating to the products of prison labour;

(f) imposed for the protection of national treasures of artistic, historic or archaeological value;

(g) relating to the conservation of exhaustible natural resources if such measures are made effective in conjunction with restrictions on domestic production or consumption;

(h) undertaken in pursuance of obligations under any inter-governmental commodity agreement which conforms to criteria submitted to the contracting parties and not disapproved by them or which is itself so submitted and not so disapproved;

(i) involving restrictions on exports of domestic materials necessary to ensure essential quantities of such materials to a domestic processing industry during periods when the domestic price of such materials is held below the world price as part of a governmental stabilisation plan; provided that such restrictions shall not operate to increase the exports of or the protection afforded to such domestic industry, and shall not depart from the provisions of this Agreement relating to non-discrimination;

(j) essential to the acquisition or distribution of products in general or local short supply; provided that any such measures shall be consistent with the principle that all contracting parties are entitled to an equitable share of the international supply of such products, and that any such measures, which are inconsistent with the other provisions of the Agreement shall be discontinued as soon as the conditions giving rise to them have ceased to exist. The Contracting Parties shall review the need for this sub-paragraph not later than 30 June 1960.

These subjects are exempt from the restrictions of the WTO multilateral system, so that in these areas can be introduced and maintained such measures that can influence or affect foreign or international trade and can be sustained without breaching international legal obligations.

It should be noted that these exceptions are related to the extraordinary nature of goods (and services) and to trade or economy emergencies. Hence, these exceptions strengthen the general basic rules of trade principles.

2.4.2.1   Free trade agreements

Under the exemption in point(h) of Article XX of the GATT, the establishment of free trade agreements is one of the most widely used tools for influencing international trade. The general exception provided for the free trade agreements and customs unions is not only suitable for the original goal of the GATT, the duty-free trade, but also for using trade affecting measures.

The EU is currently pursuing a policy of active engagement with its partners, sometimes within regional groupings, to negotiate comprehensive free trade agreements. These grant privileged access to the markets of the countries concerned and are an accepted exception from the basic World Trade Organisation principle that all trading partners should be granted equal treatment.

Agreements vary depending on the level of ambition and capacities of the country, or group of countries, the EU is negotiating with. Since the EU's many partners have different interests, the contents are tailored to each specific situation. Free trade agreements with developed countries and emerging economies are driven by economics and generally based on reciprocal market opening. Economic partnership agreements with African, Caribbean and Pacific countries combine both trade and development objectives.

The EU trade policy is focusing on key partners such as the US, Canada and Japan, although attention is also being paid to emerging economies such as the BRICS(Brazil, Russia, India, China and South Africa) , which are seen as the new drivers of the world economy. The benefit of agreements with such countries for EU exporters is clear. The average tariff they face when selling to the rest of the world is still around five percent. In some countries, tariffs are considerably higher.

A typical agreement covers different sectors and issues and specifies a timetable for individual product tariff reductions. Modern(EU) trade agreements include non-tariff matters ranging from intellectual property to public procurement. They contain various provisions, such as rules of origin, to determine which products are eligible for the tariffs being reduced or eliminated.

These agreements strengthen the EU's rules-based system which goes beyond the WTO by embedding this in the international contractual arrangements so that trade and investment are protected and can thrive. ①

2.4.2.2　Licensing system

In the global trade regime set up by the WTO agreements, in principle, trade is free and not to be restricted in any way. The agreements provide unrestricted, worldwide movement of goods, services and capital across borders and continents. At the same time, in the subject-matters laid down in Article XX of the GATT such measures can be introduced and maintained that bind this free movement to conditions and criteria. The classic form of these measures is the licensing system, which in

---

① http://europa. eu/pol/pdf/flipbook/en/trade_en. pdf.

most cases(e. g. weapons, nuclear materials, cultural treasures, etc.) is understanda-
ble.

The operation of the licensing system in the EU largely remained in the compe-
tency of Member States. In Hungary the rules on the licensing system include Government Decree 52/2012 (III. 28) , with the exception of the goods of defence industry, dual-use items(items that may be used for civil as well as military purposes)
and goods which can be used for executing death penalty, torture or other cruel, inhuman or degrading treatment or punishment.

This governmental decree maintains a licensing system on goods that are exempt from general trade regulations by Article XX of the GATT: fissile materials,
explosives, particularly dangerous products on public safety and security papers. In
general to start an import, export or re-export trade activity in relation to these
goods, an operational licence must be obtained. The governmental decree also requires separate licences for each foreign trade transaction of such goods such as in
export, import or re-export.

A similar operational and export, import or re-export licensing system is applicable to goods of defence industry, dual-use items and goods which can be used for
executing death penalty, torture or other cruel, inhuman or degrading treatment or
punishment.

Licensing procedures in Hungary are within the competence of the Hungarian
Trade Licensing Office. ①

2.4.3　Legal tools that cannot be applied directly to foreign trade, but affect it

Foreign trade cannot be easily distinguished from other areas of economy: it is
just a part of the economic system. It is particularly true in a very open economy
like Hungary, where the importance of foreign trade is much higher than usual. It is
also true in the EU, because its economy is largely based on the contribution of international trade to economic results.

Accordingly, public law as well as private law and private aspects of legislation
on the economy have a great impact on foreign trade issues.

2.4.3.1　Official prices

A very drastic economic regulatory measure is determining by the state of a

---

① http://mkeh. gov. hu/hivatal.

minimum, maximum or an exact price of goods or services, which drives market competition to a minimum regarding the product or service. Official prices are usually employed by states for products such as liquor and tobacco products which are unlikely go out of production because of controlling measures, or in respect of certain services such as supply of energy for which there is some social or other rational reason. Free-market countries usually apply official prices rarely and Hungary is no exception. In Hungary, Act LXXXVII of 1990 contains the general rules of the application of official pricing.

2.4.3.2   Regulation of some private law areas with public law significance: competition, consumer protection

Although these areas of activity are regulated in a context outside the regulation of foreign trade, they undoubtedly have an impact on international economic relations. The law relating to these areas of activity such as consumer rights and competition, which has elements of both private and public law, creates legal standards, such as by making imports expensive, having the potential to act as barriers to trade. It is not a coincidence that the EU has taken great strides in unifying and harmonising law in these private law areas.

2.5   Summary

Thanks to the WTO multilateral system, world trade is now freer than ever and the few remaining barriers of international trade are continuously disappearing. In Hungary, EU legislation take primacy in relation to regulating foreign trade. There are almost no powers left for Hungary to regulate this field of law. The EU as an independent entity participates in the world trade using the powers of its member states.

Chapter 3   Foreign Direct Investment System and Law

Benedek Tóth

3.1   Hungary and foreign investments

Since the fall of the Iron Curtain more than two decades ago, foreign direct investments (FDI) have played a very important role in the operation and development of the Hungarian economy. The presence of foreign investments and the purpose of alluring new ones are the main priorities of economic policy. Accordingly, foreign investors are present in large numbers with an outstanding value of investments. [1] Their presence has resulted in a highly open and export-oriented economic structure.

There are several historical, economic and social reasons making Hungary a desirable destination for such a large number and high amount of foreign direct investment.

The country's legislation not only followed, but also proactively contributed to the inflow and successful operation of foreign investment, which resulted in a highly advanced and investment-friendly legislation. Hungary has, in the last two and a half decades, recognised the fact that foreign investment is able to produce a favourable and essential impact on the country's economy only if there are in place stable and predictable social and legal structures conducive to investment.

3.2   Influences of non-legal factors on foreign direct investment in Hungary

Economic and social-legal factors affect foreign direct investment. It is mainly the economic factors that determine the investment environment, including the profit and payback time of the investment. Socio-legal factors define the security and sta-

---

[1]   For the data about the foreign investments in Hungary, see the webpage of OECD: http://www. oecd. org/hungary/.

bility of the investment.

3. 2. 1   The historical reason for foreign investment in Hungary

After World War II Hungary came under the Soviet sphere of influence as part of the Central and Eastern European Region, bringing with it Hungary's communist state and its socialist economic and social system. Private businesses were expropriated, and the only player in the economy became the state and its affiliates.

The centralised and planned economy was without precedent in Hungary and could be sustained only because of strong foreign pressure. By the second half of the 1960s, Hungary had already started a cautious economic opening and an internal reform of the economic policy, which was met with vehement disapproval of the Soviet leadership. This process of liberalisation peaked in 1989 when Hungary broke ranks with the Soviet interest sphere, the first country in the region to do so. Hungary immediately introduced a socio-economic system based on its own European-type democratic traditions, private property and comparative private economy. Hungary was quickly followed by other countries in the region.

In the past two and a half decades, the Eastern-Central European Region and Hungary have constantly been evolving significantly in both economic and social terms. This process was greatly stimulated by their association and membership of the European Communities (now the EU). This process of assimilation into the Union was fully accomplished when almost all the Eastern-Central European countries became members of the EU on 1 May 2004.

These changes made Hungary and the other countries of the Eastern-Central European Region the world's number one target for foreign investment in a short time, and at present they are among the world's most important regions for foreign investment.

The replacement of the communist-type economic system and the subsequent vigorous programme of privatisation meant for foreign investors an unexpected access to cheap means of production including cheap skilled labour.

3. 2. 2   Geographical location

Hungary's success in attracting foreign direct investment is due in no small measure to its geographical location on the East-West and North-South main intersection of trade routes over its more than 1,100 years of history.

As a target country of foreign investment, its importance is beyond what would be expected based on its approximately 94,000 km^2 area and a population of 9.8 million. This geographical position makes the country a significant part of the economically and socially homogeneous Eastern-Central European Region with a population of about 100 million.

3.2.3   Other economic factors

One of the major attractions is the availability of a cheap[①] but highly skilled labour force, supported by a well-established system of competitive, free or inexpensive educational and health care. The constantly developing transport infrastructure is also worth highlighting.

3.2.4   Tax system and government subsidies

Although the tax system is described as a part of the legal structure, in the past few years Hungary has recognized the importance of tax competition among the states, and that it behaves as a comparative economic factor. Therefore the country has made and continues to make great efforts to relocate the tax burden from manufacturing to consumption, so far as it is financially efficient, thereby making production activities much less expensive. In addition, export for sale is exempt from taxes which are imposed on domestic sales, which also contributes to foreign investments' higher profit rate.

EU rules provide that in taxation matters investments cannot be treated preferably only because of their foreign nature, but the country usually grants government subsidies for new foreign investments in great value and in extreme cases for the already operating investments too.

3.3   Legislation on foreign investment in Hungary

Hungary's attraction to inflow of foreign capital includes the institutional and legal stability of public bodies, the quality and predictability of legislation, a reliable judicial and administrative system, and the smooth operation of special protective legislation on foreign investments.

---

① For example, the minimum wage is HUF 111,000 (appr. EUR 358), and the guaranteed minimum wage (for skilled persons) is HUF 129,000 (appr. EUR 416) in 2016.

3.3.1   Brief outline of the public power structure in Hungary

The public power structure of the country is based on its constitution. [1] Hungary has a parliamentary structure which is quite similar to the German system. The public power is divided into legislative, executive and judicial powers, and this structure is supplemented by several constitutional bodies, such as the Constitutional Court and the Ombudsman, providing checks and balances. The head of the state is the President of the Republic with relatively limited powers. The stability of the state is provided by free and democratic elections and wide-ranging constitutional protection of fundamental rights. The EU membership contributes greatly to the strength of the state as well.

3.3.2   Legislation on economy

It is significant in relation to the protection and operation of foreign investment that Hungary is very significantly "international" both economically and legally. The framework of both public and private law systems on economic legislation is to a great extent determined by international and EU legislation. Within defined limits Hungarian courts, as do their counter parts in other modern societies, interpret and implement legislation, so far as possible, giving effect to internationally accepted standards.

For historical reasons Hungary only became a member of the United Nations in 1955[2] and has since then permanently joined existing specialized organizations and became a founding member of the subsequently created ones, such as UNCTAD, World Bank Group organisations, joined the GATT in 1973,[3] and became a founding member of the WTO. [4]

Hungary became a member of the Council of Europe in 1990[5] and is a contracting party of the European Convention on Human Rights and other Council of Europe conventions.

In order to comply with its obligations under international law, Hungary is o-

---

[1]   For the Fundamental Law of Hungary in English visit:

http://www. kormany. hu/download/e/02/00000/The%20New%20Fundamental%20Law%20of%20Hungary. pdf.

[2]   It was promulgated in Hungary by Act I of 1956.

[3]   The accession is promulgated in Hungary by the 23/1973(IX. 9)MT regulation.

[4]   https://www. wto. org/english/thewto_e/countries_e/hungary_e. htm.

[5]   The accession is promulgated in Hungary by Act LXXI of 1991.

bliged to ensure that Hungarian law is in conformity with international law. Furthermore, Hungary must accept the generally recognised rules of international law. Other sources of international law may become part of the Hungarian legal system by incorporation, that is, by their promulgation in legal regulations. International treaties rank above all domestic legal sources and are second only to the Hungarian Constitution. ①

Another decisive condition of economic regulation is Hungary's EU membership. The law of the EU is part of the legal system, which ranks above domestic legal sources. ② International investment is not regulated by EU law, but it is important to keep in mind that two of the oldest exclusive powers of the EU are the common policy of trade and the customs union. So, to a great extent the legislative powers on public economic regulation are with the EU bodies, not with member states. In these important areas EU rules must be applied and implemented.

Within these frameworks, foreign investors are treated as equals to domestic entities, regardless of whether the investors are from other EU member states or from outside the EU. Hence, any disadvantageous distinction based on origin is strictly prohibited.

Hungary complies with the international practice not only in the area of public legislation. It conforms to international standards also in the area of private legislation. Hungary initiated the founding of UNCITRAL and also the drafting of Vienna Sales Convention which was adopted in 1980. In addition, Hungary is a party to many international treaties, most of which were signed at the time of their original adoption including in the area of intellectual property rights and the international law of carriage.

3.3.3   General rules for the protection of the right to property

Hungary protects the right to property as a constitutional right. Thus it protects it as a fundamental right recognised by international law, but as a constitutionally entrenched, higher level, right. ③ That means declaring the all-inclusive right to property in the Constitution on the one hand, and determining the criteria for the removal of the ownership on the other hand, also at constitutional level: " (1) Every-

---

① Fundamental Law of Hungary, Art. Q.
② Fundamental Law of Hungary, Art. E.
③ Fundamental Law of Hungary, Art. XIII.

one shall have the right to property and inheritance. Property shall entail social re-sponsibility. (2) Property may only be expropriated exceptionally, in the public in-terest and in the cases and ways provided for by an act, subject to full, unconditional and immediate compensation. " (A variant formulation in international use is "prompt, adequate and effective").

A further condition for the deprivation of property is the requirement of non-discriminatory treatment, which comes from the declaration of the right to property as a fundamental right enjoyed by everyone, but in addition this is also a constitu-tional prohibition[1] besides the international legal obligations.

The fundamental right to property and the prohibition of discrimination are also the country's obligations under international law, which can be enforced also by an external judicial redress system. The European Convention on Human Rights (Rome, 1950) [2] adopted within the framework of Council of Europe Article 14 pro-hibits discrimination, and Article 1 of Appendix 1[3] declares the right for property and the above conditions for the deprivation of property. These norms are enforced by the European Court of Human Rights in Strasbourg which are binding on mem-ber states. [4]

These constitutional and international law provisions make any legislation of general application which takes away property without complying with the above mentioned conditions unconstitutional and illegal under international law. There is recourse to the Constitutional Court and the European Court of Human Rights in Strasbourg against such legislation.

There is a specific act[5] which applies to expropriation of property. It governs the expropriation process as an administrative act of the state, and guaranties the full realization of the above described conditions. In addition to the judicial remedy in the administrative court, there is also access to the Constitutional Court and the Eu-ropean Court of Human Rights in Strasbourg procedure is available.

---

① Fundamental Law of Hungary, Art. XV(2).

② For English version visit: http://www. coe. int/en/web/conventions/search-on-treaties/-/conven-tions/rms/0900001680063765.

③ For English version visit: http://www. coe. int/en/web/conventions/search-on-treaties/-/conven-tions/rms/090000168006377c.

④ Arts. 19 – 39.

⑤ Acts. CXXIII of 2007 on Expropriation.

3.3.4   Special regulations for the protection of foreign investments

As outlined above, the country's ability to attract foreign capital is essential for Hungary. In order to maximise the safety of foreign investments and also to promote the arrival of new investments, diverse legal rules have been promulgated containing all the modern tools for the protection of foreign investments.

Beyond these remedies open to all (also for domestic entities) provided by the Constitutional Court, the European Court of Human Rights and the administrative courts, the legal instruments specifically designed to protect foreign investment can be divided into the following groups:

ⅰ. Internal instruments;

ⅱ. Bilateral investment treaties(BIT) ;

ⅲ. Investment contracts;

ⅳ. Multilateral international investment treaties.

These will be explained below.

3.3.4.1   Internal instruments

In addition to the above-described constitutional regulation on the right to property and the prohibition of discrimination, Hungary drafted a special act[1] in 1988 to protect foreign investment.

This act expressly declares as follows:

(1) The investments of foreigners enjoy total protection and security in Hungary.

(2) The foreigner shall be compensated on actual value and without delay for damages in his/her property resulting from the measures involving nationalisation, expropriation or similar legal effect.

(3) The state provides compensation over the administrative authority by which the measure was enacted. In case of infringement of the law review of public administrative decisions relating to compensation can be requested from the court.

(4) The amount of compensation shall be paid in the investment currency to the investor.

This provision accords with the absolute guarantee of the right to property. Therefore the investment or the part it may be real or movable property, or an intan-

---

[1]   Act XXIV of 1988 on the Investments of Foreigners in Hungary.

gible asset, right or entitlement. Special protection for foreign investments thus covers everything that is part of the foreign investment.

In addition, the Act states that foreign investors are entitled to the same status as Hungarian investors and that they are free to settle in Hungary in accordance with of international agreements.

3.3.4.2 Bilateral investment treaties

Hungary began entering into bilateral investment treaties in 1987,[1] and concluded a number of such agreements in a short time. Since the beginning, this practice was motivated by the intention to attract foreign investors to Hungary, and as a result Hungary has signed such an agreement with all of its economic partners. Those conventions include legal regulation for the protection of international investments, providing the backbone of substantive legislation.

These agreements include as one of its objectives implementing the Convention, to the extent possible, without any reservation, to provide highest legal protection in the territory of the Contracting States against deprivation of foreign investment. For example, the bilateral investment treaty[2] between India and Hungary includes the following:

> "The Republic of Hungary and the Republic of India (hereinafter referred to as the Contracting Parties), desiring to intensify economic cooperation to the mutual benefit of both Contracting Parties, intending to create conditions favourable for fostering greater investment by investors of one Contracting Party in the territory of the other Contracting Party, recognising that the encouragement and reciprocal protection under international agreement of such investment will be conducive to the stimulation of individual business initiative and will increase prosperity in both Contracting Parties, have agreed as follows..."

Moreover, the highly relevant content of this bilateral investment treaty defines the terms of foreign investor and foreign investment. Since both parties have fundamental interests in the investments enjoying the fullest possible legal protection in

---

① Decree-Law No. 5 of 1988 on the promulgation of agreement between the Hungarian People's Republic and the Federal Republic of Germany on promotion and mutual protection of investments.

② Act CLXXXIX of 2005 on the promulgation of agreement signed in New Delhi, 3 November 2003 between the Republic of Hungary and the Republic of India on Promotion and Protection of Investments. The text of the BIT can be found via the official open access legal database of Hungary: http://njt. hu/cgi_bin/njt_doc. cgi? docid = 95957. 135351.

each other's territory, both the terms of foreign investor and foreign investment are determined as widely as possible in the conventions. For example, in Article 1 of the bilateral investment treaty between India and Hungary this term is defined as the following:

"1. investment means every kind of asset established or acquired, in connection with economic activities by an investor of one Contracting Party in the territory of the other Contracting Party in accordance with the national laws of the Contracting Party in whose territory the investment is made and in particular, though not exclusively, includes:

(a) movable and immovable property as well as other rights such as mortgages, liens or pledges;

(b) shares in and stock and debentures of a company and any other similar forms of participation in a company;

(c) rights to money or to any performance under contract having an economic value;

(d) intellectual property rights, including patents, copyrights, trademarks and registered designs, in accordance with the relevant laws of the respective Contracting Party;

(e) any right or business concessions conferred by law or under contract and any licences pursuant to law, including the concessions to search for, exploit or extract oil and other natural resources.

Any alteration of the form in which assets are invested shall not affect their character as investment.

2. investor means any national or company of a Contracting Party who invests in the territory of the other Contracting Party. "

Hungary provides the highest level of legal protection of the widest scope for the foreign investors. For example, in Articles 2 – 5 of the bilateral investment treaty between India and Hungary specify the extent of legal protection as the followings:

"Article 2 Scope of the Agreement

This Agreement shall apply to all investments made by investors of either Contracting Party in the territory of the other Contracting Party, accepted as such in accordance with its laws and regulations, whether made before or after the coming into force of this Agreement, but shall not apply to any dispute concerning an investment which arose, or any claim which was settled before its entry into force.

Article 3 Promotion and Protection of Investments

1. Each Contracting Party shall encourage and create favourable conditions for investors of the other Contracting Party to make investments in its territory and admit such investments in accordance with its laws and regulations.

2. Investments and returns of investors of each Contracting Party shall at all times be accorded fair and equitable treatment and shall enjoy full protection and security in the territory of the other Contracting Party.

Article 4 National Treatment and Most-Favoured-Nation Treatment

1. Each Contracting Party shall accord to investments and returns of investors of the other Contracting Party, treatment which shall not be less favourable than that accorded either to investments of its own investors or to investments of investors of any third State.

2. Each Contracting Party shall in its territory accord to investors of the other Contracting Party, as regards management, maintenance, use, enjoyment or disposal of their investment, treatment which is fair and equitable and not less favourable than that which it accords to its own investors or of any third State, whichever is more favourable.

3. The provisions of paragraph 1 and 2 of this Article shall not be construed so as to oblige one Contracting Party to extend to the investors of the other the benefit of any treatment, preference or privilege which may be extended by the former Contracting Party by virtue of:

(a) Any customs union or free trade area or a monetary union or similar international agreements leading to such unions or institutions or other forms of cooperation to which either of the Contracting Parties is or may become a party;

(b) Any matter pertaining wholly or mainly to taxation.

Article 5 Expropriation

1. Investments of investors of either Contracting Party shall not be nationalised, expropriated or subjected to measures having effect equivalent to nationalisation or expropriation (hereinafter referred to as expropriation) in the territory of the other Contracting Party except for a public purpose in accordance with the laws of the Contracting Party making the expropriation, on a non-discriminatory basis and against fair compensation. Such compensation shall a-

mount to the market value of the investment expropriated immediately before the expropriation or before the impending expropriation became public knowledge, whichever is the earlier, shall include interest at a fair rate from the date of expropriation until the date of payment, shall be made without unreasonable delay, be effectively realizable and be freely transferable in a freely convertible currency.

2. The investor affected shall have a right, in accordance with the laws of the Contracting Party making the expropriation to review, by a judicial or other independent authority of that Contracting Party, of his or its case and of the valuation of his or its investment in accordance with the principles set out in this Article.

3. The provisions of paragraph 1 of this Article shall also apply where a Contracting Party expropriates the assets of a company which is incorporated or constituted under the law in force in any part of its own territory, and in which investors of the other Contracting Party own shares. "

The content of these bilateral investment treaties varies depending on the situation and the intent of the two contracting countries, but in addition to the above described parts, typically and necessarily includes the following:

  • declaration of the right to property, i. e. the inviolability of the investor's ownership of the investment and fixing the international law conditions of deprivation (public interest, non-discrimination, a regulated procedure);

  • the need to provide immediate, unconditional, total, in real value compensation;

  • non-discriminatory treatment, i. e. the national treatment and most favoured nation treatment;

  • guarantee of external, international dispute resolution by the application of a "foreign control clause". That means that foreign investors are also considered a foreign investor if the investment is made by establishing a company resident in the contacting state, which would be otherwise a resident entity not entitled to turn to an international arbitration court. This fiction reserves the international character of the investment, and therefore the possibility remains of using an international dispute resolution forum in case of deprivation; and

  • the need to provide in an arbitration agreement for an international dispute resolution form(e. g. ICSID) and mutual submission to jurisdiction.

Bilateral investment treaties are international conventions, and thus establish international legal obligations for the investment recipient country to provide maximum protection of foreign investments. Consequently, in case of deprivation or any harm to the investment, diplomatic protection is available to protect the investment.

3. 3. 4. 3   Investment contracts

Besides the bilateral investment treaties, it is becoming common to conclude individual investment contracts between the investor and the host state in case of new investments of high value and importance. Almost all of the large foreign investments in Hungary are founded on an investment contract. Hungary explicitly supports the conclusion of such investment contracts.

The function of an investment contract is to complement an existing bilateral investment treaty or to establish a new legal mechanism when there is no bilateral treaty. Investment contracts generally include provisions that are typically found in bilateral investment treaties. An investment contract, however, provides the opportunity to achieve a higher level and/or a tailored form of investment protection.

One of the commonly used techniques to provide a higher level of protection is the "freezing in clause", which provides effective protection against nationalisation by prohibiting the state from changing the law governing the economic sector of the investment. This means that the investor and the host state stipulate in the investment contract that the legal environment at the time of signing the contract will continue to be applicable if deprivation or any harm of the investment occurs regardless of any change in the domestic law. By using this technique, the investment cannot be nationalised by a subsequent legislative amendment.

When compared to bilateral investment treaties, a significant advantages of investment contracts is confidentiality. Being international conventions, bilateral investment treaties have to be published in full, whereas an investment contract is generally a confidential document. Thanks to this, parties to an investment contract are able to regulate their relations in relation to many matters without their being disclosed to the public or, quite crucially, to competitors. They can also facilitate agreement, on a confidential basis, regarding any government support, other financial (e. g. favourable state loans) or other types of advantages granted by the host State (e. g. exemption of administrative licensing procedures), or taxation agreements.

3.3.4.4   Multilateral conventions

Hungary is a member of the Council of Europe and a contracting party in the European Convention on Human Rights (Rome, 1950) and has joined international organizations and international conventions specialising on investment protection. In 1987 Hungary joined the International Centre for Investment Disputes (ICSID) establishing the Washington Convention 1965[1] and in 1988 to the Seoul Convention 1985 on establishing the Multilateral Investment Guarantee Agency (MIGA). [2]

The 1965 Washington Convention established the International Centre of Investment Disputes (ICSID) within the World Bank Group. This is a permanent international arbitration tribunal specialising on deprivation of foreign investments. In addition to the Washington Convention, Hungary has its own investment dispute settlement procedure rules.

Typically, Hungarian bilateral investment treaties, and sometimes the investment contracts, recognize the jurisdiction of ICSID, and it fulfils its obligations under international law coming from the Washington Convention to ensure the implementation of ICSID's decisions. Some bilateral investment treaties or investment contracts may agree on an arbitration clause providing for an arbitration court other than ICSID.

It should be noted that Hungary is a member of the Multilateral Investment Guarantee Agency (MIGA), which is also part of the World Bank Group. Among others, the MIGA provides insurance for investments in developing countries against non-commercial (war, civil war, insurrection, expropriation, etc.) risk. However, Hungary is not considered to be a developing country, so MIGA does not provide insurance for investments in Hungary.

3.4   Summary

Hungary has been an important destination for foreign investment for already two and a half decades, and that alone is reason enough for the conclusion that there is a mutually beneficial long-term partnership between investors and the state. Foreign investments play a very important, or the most important, role in the economy and

---

[1]   The accession was promulgated in Hungary by Decree-Law No. 27 of 1987.

[2]   The accession was promulgated in Hungary by Decree-Law No. 7 of 1987.

these investments are the engine of development. Accordingly, a very open economic system has developed, which is supported by the legal system for the fullest possible protection for foreign investments.

The substantive rules in domestic legislation, bilateral investment treaties and investment contracts supplemented by organisational and procedural rules established by the Washington Convention provide in Hungary the highest legal level of protection available for foreign investment.

Chapter 4   Monetary and Banking System and Law

Klára Gellén

Monetary policy means financial policy and practice which aims to achieve the supply and demand balance of money and credit in the financial and capital market. Hence its priority is to safeguard economic stability. Monetary policy aims to achieve financial balance primarily through the supply and demand for money. The Hungarian Central Bank Council is responsible for conducting monetary policy.

In Hungary there is a dual-level banking system which includes monetary authorities, commercial banks and non-monetary financial institutions. In a dual-level banking system the central bank is not directly related to economic entities; it is only related to banks at the second level of the banking system. Characteristics of financial institutions at the second level of the banking system are as follows: they are profit oriented, they have independent budget, they adopt a form of a limited company, they are of mixed profile with no regional limitations and they are competition centered. Non-monetary financial institutions include bank-like institutions (savings bank, investment funds, mortgage banks) and non-bank institutions (insurance companies, pension schemes).

The main legal sources regulating the Hungarian financial sector are as follows: Act CXXXIX of 2013 on the National Bank of Hungary, Act CCXXXVII of 2013 on Credit Institutions and Financial Enterprises, Act LXXXV of 2009 on the Pursuit of the Business of Payment Services.

4.1   The National Bank of Hungary (MNB)

The National Bank of Hungary functions as a central bank and a bank of issue. Bank of issue means that this central bank has the monopoly of issuing banknotes. The National Bank of Hungary is a legal entity which operates as a public limited-liability company owned by the State of Hungary and established in Budapest. [1] Its ac-

---

① Article 5 of Act CXXXIX of 2013 on the National Bank of Hungary.

tivity and operation are regulated by Act CXXXIX of 2013 on the National Bank of Hungary.

The primary objective of the MNB is to achieve and maintain price stability. Without prejudice to its primary objective, the MNB aims to maintain the stability of the financial intermediary system, to increase its resilience and to ensure its sustainable contribution to economic growth, and to support the economic policy of the Government using the means at its disposal.

The MNB also defines and implements monetary policy and supervises the financial intermediary system. It also aims to carry out the settlement of disputes via the Financial Arbitration Board between consumers and the persons and bodies relating to the conclusion and performance of contracts for the supply of services with a view to reaching an out-of-court settlement. ①

The bodies of the MNB are: the Monetary Council; the Financial Stability Board; the Executive Board and the Supervisory Board. ②

4.2 Financial auxiliary services and financial institutions in Hungary

Act CCXXXVII of 2013 on Credit Institutions and Financial Enterprises describes what are financial services and financial auxiliary services. Particular financial services and financial auxiliary services may be performed subject to authorization by the MNB(referred to as Authority) acting within its function as a supervisory authority of the financial intermediary system.

4.2.1 Financial services

Financial services mean taking deposits and receiving other repayable funds from the public, credit and loan operations, financial leasing, money transmission services, issuance of electronic money, issuance of paper-based cash-substitute payment instruments(for example traveler's cheques and bills printed on paper) and the provision of the services related thereto, which are not recognized as a money transmission service, providing surety facilities and guarantees, as well as other forms of banker's obligations, commercial activities in foreign currency, foreign exchange other than currency exchange services, bills and cheques on own account or as com-

---

① Ibid., Article 4.

② Ibid., Article 8.

mission agents, financial intermediation services, safe custody services, safety deposit box services, credit reference services and purchasing receivables. ①

Financial auxiliary services include currency exchange activities, operation of payment systems, money processing activities, financial brokering on the interbank market as well as activities for the issue of negotiable credit tokens. ②

The difference between financial services and auxiliary financial services is that auxiliary financial services may generally be pursued along with, complementary to or related to a particular financial service. Both financial service and auxiliary financial service activities may be pursued in Hungarian Forints or other currencies. Authorisations issued to allow such activities do not name specific foreign currency or foreign exchange in which such activities may be pursued.

4.2.2   Financial Institutions

Financial services may be offered exclusively by financial institutions. Financial institutions include credit institutions and financial enterprises. These two types of institutions are authorised to offer financial services exclusively by way of business provided that they have obtained prior authorisation. There is a difference between credit institutions and financial enterprises as particular financial services may be offered exclusively by credit institutions, however, they may not be pursued by financial enterprises. ③

4.2.2.1   Credit institutions

Credit institution means a financial institution whose business *inter alia* includes taking deposits or other repayable funds from the public with the aim of public fundraising which may also issue bonds and deposit certificates. It means that a credit institution must pursue both activities. It is only a credit institution that can take deposits and other repayable funds from the public in excess of their own funds (without a guarantee or without any surety facilities provided by a credit institution or the State for guaranteeing repayment) as well as to provide currency exchange services. The MNB may not authorise a financial institution which is also not a credit institution to pursue such activities. ④

---

① Part 1., Article 3 of Act CCXXXVII of 2013 on Credit Institutions and Financial Enterprises.
② Ibid., Part 2., Article 3.
③ Ibid., Article 7.
④ Ibid., Article 8.

There are three types of credit institution:

• *Banks* are credit institutions which are authorised to perform all financial services including taking deposits, credit and loan operations and money transmission services by way of business. Only banks may be authorised to perform all the financial service activities and they are exclusively entitled to use the expression "bank" in their company name.

• *Specialised credit institutions* may not be authorised to perform all the financial services. Each specialised credit institution must operate in accordance with the relevant provisions which include all information specific to the particular specialised credit institution. "Specialised" means that the particular credit institution performs one or more financial services in a special and unique way.

—*Building savings bank*: the basic activities of such savings banks may be considered to include taking deposits and credit operations in accordance with the building savings contract.

—*Mortgage bank*: a mortgage bank basically performs activities such as loans on real estate secured by a mortgage as well as issuing mortgage bonds as a loan.

• Credit institutions set up as a "cooperative society" may perform financial service activities within an even more limited scope than specialised credit institutions.

Banks and specialised credit institutions may only operate as limited companies, the other financial institutions may be limited companies or set up as cooperatives.

4.2.2.2   Financial enterprises

A financial enterprise is authorised to provide financial services which are not exclusively reserved for credit institutions. In practice, leasing companies, factoring service companies and various claim handlers operate as financial enterprises. A financial enterprise may exclusively perform financial brokering on the interbank market. ①

4.2.3   Financial services provided by foreign companies in Hungary

A foreign company may provide financial services or engage in financial auxiliary service activities solely through its Hungarian branch with the exception of a

---

① Ibid., Article 9.

foreign financial institution which is established in a member state of the Organisation for Economic Cooperation and Development. Such institution may engage in credit and loan operations, financial leasing and financial brokering on the interbank market in the form of cross-border services, if it has been authorised to engage in such activities by the competent supervisory authority of the state where established. As the financial institutions of European Economic Area (EEA) member states may establish branches in other EEA member states without undergoing the authorisation procedure, legal provisions regulating the establishment of branches only apply to third-country financial institutions.

Third-country (that is, non-EEA) financial institutions may operate in Hungary through their branches and may perform practically the same activities as a bank. They must, however, be authorised by the competent supervisory authority to engage in such activities. Legislators have also built some additional requirements into the system, as the legal environment and particular rules relating to financial institutions of non-EEA states may completely differ from EU requirements. The parent company operating as a financial institution must submit a claim for establishing a branch, and present its authorisation by the competent authority of the state also indicating the financial service activities and auxiliary financial activities in which the company is engaged. The company must demonstrate that the company has been registered, and has paid all its dues to taxation and customs authorities, health insurance bodies and pension insurance administrative agencies. Only those third-country financial institutions which are capable of fulfilling such strict criteria may establish branches in Hungary.

Some of the requirements must be established by the State. For instance, the state where the foreign financial institution is established must establish that it has regulatory provisions to combat money laundering and terrorist financing in accordance with the requirements defined by Hungarian laws. Another broader, less concrete criterion is that the laws of the state where the company is established must ensure safe and prudent operation of financial institutions.

From January 2015, the criteria relating to branches have become less strict as a branch may be relieved of numerous prudential regulations. If a credit institution has been operating in Hungary in a safe manner for some years evidencing its prudent operation, it must be given the opportunity to establish a branch under more favourable conditions. Article 105/A sets out the circumstances when the MNB may make an exception for branches arriving from a third-country state to comply with prudential rules. It also sets out what those prudential rules are. There are other requirements that must be satisfied by a financial institution. It is the responsibility of the requesting institution to provide proof of the existence of its data processing rules which meet the requirements defined by Hungarian laws, and to guarantee that it takes full responsibility for all the activities performed by the branch under the company name. The requesting institution must also prove that it has been authorised by the competent supervisory authority of the state where it is established to establish a branch.

A foreign financial enterprise may also establish a branch in Hungary to provide a particular financial service if it has been authorised by the competent supervisory authority of the state where it is established to engage in such activity. [1]

4.2.4   Cross-border financial services of foreigners

Besides establishing a branch, credit institutions may also engage in activities in EEA member states by way of cross-border activities which they may perform under the principle of freedom to provide services. Cross-border activities may be performed by only EEA member states: however, a third-country financial institution may establish a branch in an EEA member state. Similarly, an EEA member state financial institution may establish a branch in a third-country state. In contrast to cross-border financial services may only be provided within the single market of EEA member states.

The same rule applies to cross-border services as to establishing branches: according to the single passport principle, a credit institution already authorised is not subject to another authorisation procedure to provide cross-border services: all that is required is to comply with a notification procedure. According to the definition of cross-border services, two conditions must be met in order to consider activities as cross-border activities. One condition is that the services must be provided by the financial institution in a country which is different from the country where the institution is established or where its other establishment, head office or branch is located. The other condition is that the service users' establishment or residence must be situated in a country that differs from the country where the financial institution provi-

---

[1]   Ibid., Article 9 and Articles 36 – 40.

ding services is established.

All findings relating to the general nature of cross-border financial services, notification procedures and other procedural rules relating to credit institutions too, apply to cross-border services supplied by financial enterprises. The only difference is that not all financial enterprises are authorised to supply cross-border financial services; only those enterprises which comply with the requirements included in the law are authorised to supply such services. ① (The requirements are as follows; The financial enterprise is established in an EEA member state, and the financial enterprise; (a) is the subsidiary, or a jointly controlled entity, of a credit institution that is established in the same EEA member state as the financial enterprise, or(b) is the subsidiary, or a jointly controlled entity, of a financial enterprise that meets the condition set out in Subparagraph(a) and is established in the same EEA member state as its subsidiary; and performs its activities in the EEA member state in which it is established; the parent company controls at least ninety per cent of the voting rights; the parent company provides the Authority with a certificate from the competent supervisory authority of the EEA member state in which it is established that the financial enterprise is managed in a prudent and circumspect manner; the parent company, with the consent of the competent supervisory authority, undertakes full responsibility for the financial enterprise's obligations; and the financial enterprise is subject to supervision on a consolidated basis with the parent company). ②

4.3   The definition of the credit and account agreements in the Civil Code(Act V of 2013)

4.3.1   Credit agreements

Under a credit agreement, the creditor undertakes to ensure the availability of credit up to a specific limit, and to conclude a loan agreement, contract of suretyship, guarantee contract or conduct other loan operations up to the said credit limit, and the debtor undertakes to pay the fee agreed upon. The creditor shall enter into a contract for loan operations when so requested by the debtor, if the conditions set out in the credit agreement are met. The debtor shall be entitled to call upon the

---

①   Ibid. , Article 41.

②   Ibid. , Article 15, paragraph 4.

creditor to conclude a contract during the period of availability fixed in the credit a-greement. ①

4.3.2   Loan agreements

Under a loan agreement, the creditor undertakes to make available a specific sum of money, and the debtor undertakes to repay that sum to the creditor at a later date with interest. ②

4.3.3   Deposit account contracts

Under a deposit account contract, the deposit holder is entitled to deposit a specific amount of money to the bank, and the bank undertakes to accept the sum of money offered by the deposit holder and to repay the same amount at a later date with interest. ③

4.3.4   Current account contracts

Under a current account contract, the parties assume an obligation to record and settle their enforceable monetary claims arising from a specific relationship in a consolidated account. ④

4.3.5   Payment account contracts

Under a payment account contract, the account keeper undertakes to open a current account for the account holder for handling his financial transactions, and the account holder undertakes to pay the fee agreed upon. ⑤

4.3.6   Payment service contracts

Under a payment service contract, the agent undertakes to pay a certain a-mount of money to the payee according to the payer's instructions, and the payer undertakes to pay the fee agreed upon. ⑥

4.3.7   Factoring contracts

Under a factoring contract, the factor undertakes to pay a certain amount of money, and the debtor undertakes to assign his claim from a third party to the fac-

---

① Article 6:382 of Civil Code.
② Ibid. , Article 6:383.
③ Ibid. , Article 6:390.
④ Ibid. , Article 6:391.
⑤ Ibid. , Article 6:394.
⑥ Ibid. , Article 6:400.

tor; if the obligor fails to satisfy the assigned claim at the time when due, the debtor shall be liable to repay the funds received with interest, and the factor shall be liable to re-assign the claim. ①

4.3.8   Financial leasing agreements

Under a financial leasing agreement, the lessor undertakes to make available for use, for a limited period of time a thing or a right he/she owns, and the lessee undertakes to accept the leased asset and to make lease payments if the lessee is given the right under the agreement to use the leased asset up to or surpassing its economic lifetime; or, if use is stipulated for a shorter period, to acquire the leased asset at the end of the term of the contract without any consideration or at a price considerably lower than the market value prevailing at the time of conclusion of the contract, or the total sum of lease payments reaches or exceeds the leased asset's market value prevailing at the time of conclusion of the contract. ②

4.4   The rules of payment services

According to Act LXXXV of 2009 on the Pursuit of the Business of Payment Services, in addition to payment transactions made in cash, the following means of payment are recognised:

A. payment between payment accounts;

B. cash payment to or from a payment account;

C. and payment transactions without any payment account. ③

The Decree No. 18/2009 (VIII. 6) MNB of the Governor of the National Bank of Hungary on Payment Services Activities determines the terms and contains the details of particular payment types. The following means of payment are be recognized according to the Payment Services Act:

A. Payment between payment accounts

• Credit transfer

A payment order for the transfer of funds (transfer order) means any instruction by a payer to his/her payment service provider requesting the execution of a pay-

---

①   Ibid. , Article 6:405.

②   Ibid. , Article 6:409.

③   Article 63 of Act LXXXV of 2009 on the Pursuit of the Business of Payment Services.

ment transaction for the transfer of a specific amount from his/her payment account to the payee's payment account. The payer must give the transfer order to the payment service provider carrying his/her payment account. If so agreed with the payment service provider, the transfer order may be submitted with the debit day indicated. Transfer of funds shall, in particular, mean:

(a) *group transfer*

Group transfer is any instruction by a payer under agreement with his/her payment service provider requesting the execution of payment transactions by giving, at the place and in the manner specified in the framework contract, transfer orders of the same title codes in batches for the transfer of specific amounts to different payees. [1]

(b) *periodic credit transfer*

Periodic credit transfer is an instruction by a payer to his/her payment service provider requesting the execution of a payment transaction for the transfer of a specific amount on specific days(debit days) periodically. The payment service provider must continue to execute a periodic credit transfer order until it is withdrawn by the payer or until the last debit day indicated on the transfer order. [2]

(c) *official transfer and remittance summons*

In connection with an official transfer order initiated by the payee through his/her payment service provider, the payment service provider carrying the payee's payment account must proceed after receipt of the official transfer order to verify that the account identification number does in fact belong to the payee indicated in the official transfer order as the account holder, and shall check the signature of the authorised signatory as registered with the payment service provider. The payment service provider carrying the payee's payment account must forward the information contained in the official transfer order to the payment service provider carrying the payer's payment account. The payer's payment service provider must proceed immediatcly upon receipt of the official transfer order and remittance summons to verify the account identification number of the payer indicated in the payment order as the account holder. [3]

---

[1]   Article 29 of Decree No. 18/2009(VIII. 6)MNB of the Governor of the National Bank of Hungary on Payment Services Activities.

[2]   Ibid., Article 30.

[3]   Ibid., Article 31.

• Direct debit

A direct debit is any instruction by a payee to the payment service provider carrying his/her payment account for debiting a payer's payment account with a specific amount and credit this amount to his/her payment account. ① Direct debit, in particular, means:

(a) *collection based on a letter of authorisation*

In the power of attorney (letter of authorisation), the payer (account holder) gives consent, in the manner notified to the payment service provider, to the payee to execute the direct debit payment transaction. The letter of authorisation may also lay down conditions for submission if so agreed between the payer and his/her payment service provider. Unless otherwise provided for by the letter of authorisation, the payment service provider must receive and execute a collection order based on a letter of authorisation until the payer withdraws the authorisation in writing. ②

(b) *bill collection*

Where a direct debit request is for the collection of a claim based on a bill of exchange, consent of the original drawee is embodied by the bill itself. With a collection order based on a bill of exchange the original draft must be enclosed. ③

(c) *check clearing*

Where a direct debit request is for cashing a check, consent of the issuer of the check is embodied by the cheque itself. With a cheque clearing order the original copy of the check must be enclosed. ④

(d) *automatic debit transfer*

By authorisation of the payers concerned, if agreed between the payee and payment service provider carrying his/her account, the payee must submit direct debit requests of the same title codes for the transfer of sums from the payment accounts of a large number of payers on a specific debit day, grouped in batches. The payment service provider carrying the payer's payment account must notify the payee, through the payment service provider carrying the payee's account, upon receipt of authorisation from the payer for the execution of automatic debit transfer, including any amendment to or the withdrawal thereof within four business days of receipt.

---

①   Ibid., Article 32.

②   Ibid., Article 34.

③   Ibid., Article 35.

④   Ibid., Article 36.

Where the transaction amount is limited, the payment service provider must be authorised to notify the payee concerning such amount limit only upon the payer's prior consent. ①

(e) *deferred payment documentary collection*

Deferred payment documentary collection order means the payee's instruction to the payment service provider carrying his/her payment account to have a specific amount collected and credit the said amount to his/her payment account from a payer who has an account at the Treasury for the purpose of enforcing a contractual payment obligation. On the deferred payment documentary collection order, the payee must set a deadline for the payer within which to file an objection against the payment collection(hereinafter referred to as "objection deadline"). The last day of the time limit for the objection must be set past the tenth business day following the date upon which the payee submits the order to the payment service provider carrying his/her current account. ②

(f) *documentary collection*

The beneficiary of the underlying transaction must submit to his/her payment service provider carrying his/her payment account the documentary collection order and the documents on which the claims are based, to be released to the payer(addressee) only upon payment, acceptance of a bill of exchange or upon the satisfaction of other conditions. ③

• Payment initiated by the payer through the payee

Where any payment is transacted by way of bank card in Hungary, if the currency in which the receipt is denominated corresponds with the currency of the payment account to which the bank card is linked or the line of credit linked to the credit card, the amount charged to the payment account or the line of credit must in all cases be the same as the amount indicated on the receipt. The payer's payment service provider must identify the payment transaction executed in Hungary by way of the country code disclosed by the payee's payment service provider, assigned to the payee in connection with the given payment transaction as specified in the payment order statement. ④

---

① Ibid., Article 37.
② Ibid., Article 38.
③ Ibid., Article 39.
④ Ibid., Article 40.

• Documentary credit(letter of credit)

Documentary credit means the payment service provider's (the opening payment service provider's) commitment, on the basis of the order submitted by the payer of the underlying transaction, made in his/her own name for paying the amount specified in the documentary credit if the payee submits the required documents within the deadline specified, provided that they are acceptable and in compliance with other conditions set out in the letter of credit. ①

B. Cash payment to or from a payment account

• Transactions with cashier's cheques(issue and acceptance)

The account holder may issue a cashier's cheque if he/she has concluded a cheque contract with his/her account carrier payment service provider. Unless otherwise agreed, the payment service provider must accept a cheque made out to the payment service provider up to the amount covered by the payment account indicated on the cheque by the account holder issuing it. When a payment account is terminated, the account holder must return all unused cheques (the cheque book) in his/her possession to the issuing payment service provider. The payment service provider must require the payee whose name is shown on the cashier's cheque or the bearer to sign the back of the cheque, acknowledging receipt of the money. ②

• Cash placed on a payment account

Apart from the account carrier payment service provider, other payment service providers may also accept cash deposits to payment accounts on the basis of an agreement between the payment service providers involved. ③

• Cash withdrawn from a payment account

Cash may be withdrawn from a payment account at the payment service provider carrying the account, or at another payment service provider acting under contract on his/her behalf. Cash may be withdrawn from a payment account at any of the designated tellers of the account carrier payment service provider by using a cash withdrawal form(e. g. cash withdrawal slip, cash withdrawal ticket) or by signing the cash desk voucher, or, outside of cheques, by way of a cash withdrawal voucher. Furthermore, cash may be withdrawn from a payment account by way of

---

①   Ibid. , Article 41.

②   Ibid. , Article 42.

③   Ibid. , Article 43.

the postal services (postal delivery) using a cash disbursement voucher. ①

C. Payment in the absence of a payment account

In connection with the use of cash withdrawal vouchers, the agreement between the account holder and the payment service provider carrying his/her payment account must determine: the procedures relating to supplies of cash withdrawal vouchers (cash withdrawal book), including application, delivery and return, and the formal and content requirements for cash withdrawal vouchers, and the rules for making out and signing them. ②

4. 5. Supervision and insurance of deposits

4. 5. 1   The National Bank of Hungary as a supervisory body

The MNB is responsible for the supervision of the financial sector. The rules relating to the supervisory procedure are contained in the MNB law. Within the framework of its responsibilities the MNB evaluates the applications submitted for authorization and other petitions, it maintains the records and registers assigned to its scope of competence, inspects the systems of the persons and bodies for the provision of information and oversees the data disclosure, moreover, it oversees the enforcement of national laws and the relevant EU legislation and the implementation of resolutions, it also opens market surveillance procedures identifying any operations conducted without authorization or in the absence of notification. The MNB collaborates with foreign financial supervisory authorities, in particular with the competent authorities of the EEA member states exercising financial supervision. ③

4. 5. 2   The National Deposit Insurance Fund(OBA)

It is the OBA's responsibility to indemnify persons entitled to compensation in case of frozen deposits. The insurance provided by the Fund is limited to registered deposits. The OBA must indemnify persons entitled to compensation for the principal and for the interest on frozen deposits up to a maximum amount of one hundred thousand euro per person and per credit institution on the aggregate. ④

---

①   Ibid. , Article 44.

②   Ibid. , Article 47.

③   Articles 39-44 of Act CXXXIX of 2013 on the National Bank of Hungary.

④   Articles 212-214 of Act CCXXXVII of 2013 on Credit Institutions and Financial Enterprises.

Chapter 5   Laws Relating to Infrastructure Construction in Hungary

Orsolya Johanna Sziebig

Development, sustainability, financing are the core issues of the 21st century for the international community on a national, regional and global level. Construction of infrastructure, that is, developing and creating additional value for a country usually guided by long-term program, is influenced by various factors, such as the existing legal background of the State and financial measures.

The main aim of this part is to summarise the relevant legal and financial issues and highlight restrictions and fault lines that affect investments into the Hungarian economy. The related area has three main legal pillars: international obligations, the European Union's rules and local regulations. The national law always has to be in line with the self-imposed international norms and the obligations that arise from our EU membership. In this chapter the international and EU law measures will be mentioned when it is a necessity to understand the Hungarian context.

5.1. The legal measures relating to investments in Hungary

The creation of a new infrastructure is a complicated process, technically and economically. Investment is defined as the development or purchase of a means of production, and in this way economical performers are able to gain benefits in order to help the production of other benefits. "Investment" is a way to gain profitable returns, as interest, income or appreciation in value. In this way the production of other benefits and values are supported by the investor. One important area is the investment into construction which is secured by the legislation. Historically, in the 20th century the main legal rules were in the Constructional Investment Codex (in force till the end of the 1960s). The definition of construction was set out in Governmental Decree No. 45/1961 (09. XII). The operational legal act is Act LXXVIII of 1997 on Formation and Protection of the Built Environment. My aim here is just to provide an overview of the legislation. The aim of the Act is to provide a proper legislative background for the "Built Environment". The Act has general and special rules regarding to the above mentioned topic as follows:

Part I . general regulations such as the effect of the legislation;definitions;
general requirements(development and protection of the built environment);
the building tasks of the State,building tasks of the local authorities.

Part II . urban development and urban design with specialized rules of the
development of the capital city and advantaged areas (Danube-coast and
"Városliget").

Part III. rules of the process of construction.

Part IV. the reservation,use,protection of the built environment.

Part V . other and closing regulations.

The general requirements of the creation and protection of the built environment are specified at Part I of the Act as follows:

The urban development concept has to be

  • in accordance with the legislation by the integrated urban development
strategy, urban development instruments and architectural-engineering documentation.

  • in accordance with the architectural,engineering,safety,hygiene,desti-
nation and use and the rules of environment and nature protection legislation.

  • considering the humane environment and esthetic creation.

  • on the basis of participants' cooperation.

Some investments are productive (e. g. industry, agriculture) and others are
non-productive(e. g. health service,education,culture,social supply and other com-
municational services). ①

5.1.1 Forms of public-private partnerships

The output focused forms of public-private partnerships(PPPs) are the(a)con-
cessions②, (b)the Build-Operate-Transfer(BOTs) and(c)the Design-Build-Oper-
ate (DBOs). The BOTs and DBOs are used both in the areas of greenfield and

---

① Ágfalvi,Mihály:*Mérnökgeodézia* 1.2010.

② Concession means that the state or the local government enters into a contract with the winner of the competition in order to provide activities defined by the relevant legislation.

brownfield projects[1] as part of long-term projects and operations. [2] The existing form of the concession was read into the Hungarian law regulated by Act XVI of 1991 on Concessions. [3]

Natural and legal persons as well partnerships without legal personality who are qualified as foreign entities under the foreign currency rules can be a partner to concessional contract under the same conditions and opportunities as the local entities. The concession is based on the idea that even outside the framework of the market economy there are several activities which are reserved for the government on grounds of public interest. The concessional act was written to define the monopoly of the government regarding the above mentioned activities and to create the framework for those activities which can be open to the private sector. The treaty of concession is connected to the exclusive property or authority of the state, the local government or the association of local governments. By creating concessional treaties, the states or local governments yield the possession, use and the right of profit-taking to the winner of the competition. The treaty of concession can be created for maximum 35 years and must be definite in term. The activities under the concession act can be divided into two main parts: (a) the actuation of things which belong exclusively to the state(e. g. public roads), and (b) the exclusive economic activity of the state(e. g. gambling, mining, trade in tobacco products). [4] In Hungary, the trade in tobacco products is an exclusive governmental activity which can be yielded under the legislation of the concession act for a defined term. In the last couple of years, the new Hungarian governmental measures[5] regulating the trade on tobacco

---

① Greenfield and Brownfield projects are the two main types of foreign direct investment(FDI). During the greenfield projects "a parent company begins a new venture by constructing new facilities in a country outside of where the company is headquartered", besides at the brownfield projects "a company or government purchases an existing facility to begin new production." See http://www. investopedia. com/ask-/answers/043015/what-difference-between-green-field-and-brown-field-investment. asp.

② http://ppp. worldbank. org/public-private-partnership/agreements/concessions-bots-dbos (13 March 2016).

③ Act XVI of 1991 on concession; see
http://net. jogtar. hu/jr/gen/hjegy_doc. cgi? docid =99100016. TV(in Hungarian).

④ Várhomoki-Molnár, Márta: The Hungarian Model of Concession and the European Law. http://epa. oszk. hu/02600/02687/00006/pdf/EPA02687_jogi_tanulmanyok_2014_635-644. pdf(13 March 2016).

⑤ Act CXXXIV of 2012 on the roll-back of minor's smoking and the trade in tobacco products.
See http://net. jogtar. hu/jr/gen/hjegy_doc. cgi? docid = A1200134. TV(in Hungarian).

products were questioned by several participants of the market. A new tobacco distribution system was implemented in 2013 such as the National Tobacco Stores. ①
Under the new Tobacco legislation, the operation of the Tobacco Shops are in the hand of private investors but they won the right to open and operate the Shops by a competition procedure that was questioned by several parties, because of the confiscation of the applications(the method of judging applications) , and besides, several winner applicants were "close" to the governmental power.

Another disputed issue was the new gambling legislation and the concession treaties with the Las Vegas Casino Ltd. ②

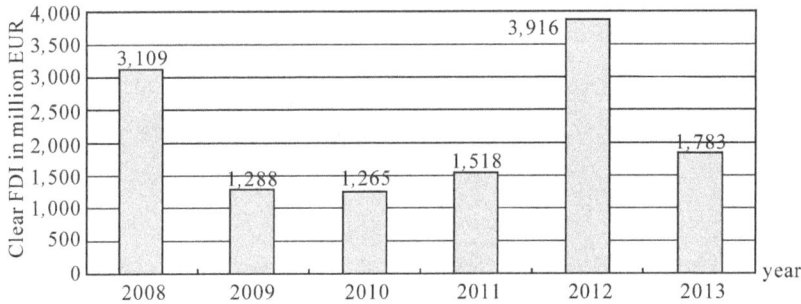

Figure 1. Clear FDI to Hungary

Source : The author's own tabulation.

To express the Hungarian investment situation, let us examine the FDI numbers. The capital attraction activity has changed in the recent years regarding the Hungarian economy. The foreign direct investment was EUR 10. 85 billion in 2012 and EUR 2. 3 billion in 2013, but a significant part of the capital was just flown through the Hungarian economy(e. g. a foreign parent company buys another foreign company through a Hungarian subsidiary company) , so if we highlight those factors and clear up the FDI with the bank capital flow, the clear FDI is less than the "official" numbers. In this way the clear FDI was around EUR 4 billion in 2012 and

①   http://www. euromonitor. com/tobacco-in-hungary/report(13 March 2016).

②   The treaties are available on the website of the Ministry of National Development only in Hungarian. http://www. kormany. hu/en/ministry-of-national-development/information-in-the-public-interest.

EUR 1. 8 billion in 2013 (see Figure 1). ①

5.1.2   Public procurement(PP)

Public procurement is defined as an act of obtaining or buying goods or services by the government. The process includes the preparation and processing of a demand, receipt of goods or services and payment approval. ② The Hungarian PP rules have to correspond with the WTO Agreement on Government Procurement (GPA) measures③ and with the EU legislation. ④

The characteristics of the procurement process are the following: the Hungarian Public Procurement Rules are found in hard law (legislation) and soft law (such as the President's Briefings and the Authority's Guidelines).

5.1.2.1   The Hungarian public procurement legislation

The hard law consists of Act CXLIII of 2015 on Public Procurement, ⑤ the so-called PPA(Public Procurement Act). ⑥ The new PPA incorporates all the new EU directives(EU Directives 2014/23,24,25) relating to public procurement procedures

---

①   http://www. portfolio. hu/gazdasag/jon-e_a_mukodotoke_magyarorszagra. 198024. html(13 March 2016).

②   See http://dictionary. cambridge. org/dictionary/english/public-procurement and
http://www. businessdictionary. com/definition/government-procurement. html(13 March 2016).

③   See for the Protocol Amending the Agreement on Government Procurement Protocol:
http://kozbeszerzes. hu/data/attachments/2014/05/14/Protocol_amending_the_GPA. pdf.

④   The European Commission accepted the new PP related legislation on 20 December 2011 that built from three pillars to replace the existing Directive 2004/17/EC and 2004/18/EC: two directives relate to the classic and public service sector and another directive is connected to the rules of concessions. The new regulations were accepted on 15 January 2014 and had to be implemented by the Member States in 24 months. The normative laws of the EU are the following: Directive 2014/55/EU of April 2014 on electronic invoicing in public procurement; Directive 2014/24/EU of 26 February 2014 on public procurement and repealing Directive 2004/18/EC; Directive 2014/25/EU of 26 February 2014 on procurement by entities operating in the water, energy, transport and postal services sectors and repealing Directive 2004/17/EC; Directive 2014/23/EU of 26 February 2014 on the award of concession contracts; Directive 2004/18/EC of 31 March 2004 on the coordination of procedures for the award of public works contracts, public supply contracts and public service contracts and Directive 2004/17/EC of 31 March 2004 on the coordination of the procedures for awarding public procurement in the water, energy, transport and postal services sectors. EU legislation http://www. kozbeszerzes. hu/jogi-hatter/eu-s-szabalyozas/(13 March 2016).

⑤   Most of the regulations of the PPA entered into force on 1 November 2015. However, the rules on mandatory electronic procedure will be applicable later: for centralised purchasing activities from 1 November 2016 and for all public procurement procedures from 1 February 2017.

⑥   The English version of the PPA is available at the following link:
http://kozbeszerzes. hu/data/documents/2015/07/03/PPA_2015_07_01. pdf.

and aims to implement EU rules regarding concessions and procurement by classic contracting authorities as well as in the utilities sector. ① The classic fields of the PPA are the public works contracts, public supply contracts and public service contracts. On the other hand, the utility sector means: the PP procedures at the field of the water, energy, transport and postal services sectors and repealing. The differentiation is more about the sector of the PP and less about the contracting parties. The aim of the act is defined in Article 1 : "This Act regulates contract award procedures and rules concerning the legal remedies related thereto for the sake of a reasonable and effective use of public funds and with the aim of providing for the public control thereof and furthermore with the aim of ensuring fair competition in public procurement. In addition, the purpose of this Act and the legislation based on its execution is to enhance access of small and medium-sized enterprises to contract award procedures, to promote sustainable development, social considerations of the State and lawful employment. " ②

As for quality matters, among the major changes is the need to consider not only the price but also other relevant factors when weighing bids. ③ Winning tenders should ultimately be chosen in accordance with what the contracting authority considers to be economically the best solution among those offered. The legislation should guarantee transparency, non-discrimination and equal treatment through various channels. The best price-quality ratio should always include a price or cost element, which is objective. Furthermore, during the evaluation process, contracting authorities should rely on professional evaluation methods. Such methods would be elaborated by the legislature in cooperation with professional bodies. These methods would be either obligatory for contracting authorities or may serve as non-binding guideline to follow.

Now is the time for professionals to lobby, so that they have a chance to help determine what the quality determinants will be. Tenderer's lobbying activity will be vital in relation to new professional quality criteria. Through the related professional bodies, powerful companies may submit their recommendations on the new evalua-

---

① Rather than simply amending its laws, Hungary has undertaken to create a whole new Public Procurement Act, which must be in place by the end of 2016. The government has already shared its concept of what the law might look like, and is now using that concept to make draft of legislation.

② PPA Article 1.

③ Note that the EU directive calls for changes to ensure the "best price-quality" ratio.

tion criteria and even have an influence on the government's different professional policies. Therefore, in the future, the companies' success may depend on the initial lobbying activity.

Another change is the opportunity for firms who might otherwise not be allowed to bid to change their status by "self-cleaning" their past record, so they can participate in current tenders. If a tenderer committed a serious breach of a previous public contract, they must be excluded from bidding for new tenders. According to the new rules, however, if such a tenderer can prove their reliability despite the previous breach, they should not be excluded from making a bid. According to the concept, an independent authority would decide on the reliability of the tenderer in such a case. This should guarantee the fairness and transparency of the procedure.

Overall, the changes bring transparency, something that will be a welcome change to many market players in Hungary. From a public procurement perspective, the new rules aim to ensure a more effective and transparent use of EU funds which have been already granted. The concept highlights the problem of contract awards where there was only one bidder, and offers certain solutions for that. The one-bidder issue takes place mostly in negotiated procedures launched without prior notification. This type of procedure is heavily criticized by the EU.

The new rule is that in procurements the value of which exceeds a certain threshold a summary sheet of the most important data of the given procurement procedure should be published on the website of the Public Procurement Authority① at least three days before the start of the procedure. If, on the basis of such information, a potential bidder notifies the contracting authority of its willingness to participate, the contracting authority would have to ensure the participation of all potential bidders on an equal footing. ②

5.1.2.2   Complaints and remedies

a. Complaints

According to Act CXLIII of 2015 on Public Procurement, a Public Procurement Arbitration Board (hereinafter referred to as the Arbitration Board) was created in order to deal with complaints regarding to the PP procedure. The Arbitration Board is empowered to conduct proceedings instituted against any infringement of the legislative provisions applicable to public procurement or contract award procedures. The infringement might include the proceeding initiated against the rejection of the request for prequalification specified in a separate act of legislation and the deletion

---

① The Public Procurement Authority was established by Act XL of 1995 on Public Procurement and was defined as a central budgetary organ. Act CXLIII of 2015 on Public Procurement basically left its structure intact. Within the framework of the Public Procurement Authority, a Council of 19 members operates. The Council operating within the framework of the Authority includes all three segments of the major actors of public procurements, thus, all the interest groups may take part in the decision making process. The enforcement of the principles of the PPA and specific objectives in the public interest, the interests of contracting authorities and of tenderers shall be the responsibility of the persons stipulated in the PPA. The Authority's manifold duties are stipulated in the PPA. Among others the Authority:

(a) monitors the application of the law and formulates its opinion on draft legislations,

(b) makes guidelines (without legal force),

(c) collects and publishes statistical data on public procurement,

(d) edits the Official Journal of the Authority (the Public Procurement Bulletin), verifies and publishes the notices related to the contract award and design contest procedures,

(e) maintains the Public Procurement Database, which is the central register of contract award procedures,

(f) maintains relationships with public procurement bodies of other EU Member States,

(g) organizes conferences, trainings, professional courses,

(h) monitors the amendment and execution of public procurement contracts,

(i) is responsible for the tasks related to the operation and maintenance of the electronic public procurement system.

② http://globalcompliancenews.com/hungary-new-bidding-law-likely-to-increase-transparency-20150306/.

from the prequalification list. The Arbitration Board may open a procedure upon a claim① or *ex officio*.

Before commencing the proceeding of the Arbitration Board, the tenderer may apply to the contracting authority to review its decision(preliminary dispute settlement). ② As a rule a claim must be made to the Arbitration Board within 15 days of becoming aware of the infringement of the PPA, but in case the claim is related to the closure decision of the contract award procedure, the proceeding must be launched within 10 days. In any event, it is not possible to make a claim 90 days after the occurrence of the infringement.

The application has to include all the relevant information as stipulated in Article 149(1) of the PPA and an administrative service fee has to be paid. The Arbitration Board may take interim measures, upon request or of its own motion, before the conclusion of the contract, if there is indicative evidence that an infringement of the rules of the contract award procedure has been committed or a risk thereof is detected. ③

The Arbitration Board holds a hearing if it considers it necessary for the clarification of the cause of action. The hearing must be held in public.

The Arbitration Board may impose a fine, ranging from HUF 50, 000 to 500,000, on the applicant or any other person taking part in the review procedure if they:

• disclose wrong or false data, relevant to the judgment of the case;

• fail to supply information at all or within the deadline;

• hinder access to documents related to business or public procurement activities;

• make a clearly unsubstantiated statement with respect to exclusion, or make a repeated unsubstantiated statement against the same public procurement commis-

---

① The claim can be submitted by a contracting authority, a tenderer(and in the case of a joint tender any of the tenderers) , a candidate(and in the case of a joint request to participate any of the candidates) , or any other interested person whose right or legitimate interest is being harmed or risks being harmed by an activity or default which is in conflict with the PPA.

② If, after the opening of tenders, the tenderer has applied for a preliminary dispute settlement, the contracting authority is not allowed to conclude the contract before the expiry of 10 days from sending its answer.

③ As an interim measure the Arbitration Board may order the suspension of the public procurement procedure or request the contracting authority in charge of the contested procedure to invite the applicant to take part in the procedure.

sioner during the same procedure.

The Arbitration Board's decisions have to be taken within 15 days if a hearing is not held, 25 days if a hearing is held, and 60 days if the proceedings initiated against the amendment or performance of a public procurement contract allegedly in a manner violating the PPA. An additional 10 days extension can be granted if justified.

Decisions are delivered to the parties and other interested parties. They are also published in the Public Procurement Bulletin.

The application of the legal consequences required by the PPA does not preclude the application of the Civil Code, according to which a contract awarded in violation of the PPA can be declared void. ①

b. Legal remedy-procedure of the court

No direct appeal can be lodged against the Arbitration Board's decisions. The courts can review these decisions only if so requested in the form of a statement of claim. The reason for reviewing the decision of the Arbitration Board can be not only for an infringement of the law, but also if the plaintiff has found that the Arbitration Board—in accordance with the PPA—had assessed, qualified the previous proceeding in an appropriate way. The Arbitration Board has to measure various sides of the PP procedures with regard to all circumstances of the case. The Arbitration Board has to measure two highlighted factors, namely whether(ⅰ)the injurious act has directly affected the petitioner; and(ⅱ)the correct and lawful procedure would make a difference to the legal position of the petitioner.

The procedure for invoking judicial assistance is as follows:

• a statement of claim must be submitted to the Arbitration Board within 15 days from the service of the Board's decision;

• the Arbitration Board must send the statement and the documents of the proceeding to the court within five days;

• the court must serve the statement of claim within eight days, simultaneously informing the plaintiff and the parties involved, in case they wish to intervene;

• the statement does not have a suspending effect on the enforcement of the Board's decision. However, if the application contains a request for the suspension of the enforcement of the decision, the court takes a decision within five days fol-

---

① http://www. kozbeszerzes. hu/nyelvi-verziok/complaints-and-remedies/.

lowing the receipt of the documents at the court and it must send its decision to the parties without delay.

The court may overrule or annul the Arbitration Board's decision and order a new procedure to be conducted by the Arbitration Board. Furthermore, the Regional Court may review decisions of the court if the PPA allows further remedy.

The decision of the Arbitration Board may not be annulled by the court unless an infringement of the substantial rules on legal remedy proceedings having an effect on the substance of the case occurred in the proceeding of the Public Procurement Arbitration Board. [1]

Table 1. Total Number of PP Procedures in Hungary

	2009	**2010**	**2011**	**2012**	**2013**	**2014**	**2015**
Number of procedures	6611	10685	10918	8451	12351	14197	14127
EU supported	1067	778. 2	645. 5	721. 7	1462. 1	1050. 8	735. 6
Total value (Billion HUF)	1809. 8	1496. 5	1457. 3	1333. 5	2394. 3	2135. 9	1931. 6

The rate of successful foreign offers has not changed significantly since Hungary joined the EU, the rate is getting lower, indeed. In 2004 the indicator was 2. 4 percent and in 2013 it was only 0. 9 percent. On the other hand, as compared to the total value of successful PP procedures (see Table 1), the participation of foreign capital has risen from 3. 6 percent to 5. 9 percent. [2]

5.2   Participation of foreign capital in Hungary

The participation of foreign capital is generally influenced by legislation on foreign capital investments. The most important regulations in Hungary fall into three categories: the international legal norms, EU norms and Hungarian legislation. Of international norms mention may be made of the OECD "Guidelines for Multi-

---

[1]   http://www. kozbeszerzes. hu/nyelvi-verziok/complaints-and-remedies/.

[2]   The numbers are based on the statistical reports of the Hungarian Public Procurement Authority.

national Enterprises", the latest of which has been in effect since 2011. ① Regarding the EU norms, ② the following deserves special mention: the rules of European Company (SE). ③ The relevant national sources are the basic rules of economic corporation as part of Act V of 2013 on the Civil Code, Act XXIV of 1988 on foreigners' investments in Hungary and Act XCIII of 2001 on the abolition of foreign currency limitation, which define the term of foreign investor. For foreign investors, the most important area is the protection of investment, which is governed by Act XXIV of 1998 generally, and supplemented by the Bilateral Investement Treaties (BIT) and Multilateral Investment Treaties (Multilateral Investment Agreement (MIA)).

5.2.1 Restrictions and facilitations

During the mid 20th century, Hungary had to deal with a significant lack of capital that led to serious indebtedness. Hungary has been open to foreigners' investments since 1972 but till 1988 – 1989 with severe restrictions (the interest rate had to be under 50 percent), they were not allowed to conduct producer activity and a complicated permission system existed. After the change of the regime, the economic borders were dismantled to clear the way for foreign capital inflow into the Hungarian economy by granting legal guarantees, such as the national treatment principle. After the adoption of Act XIII of 1989 on the Transformation of Business Organisations, there began a huge privatisation wave. At the beginning of the 1990s, besides the foreign state capital, foreign private capital started to flow into the Hungarian infrastructure. ④

5.2.2 The new Land Act

One important restriction on foreign capital is the restriction on "field land" ownership. The relevant legislation is Act CXXII of 2013 (New Land Act) on the definition of field and forestry land that replaced the old land act, Act LV of 1994 on Field land. After Hungary joined the EU, there was a transition period regarding

---

① http://www. oecd/daf/inv/mne/48004323. pdf.

② http://eur-lex. europa. eu/legal-content/EN/TXT/PDF/? uri = CELEX: 32001R2157&from = EN.

③ Council Regulation No 2157/2001 of 8 October 2001 on the Statute for a European Company (SE) and Council Directive 2001/86/EC of 8 October 2001 supplementing the Statute for a European Company with regard to the involvement of employees.

④ http://www. xn-klker-kva. hu/dokumentumok/(14 March 2016).

the ownership of field land for a terminated seven years and the citizens of the EU were restricted in getting field lands in the territory in Hungary as other foreigners. The moratorium ended in 2014 at the 10th anniversary of the Hungarian EU membership.

After that time we have to divide the category of "foreigners" into EU citizens and third parties(non-EU members/not party to the European Economic Area). Regarding to the third parties the State can create restrictions. Under the legislation of the old land act, a natural person or a legal entity who was regarded as a foreigner could not own field or protected natural land subject to a few of exceptions, such as buying a separate homeland as a real estate not more than 6,000 square meters in extent. On the other hand, because of the New Land Act the EU has started an infringement procedure against Hungary in 2014 because in the Commission's opinion the new regulation still means restriction for the EU citizens. Under the rules of the New Land Act, foreign natural and legal persons(from a non-member State/non-EEA country) cannot gain the ownership of filed land in Hungary. After the new Act only that person can have land ownership who registered as farmer—this rule concerns the foreign and Hungarian owners as well.

Hungary facilitates foreign and national investment such as by offering tax incentives. [1]

5.3   Funding and state involvement

Investment by the state became extremely important in the last couple of years and in 2015 the state-financed investments increased by 36.9 percent. The private investment sector is shrinking, and the state participation in national economy is around 22 percent. [2]

Since Hungary has been a member in the EU for more than a decade, EU funding has an important role to play in Hungary's financial management. EU guide-

---

[1]   Some recent examples are: The Hungarian government supported the Richter's biotechnological capacity building investment, which would create 125 new workplaces, with 5 billion HUF; It will support the Master Good slaughter-house with more than 8 billion HUF and will provide another HUF 1.2 billion for two car industrial investments of German companies. Mercedes Company received around HUF 40 billion endowment to support their investment in Kecskemét. http://www. mfor. hu/dossziek/84. html(14 March 2016).

[2]   See http://mfor. hu/cikkek/makro/Soha_ekkora_kulonbseg_nem_volt_az_allam_es_a_piac_kozott. html(14 March 2016).

lines provides that EU funding is available "for a broad range of projects and pro-grams" in several fields, such as: (a) development at regional and urban level; (b) social and employment inclusion; (c) developing agriculture; (d) research and inno-vation and (e) humanitarian aid. Tight control, accountability are the most important rules of EU funding. ①

To create the framework of investments and infrastructure building, long-term programs have been developed both at national and EU levels. At EU level, the Eu-rope 2020 Strategy has five central aims on employment, innovation, education, so-cial inclusion and climate/energy for this decade. ② The financial background is provided by five structural funds within the European Structural and Investment Funds. ③ At national level a vehicle infrastructural development plan was adopted for the term 2014 to 2050 to maintain economic growth by providing the suitable conditions for economic and welfare mobility. ④ The EU will grant EUR 20. 5 bil-lion to Hungary and another EUR 4 billion in the form of agrarian and other sup-port.

5. 4   Summary

As can be seen, the Hungarian legislation on infrastructure building has three main pillars: international, EU (regional) and national, all of which have to be taken into consideration. The EU membership means significant cash flow into Hungary for infrastructure building, since the country usually gets seven times the money that Hungary pays into the EU back from it. On the other hand, unfortunately the Hun-garian governmental decisions and investment related statutes have received some criticism, particularly in connection with the use of EU sources and transparency as the report of the Transparency International has highlighted⑤ and mentioned by the EU country report. ⑥There is also a high possibility of corruption: the Anticorrup-

---

① EU funding http://europa. eu/about-eu/funding-grants/(14 March 2016).

② EUROPE 2020 http://ec. europa. eu/europe2020/index_en. htm.

③ http://ec. europa. eu/regional_policy/en/funding/.

④ The Strategy is available only in Hungarian.

http://www. kormany. hu/download/b/84/10000/Nemzeti% 20K% C3% B6zleked% C3% A9si% 20Infrastrukt% C3% BAra-fejleszt% C3% A9si% 20Strat% C3% A9gia. pdf.

⑤ The opinion of the Transparency International Hungary regarding the new PP act http://transparency. hu/uploads/docs/transparency_international_ujkbt_velemenyezes_20150519. pdf.

⑥ http://ec. europa. eu/europe2020/pdf/csr2015/cr2015_hungary_hu. pdf.

tion Report of the EU① mentioned in 2014 that in half of the PP procedures there was only one applicant!

Obviously, Hungary has a lot to do in the area of investments and infrastructure building.

---

① See http://ec. europa. eu/dgs/home-affairs/e-library/documents/policies/organized-crime-and-human-trafficking/corruption/docs/acr_2014_en. pdf and http://korrupciomegelozes. kormany. hu/download/4/49/90000/EU% 20Antikorrupci% C3% B3s% 20Jelent% C3% A9s% 20-% 20Mell% C3% A9klet% 20Magyarorsz% C3% A1 gr% C3% B3l. pdf.

Chapter 6   Law Relating to Labour Management and Treatment in Hungary

József Hajdú

6.1   Employer-Employee Relationship

Employment law is found primarily in the Act No. 1 of 2012 on the Labour Code(hereinafter,"Labour Code"). ① The Labour Code is very similar in content to the labour laws of other European countries in that it prescribes only the minimum requirements of the content of an employment contract. ②

There are some very important "deviation provisions" in the Labour Code, which must be kept in mind during everyday practice. In general, the parties may deviate from the rules laid down in the Labour Code to the benefit of the employee. At the same time, there are also provisions from which the parties may not deviate. Furthermore, there are certain provisions from which the parties may deviate even to the detriment of the employee. These deviation provisions are precisely inserted in the relevant part of the Labour Code.

The Labour Code covers: (a) employers, (b) employees/workers, (c) employers' interest groups, (d) works councils, and (e) trade unions. ③

Employment contracts are usually concluded for an indefinite period of time. Employment contracts may also be signed for a definite period(fixed-term contract) but the extension thereof requires the existence of the legitimate economic interest of the employer, and the period thereof may not exceed five years together with the extension of the contract. ④

An employment relationship can only be established by a written employment contract, regardless of the anticipated duration of the employment. At the beginning of the employment relationship, the parties may specify a probationary period of not

---

① Adopted by Parliament on 13 December 2011 and came into effect on 1 July 2012.
② József Hajdú, *Labour Law in Hungary*(Wolters Kluwer Law International, 2011).
③ Labour Code, s3.
④ http://eugo. gov. hu/doing-business-hungary/labour-law.

more than three months, or in case of a collective agreement, not more than six months.

The employment contract must specify the (1) employee's basic salary and (2) the employee's assignment. ① After the employment contract has been signed, the employer must, within 15 days, provide the employee with a written description of his/her most important rights and obligations.

Atypical(flexible) employment: Atypical or flexible employment refers to the following: (1) fixed term employment, (2) part-time work, (3) teleworking, (4) outworkers, (5) simplified employment, (6) occasional work relationships, (7) employment relationship with public employers, (8) agency work, (9) executive employees and (10) incapacitated workers. For instance to job sharing, employee sharing and teleworking. These methods are not, however, widely used in the practice. ② Legislators have collected these into a single chapter in the recent revised version of the Labour Code, with three new categories added. ③

Discrimination: The main legal sources of discrimination and equal treatment are the Constitution(Fundamental Law) , the Act on Equal Treatment④and the Labour Code. Hungary prohibits discrimination against employees on the grounds of sex, racial origin, colour, nationality, origin of national or ethnic minority, mother tongue, disability, state of health, religious or ideological conviction, political or other opinion, family status, motherhood(pregnancy) or fatherhood, sexual orientation, sexual identity, age, social origin, financial status, part-time nature or definite term of the employment relationship or other relationship aimed at work, membership in an organisation representing employees' interests, any other status, characteristic feature or attribute. It also prohibits discrimination with regard to establishing or terminating employment, application procedures, training and the determination of working conditions. ⑤

Restraint on freedom of trade or non-competition clauses: during the life of the

---

① These are mandatory legal requirements for validity of an employment contract.

② http://eugo. gov. hu/doing-business-hungary/labour-law.

③ Chapter XV of the Labour Code. Previously these provisions were contained in separate chapters. The three new categories are: call for work, job sharing and employee sharing.

④ Act CXXV of 2003 on Equal Treatment and Promotion of Equal Opportunities.

⑤ https://www2. deloitte. com/content/dam/Deloitte/global/Documents/Tax/dttl-tax-hungaryguide-2015. pdf.

employment relationship, workers must not engage in any conduct to jeopardize the legitimate economic interests of the employer, unless so authorised by the relevant legislation. Workers may not engage in any conduct during or outside their paid working hours that, stemming from the worker's job or position in the employer's hierarchy, directly and factually has the potential to damage the employer's reputation, legitimate economic interest or the intended purpose of the employment relationship. The actions of workers may be restricted if deemed strictly necessary for reasons directly related to the intended purpose of the employment relationship and if proportionate for achieving its objective. The means and conditions for any restriction of personal rights, and the expected duration must be communicated to the workers affected in advance. However, when exercising such restriction, the workers affected must be informed in writing in advance. ①

Workers may not exercise the right to express their opinion in a way where it may lead to causing serious harm or damage to the employer's reputation or legitimate economic and organizational interests. Workers must maintain confidentiality in relation to business secrets obtained in the course of their work. Moreover, workers must not disclose to unauthorised persons any data learned in connection with their activities that, if revealed, would result in detrimental consequences for the employer or other persons. The requirement of confidentiality must not apply to any information that is declared by specific other legislation to be treated as information of public interest or public information and as such is rendered subject to disclosure requirement. ②

A worker may be requested to make a statement or to disclose certain information only if it does not violate his/her personal rights, and if deemed necessary for the conclusion, fulfillment or termination of the employment relationship. An employee may be requested to take an aptitude test if one is prescribed by employment regulations, or if deemed necessary with a view to exercising rights and discharging obligations in accordance with employment regulations. ③

Non-competition agreement: The Labour Code makes provision to ensure that an employee does not engage in competitive activities which violate unfairly the le-

---

①   Labour Code, Article 8(1) – (2).

②   Ibid., Article 8(3) – (4).

③   Ibid., Article 10.

gitimate interests of the employer. By agreement of the parties, the employee must not engage in any conduct-for up to two years following the termination of the employment relationship-by which to infringe upon or jeopardize the rightful economic interests of the employer. ① The employer must pay appropriate consideration in exchange for the non-competition undertaking. When it comes to determining the amount of appropriate compensation, one must examine particularly the extent to which the non-competition agreement prevents the employee from getting a new job and also take into account his/her qualification and experience. The amount of appropriate compensation may not be less than one-third of the employee's basic wage, payable for a period equal to the length of the non-competition period. We note that this amount is only a minimum amount and that the stricter the non-competition undertaking, the higher the amount which has to be paid as compensation. ② It must be stated that non-competition agreements of ordinary employees and executive employees differ because of the different levels of their engagement in and exposure to employer's work.

Legal succession: The Labour Code provides for situations when there is a succession of employers. The Labour Code makes it clear that in the event that there is a legal succession on the employer's side, the rights and obligations of the employer will pass on to the new employer.

Working hours and rest periods: Working time conditions (e. g. permitted maximum hours of work), extra payment for overtime and periods of rest are strictly regulated by the law. ③ Standard working hours for full-time employment are 40 hours per week (usually from Monday to Friday), or eight hours a day, but may go up to 12 hours, including overtime. ④ Employers may not demand more than 250 hours of overtime a year, or more than 300 hours if a collective agreement is in place. The employer may set out a variable work schedule within a certain period of time, which allows an unequal allocation of working hours for a given employee. This period may last for four months or 16 weeks in general, but in specific cases, for instance seasonal work or standby it can reach six months or 26 weeks. A specif-

---

① Ibid. , Article 228.
② http://www. szecskay. hu/dynamic/non_competition_agreement_labour_law. pdf.
③ http://eugo. gov. hu/doing-business-hungary/labour-law.
④ https://www2. deloitte. com/content/dam/Deloitte/global/Documents/Tax/dttl-tax-hungaryguide-2015. pdf.

ic provision in the collective agreement may extend this period to 12 months or 52 weeks. ①

Employees are entitled to two non-working days per week(usually Saturday and Sunday). Sunday workers,i. e. if Sunday work is performed during their regular working hours,must receive 150 percent of their regular daily salary and be provided with another day off. Exemptions to this rule may apply to special work schedules,but employers must provide adequate rest time for employees. Employees must be paid minimum premiums of 15 percent for night work and 50 percent for overtime work. ②

The statutory minimum amount of paid annual leave is 20 days,which increases with the employee's age(the first increase is when the employee reaches the age of 25). The maximum amount of paid leave is 30 days,which applies to employees over 45. The paid leave days must be granted in the year in which they are due;exceptionally,an employee may be permitted to carry over unused holidays to the following year.

Minors and employees with children are entitled to additional days of annual leave is granted in certain situations,such as when the employees is younger than 18 years of age(five days)or where both parents are in employment(extra two days of paid leave per child subject to a maximum of seven days a year). ③

Maternity and family benefits:There are two types of financial assistance for parents with children:(1)the subsidies employed parents are eligible for(insured), and(2)those allowances(generally small)which are granted to parents whether they are in employment or not(social insurance). ④

Parents who satisfy social insurance contribution conditions(at least 365 days of employment within the last two years) are entitled to parental leave up to the child's third birthday. In the first 24 weeks following childbirth,the mother is eligible for maternity benefit(called:csecsemögondozási díj),which is equal to 70 per-

---

① http://www. pwc. com/hu/hu/publications/investing-in-hungary/assets/investing_guide_en_2014. pdf.

② https://www2. deloitte. com/content/dam/Deloitte/global/Documents/Tax/dttl-tax-hungaryguide-2015. pdf.

③ Ibid.

④ http://europa. eu/epic/countries/hungary/index_en. htm.

cent of average gross earnings. ① After this period, until the second birthday of their child, both parents can be eligible for parental benefit(called GYED) amounting also to 70 percent of their earnings but with an upper limit not exceeding HUF 147, 000 per month(about EUR 474).

In addition to these allowances which only parents with employment(social insurance coverage) are eligible for, there are other types of child-care subsidies that every parent is entitled to(universal family benefit). The monthly family allowance in 2016 for one child is HUF 12,200(about EUR 40), HUF 13,300 (about EUR 43) per child for two children and HUF 16,000 (about EUR 52) per child for three or more children. This support is available until the child is beyond school age(e. g. about 18 years of age).

As to the amount of the child allowance for parents or grandparents caring for children under three(called GYES) and the child allowance for parents with three or more children with the youngest being between three and eight years old (called GYET), both equal the minimum old-age pension of HUF 28,500 (about EUR 92). In case of twins, the age limit for the receipt of GYES is school age and in the case of disabled children, it is ten years. From 2011, the amount of GYES in case of multiple births is multiplied by the number of children born. Another favourable measure is that since 2011 parents who adopt children are eligible for GYES. ②

Sick leave and sick pay: Sick pay is a contribution based social insurance benefit. It is divided into two periods: (1) employer charged 1 – 15 working days, and (2) health insurance charged 16 days-maximum per annum. Accordingly, the employer must pay 70 percent of wages for a maximum of 15 working days per year in case of illness. After the 15 days, the employee is entitled to receive from the State sick pay is at the rate of 60 percent if the employment period has been longer than two years, and 50 percent if the employment period has been less than two years. There is a ceiling: the maximum amount of sick pay cannot exceed two times the

---

① According to the Labour Code the employer must provide maternity leave up to 24 weeks.

② After the child's first birthday, a parent in receipt of the allowance may use a crèche or other type of daycare for children without any time restriction. On the other hand, Grandparents can use the crèche only after the child's third birthday and only for a maximum of five hours a day. From September 2015, parents are obliged to take their children to a nursery from the age of three until they reach school age(currently it is obligatory only from the age of five).

minimum wage. ①

Wages and benefits: Based on the Labour Code, a Government Decree sets annually the mandatory basic minimum wage in hourly and monthly terms for all types of Effective as of 1 January 2016, the mandatory minimum gross monthly wage is HUF 111,000 (cca. EUR 358), but for workers employed in positions requiring a secondary school graduation or advanced vocational training (or higher education) it is HUF 129,000 (cca. EUR 416) per month. Employers must pay additional premiums for shifts, nightwork and overtime. ②

Wage levels: Wage levels may vary widely. Wages in the state sector or wholly Hungarian-owned enterprises generally are lower than in multinational companies. Skilled white-collar workers, in particular qualified information technology specialists command a premium. There is disparity in salary between regions of the country: for instance, wage levels in Budapest and the Western counties are higher than in certain Eastern regions.

The Labour Code adopts the principle of equal wage for equal work, meant to address discrepancies between wages for male and female employees. Hungary is a signatory to, and adheres to, ILO conventions protecting employee rights. ③

Wage guarantee fund: ④ Article 1 Paragraph 1 of Act LXVI of 1994 on the Wage Guarantee Fund states that provides as follows:

"The following accrued payroll of the undertaking under liquidation may be advanced in wage of guarantee proceedings:

(a) wage debt of undertaking (as the employer);

(b) wage debt of temporary agency (as the employer) from the fee which is agreed in the contract between the temporary agency and the user undertaking;

(c) wage debt of the school cooperative (as the employer) from the fee which is agreed in the contract between the school cooperative and user undertaking".

Employee's responsibility for damages for malfeasance or negligence: The La-

---

① https://www2. deloitte. com/content/dam/Deloitte/global/Documents/Tax/dttl-tax-hungaryguide-2015. pdf.

② http://www. pwc. com/hu/hu/publications/investing-in-hungary/assets/investing_guide_en_2014. pdf.

③ https://www2. deloitte. com/content/dam/Deloitte/global/Documents/Tax/dttl-tax-hungaryguide-2015. pdf.

④ Act LXVI of 1994 on the Wage Guarantee Fund.

bour Code provides, like the current regulation, that an employee is obliged to compensate an employer for damage caused by violation of his/her employment duties, whether intentional or negligently caused. The burden of proof is on the employer to establish the extent of the damage, misconduct(malfeasance or negligence) and causation. However, in contrast to the current 1. 5 monthly average salary limitation, the Labour Code provides for four months for negligence and unlimited liability for gross negligence or intentional wrongdoing. No compensation is provided for damage which was unforeseeable at the time it was caused or which is attributable to the culpable conduct of the employer or through an employer failing to meet his/her obligation to limit the damage.

Employers' liability for damages: The employer must provide compensation for any loss caused to an employee in connection with his/her employment. The employer is exempted from liability if he/she can prove (a) that the damage was caused by an unforeseen external circumstance beyond his/her control and which he/she could not be expected to avoid or eliminate, or(b) that the damage was the unavoidable result of the conduct of the aggrieved party. In the event of the worker being put at the disposal of another employer, both employers are jointly liable. The employer must compensate the employee for the entirety of his/her loss. No compensation is provided for damage if the employer can prove that the occurence of the damage was unforeseeable at the time it was caused. However, no compensation is payable in respect of such part of the damage that was caused by the employee's culpable conduct or which arose from the fact that the employee failed to meet his/her obligation to limit the damage.

Termination of employment: Employment may be terminated by mutual agreement, or by unilateral notice given by one of the parties, which can be(1) ordinary termination(termination with notice) or(2) immediate termination(termination without notice). ① Note that the employer is required to provide a reason for its termination of the employee's contract and that the reason must be realistic and rational. Employees may terminate their employment by notice without providing any reason. Where an employer or employee gives immediate notice of termination, he/she

---

① https://www2. deloitte. com/content/dam/Deloitte/global/Documents/Tax/dttl-tax-hungaryguide-2015. pdf.

must provide a substantial and verified reason. ① An employee cannot be dismissed without sufficient justification(except during the probationary period)which clearly describes the reason for the termination. An employee has the right to sue for damages for unfair dismissal if the reason for dismissal is untrue or unclear.

The option of immediate termination may be exercised if the other party violates an employment obligation substantially and wilfully or through gross negligence,or acts in a way that renders the continuation of the employment impossible. The reasons for termination with a notification period can be related to the employee's performance or conduct in connection with the employment, or to the employer's operations.

Special rules apply to layoffs in which numerous employees are dismissed at the same time(mass redundancy).

There are specific situations in which employment cannot be terminated(i. e. during maternity leave). If the employer terminates employment during such a period, the notice period starts only when such situation ceases to exist. There are certain consequences if the employer unlawfully terminates employment: for instance the employee may claim compensation. In the case of ordinary termination of employment, the notice period is at least thirty days, but the length of the notice period increases in proportion to the number of years the employee has spent in the employ of the employer, with 90 days as the maximum notice period. ②

Severance payment:Employees are entitled to severance payment if(a)the employer terminates the employment relationship giving notice; or(b) the employer ceases to exist without a legal successor;or(c)the successor employer which is taking over the economic activity is not governed by the by the Labour Code but by some other law(e. g. a government agency) ;or(d)the employee terminates the employment without notice ;or(e)the employer terminates the employment unlawfully and the employee would have been entitled to severance payment if he/she had be lawfully terminated. Depending on the number of years the employee has spent in the employ of the employer, the amount of the severance payment can be between one month's and six months' absence fee, which is not necessarily equal to the

---

① http://eugo. gov. hu/doing-business-hungary/labour-law.
② Hajdú József—Kun Attila:Munkajog I. (Labour Law I.) ;Bethlen-sorozat,Patrocinium Kiadó. Budapest 2012.

employee's salary. In some cases, such as when the employee would reach the relevant age for retirement within five years, it can be an even higher amount. However, the employee is only entitled to severance payment if he/she has worked for the employer for at least three years. No severance payment need be paid, (a) if the employee qualifies as retired at the time of the delivery of notice of termination, or (b) if the grounds for termination are related to the employee's conduct in connection with the employment or related to the employee's skills (except for health issues). ①

6. 2. Collective labour law (industrial relations)

Not less than 10 employees are entitled to organise a trade union. Trade unions may inform their members of their rights and obligations concerning financial, social, cultural and living/working conditions. They also may represent their members vis-à-vis the employer and before government agencies in matters concerning labour relations and employment.

Employees, as a group, are entitled to participate in company matters; these rights are exercised by the works council② or the employees' trustee elected by the employees. ③ Works councils are mandatory in all workplaces employing 50 or more persons. The appointment of an employee delegate for the workplace is mandatory for companies employing more than 15 but fewer than 50 persons. The works council is a forum for employee representation. The company's employees elect the council, which can negotiate employment terms on behalf of the employees. Often, members of works councils are union representatives as well. Employers must inform the works councils or trade unions (if any) before decisions are made regarding a mass redundancy. ④

Collective bargaining and collective agreements: Individual labour contracts are a standard practice among companies in Hungary, and the Labour Code requires

---

① http://www. pwc. com/hu/hu/publications/investing-in-hungary/assets/investing_guide_en_2014. pdf.

② Drawing heavily on the German experience, Work Councils were first introduced in 1992.

③ http://www. worker-participation. eu/National-Industrial-Relations/Countries/Hungary/Workplace-Representation.

④ https://www2. deloitte. com/content/dam/Deloitte/global/Documents/Tax/dttl-tax-hungaryguide-2015. pdf.

them to establish employment relationships. Collective agreements for employees are negotiated at the enterprise level and are rare, although trade unions have been working to establish such contracts in several industries. Works councils may negotiate works agreements① in enterprises where there are no trade unions. ②

Dispute resolution mechanisms: Basically there two mechanisms: (a) collective and (b) individual dispute resolution.

(*a*) *Collective dispute resolution mechanisms*

Collective dispute resolution mechanisms are regulated by the Labour Code (Act I of 2012) , Art. 291 – Art. 293. ③

Depending on the parties in argument or disagreement, the employer and the works council or the employer and the trade union may set up an ad hoc conciliation committee (egyeztetö bizottság) to resolve their dispute. The works agreement or the collective agreement may contain provisions for a standing conciliation committee as well. The conciliation committee is composed of an equal number of members nominated by the employer and the works council/the trade union, and an independent chairperson. The employer and the works council/the trade union may agree in writing in advance to abide by the decision of the committee. In this case the committee's decision is binding. In the case of a tied vote, the chairperson's vote is decisive.

Some collective disputes specified by the Labour Code (Art. 236 Sec 4; Art. 263) should be decided by an arbitrator.

The Labour Arbitration and Mediation Service (Munkaügyi Közvetítöi és Döntöbírói Szolgálat, MKDSZ) can be invited as an alternative dispute resolution body by the parties in dispute to assist (through conciliation or mediation) or to arbitrate.

(*b*) *Individual dispute resolution mechanisms*

According to the Labour Code (Art. 285) , the main individual dispute resolution bodies are the courts. Individual labour disputes are decided by a specialist court known as the " Administrative and Labour Court ". They operate at district

---

① The works agreement may regulate terms and conditions of employment as a collective agreement, with one important caveat: it cannot regulate wages and remuneration.

② http://www. fesbp. hu/common/pdf/Nachrichten_aus_Ungarn_june_2012. pdf.

③ It is important to note that the Labour Code uses the term " collective labour disputes " , which is interpreted as solely collective interest disputes.

court level, but only in the county seat towns. These courts are courts of first instance, and cases which are not settled in them are presented in the second instance to the civil courts. ①

Right to Strike : The right to strike is guaranteed to individual workers in pursuit of their own demands, while the right to organise a solidarity strike is granted only to trade unions. There is a prescribed seven-day conciliation period before a strike may be carried out. It is customary, but not required, for notice of a strike to be given one to two days before the strike. A national mediation and arbitration service exists to help settle labour disputes, but it is not obligatory to seek their assistance. .

In Hungary strikes are generally allowed in the private sector. The strikes are regulated by law. ② According to the amended new act on strikes, ③industrial action such as strikes will only be lawful if employers and trade unions agree in advance on the minimum level of services to be provided. ④If they fail to agree, the Labour Court will have the final say.

No strikes are allowed by members of judicial bodies, or by members of the Hungarian Defence Forces, law enforcement bodies or civil national security services. State administration employees may only strike according some special rules and in special circumstances as have been agreed between the government and relevant trade unions, but the professional staff of the National Tax Office have no right to strike. ⑤

6.3 Foreign workers

Foreign nationals can work in Hungary on a Hungarian employment contract or

---

① http://www. eurofound. europa. eu/observatories/eurwork/comparative-information/national-contributions/hungary/hungary-working-life-country-profile.

② Act VII of 1989 on Strike.

③ Act CLXXVIII of 2010.

④ As it stood, industrial action legislation required the parties involved to cooperate on the terms and conditions of minimum services that should be put in place during a strike for utilities such as electricity, gas, water supply, public transport and communication(Par. 2 , Article 4 of Act VII of 1989 on Strike). "Minimum services" were not, however, clearly defined. Where the parties could agree, a minimum service was provided; if not, there were no or limited services. During the debate of the amendment of the Strike Act, the employers wanted a more detailed definition of the "minimum services" that should be guaranteed by potential strikers, and a requirement that they set out clearly when a proposed strike would commence and end.

⑤ http://www. eurofound. europa. eu/observatories/eurwork/articles/industrial-relations/amended-strike-law-one-year-on.

as assignees(posted workers). The legal requirements for staying and working in Hungary applicable to the EEA (European Economic Area) and third-country nationals(i. e. a non-EEA country) are different, as outlined below. ① However, both EEA and third-country national individuals must submit an application for a residence permit before taking up employment. ② The following documents must be submitted along with the application; work permit, contract of employment, a document certifying availability of accommodation in Hungary, evidence of qualifications required for the position, certificate of annual income envisaged and health insurance.

These provisions also apply to EEA or third-country nationals who are employed by a foreign company and transferred to Hungary on secondment. ③

6. 3. 1   Employees from EU and EEA countries

Since 1 January 2009, citizens of EEA member states and their family members may be employed in Hungary without a work permit. For statistical purposes, the employer is required to report to the employment centre the employment data of EU citizens. The employer must notify the competent labour center of the employment that the proposed employee is not subject to a work permit. The commencement of the employment must be reported on or before the start date of employment. The termination of the employment must be reported on the day following the termination.

No residence permit is necessary for EU citizens who plan to spend more than three months in the country for employment purposes. Nevertheless, they are required to report the details of their extended stay to the Immigration Office and to apply for a residence card and address card. The company where the EEA national carries out his/her activities must report to the National Labour Office the EEA national's position and nationality. ④

---

① http://www. pwc. com/hu/hu/publications/investing-in-hungary/assets/investing_guide_en_2014. pdf.

② Residence permits are issued by the Office of Immigration and Nationality.

③ https://www2. deloitte. com/content/dam/Deloitte/global/Documents/Tax/dttl-tax-hungaryguide-2015. pdf.

④ http://www. pwc. com/hu/hu/publications/investing-in-hungary/assets/investing_guide_en_2014. pdf.

6.3.2　Third country nationals

Suject to a few exceptions, a third-country national may engage in employment in Hungary only if he/she has a valid work permit and a residence permit. Work permits are issued by the labour center upon the application of the employer, and upon showing that the individual's skills are needed in Hungary. An employment contract may be concluded only after a work permit is issued, and may last only for the duration of the period for which the permit is valid.

Individual work permits are usually valid for a maximum of two years, renewable for another two years. Officially, the employee applies for the work permit, but the employer must have certified that they had already tried to fill the vacancy with a Hungarian citizen, with the help of the employment centre. Non-EU citizens may only begin their employment in Hungary after they have obtained all permits and documents necessary for their employment. ①

The Hungarian employer must submit a workforce demand application before a work permit application can be submitted. When the workforce demand application has been accepted, the work permit application can be submitted. The permit must be obtained before commencement of the employment. A Schengen visa has to be obtained for the individual to enter Hungary. The visa application should be submitted with the work permit application at the Hungarian embassy in the individual's home country. After receiving the visa and entering Hungary, the individual needs to go to the Immigration Office to obtain the residence permit and register his/her Hungarian address. ②

6.4　Personal income tax, tax and social security liabilities

The aim of the Hungarian Government over the next few years has been to simplify administrative obligations and decrease labour costs borne by employers. Employers can provide their employees(and in certain cases the employee's close relatives) with fringe benefits such as meal vouchers, holiday cards, local travel pas-

---

① http://eugo. gov. hu/doing-business-hungary/labour-law.

② http://www. pwc. com/hu/hu/publications/investing-in-hungary/assets/investing_guide_en_2014. pdf.

ses. ① These benefits are taxed at preferential rates compared with the taxation of employment income. ② Benefits available to all employees of the employer can also be provided at preferential tax rates. Although there is no special expatriate tax regime in Hungary for assignees, they can be provided with certain tax-free benefits. ③

6.4.1 Salary-based social security contributions and tax

Employers are required to pay taxes and contributions based on the gross salary of their employees. The social tax payable by the employer and the employee generally covers pension and healthcare insurance. Based on the gross wages of an employee, the employer pays a 27 percent social tax. Companies must also pay 1.5 percent to the vocational training fund. The employee contributes 10 percent for uncapped pension insurance, 7 percent for uncapped healthcare and 1.5 percent of gross wages to the unemployment fund (see Table 2). Employee contributions are assessed and withheld by the employer. ④

There is also a health tax payment obligation for fringe benefits, which is 14 percent with a tax base adjustment of 19 percent, resulting in an effective health tax rate of 16.66 percent.

Table 2. Salary Based Social Security Contributions and Tax

To be paid by the employer	To be paid by the employee
27 percent social contribution tax	15 percent personal income tax
1.5 percent vocational contribution	10 percent pension contribution
	7 percent social security contribution
	1.5 percent employment contribution
Total:28.5 percent	Total:33.5 percent

Source: Author's own compilation.

---

① Fringe benefits can be provided to employees in the form of food vouchers, meals at workplace canteens, a "Szechenyi" holiday card(used for accommodation, food and beverages and recreation), schooling assistance, travel passes, etc.

② The tax rate for fringe benefits is 16 percent, but there is a tax base adjustment of 19 percent, resulting in an effective tax rate of 19.04 percent.

③ http://www.pwc.com/hu/hu/publications/investing-in-hungary/assets/investing_guide_en_2014.pdf.

④ http://www.doingbusinessinhungary.com/taxation.

6.4.2　Health insurance

In Hungary, there is a single type of health insurance. ① Everyone who is entitled to healthcare receives all the care their state of health requires. Generally, medical care in Hungary is free of charge. If the treatment is not prescribed by a physician, or is not provided through the normal hospital system, or if he/she chooses a doctor other than the one allocated by the healthcare system, the patient must pay fees imposed by the care provider. The patient might also pay part of the cost of medicines and medical appliances.

Sickness benefit: Sickness benefits may be granted for a maximum of one year while the person is validly insured, with the first 15 working days of the incapacity covered by the employer. The 15-day payment by the employer is known as the absence fee. The amount of absence fee is 70 percent of the daily gross earnings. Incapacity for work must be certified by a doctor. The amount of this benefit is 60 percent or 50 percent of average gross daily pay not exceeding twice the minimum monthly gross wage. Insured persons and mothers caring for a sick child who are unable to work are eligible for sickness benefit.

6.4.3　Pensions

In Hungary there is a multi-pillar mandatory old-age pension scheme. The 1st pillar is the mandatory, social insurance type pension pillar② which is a uniform, defined-benefit, pay-as-you-go system, with an earnings-related public pension combined with a minimum guaranteed pension. ③The current retirement age is 62 years and six months for both men and women. The retirement age will increase gradually until it reaches 65 years in 2022. ④ In addition, 20 years' service is required for both

---

① The law determines the legal status guaranteeing ipso facto compulsory insurance coverage.

② The mandatory social insurance pension scheme(organised and guaranteed by the State)has been in operation since 1 January 1929.

③ There is a minimum pension of HUF 28,500 per month(around 12 percent of average earnings). The amount has remained unchanged since 2009.

④ On 1 January 2012 the mandatory social insurance pension system was reformed. From this date the former early retirement pensions ceased to be operative and a pension can only be awarded after reaching the standard retirement age.

the earnings-related pension① and the minimum pension. ② A person who has reached the age of retirement, may continue in service and take late retirement, with the agreement of the employer. ③

The amount of pension paid depends on the number of years of contribution and the average salary of the claimant; 15 years of contribution entitles a person to 43 percent of their average salary, whereas 50 years of contribution or over entitles the person to 100 percent.

Survivors' pension: This is a pension paid to the widow and orphans of an insured person whose death is due to an accident at work (occupational injury). If a pensioner or a person who was eligible for a pension dies, any dependants are eligible for a pension. There are temporary and temporary widow/widower's pension. ④

Orphan's allowance: Any child, including a child of an earlier marriage or cohabitation, who is raised in the same household in the framework of a marriage or cohabitation, is entitled to an orphan's allowance.

Parental pension: A dependent parent's pension will be paid to any person whose deceased child was an old-age or invalidity pensioner at the time of his/her

---

① The earnings-related pension is calculated as 33 percent of average earnings for the first ten years of coverage, adding 2 percent for each additional year from 11 to 25 years of coverage. For each additional year between 26 and 36 years of coverage each year adds an additional 1 percent and for between 36 to 40 years of coverage each year adds 1. 5 percent. For each year of coverage above 40 years of coverage each year adds an additional 2 percent. The earnings base used to be net-gross pay in all years since 1988, moving towards the full lifetime. This was changed into net pay from 2008. Earlier years' earnings were valorised with economy-wide average earnings to a point two years before retirement in 2006. The last three years' earnings prior to retirement were entirely unvalorised. This was changed from 1 January 2008, to full valorisation. Annual adjustment rules have changed with effect from 1 January 2010. From 1 January 2012 pension payments are adjusted in line with changes in consumer price index, which is inflation-based. Until 2012 there was a ceiling of HUF 21,000 per day of pensionable earnings, but from 1 January 2013 there is no ceiling.

② 15 years' service is required to receive a partial pension.

③ It is possible to defer the earnings-related pension. The pension is increased by 0. 5 percent for each month of deferral. Since 1 January 2008, adjustment is provided for gainfully employed pensioners after completing 365 days service period. As of 1 January 2011, adjustment equals 0. 5 percent per month as a percentage of the annual income gained divided by 12. http://eugo. gov. hu/doing-business-hungary/labour-law.

④ Temporary widow/widower's pension is due for one year or for a maximum of three years if the widow/widower cares for a disabled or permanently ill orphan. Temporary widow/widower's pension is converted into a permanent pension if the spouse: (a) is above his/her relevant retirement age, or (b) is deemed to be a person with changed working capacity, or (c) has at least two minor children (who are entitled to orphan's allowance) from the deceased.

death, or was entitled to either of those pensions if, at the time of his/her death, the parent is disabled or elderly (65 years and above) and had been substantially dependent on the child during the last year of the latter's life.

The survivors' pension is mainly 60 percent of the pension the deceased received.

6.4.4   Accidents at work and occupational diseases

In Hungary, there is no specific insurance against accidents at work or occupational diseases. These risks are covered by the insurance systems for sickness, invalidity and survivors. However, the insurance does not cover injury or illness solely attributable to the victim's behaviour.

The compulsory health insurance contributions paid by workers and employers also entitle beneficiaries to healthcare benefits in the event of an accident. These are:

(a) benefits in kind in the form of healthcare;

(b) cash benefits such as accident benefits and accident allowance.

The covered risks are the following. Injury sustained in the course of work performed within the range of the insured person's profession or in relation to it, or during travel between home and work (commuting accident); work accidents sustained during the performance of charitable work or in the course of utilising certain social insurance benefits, such as in connection with an appearance at a medical examination for the determination of invalidity. Occupational diseases are recognised diseases appearing on a list created and adjusted by the National Health Insurance Fund (Országos Egészségbiztosítási Pénztár), subject to a Government Decision.

There is no qualifying period for cash benefits for accidents at work, which are work accident sickness benefit and work accident annuity. Work accident sickness benefit (Baleseti táppénz) is paid to people who, as a result of an accident at work or an occupational disease, are unable to work and cannot perform their normal work without an appliance or because of their state of health. A work accident annuity (Baleseti járadék) is paid to anyone who, as a result of an accident at work or occupational disease, suffers a loss of working capacity of more than 13 percent and is not entitled to disability benefit. These benefits, which are equal to 100 percent of income (90 percent in the case of an accident while travelling), are granted for one year, but may be extended for a further year if necessary. If the loss of working capacity is no more than 20 percent, the allowance is paid for two years; otherwise, it is paid until the person is able to work again. The amount of this allowance depends on the loss of working capacity, and represents 8, 10, 15 or 30 percent of average monthly income.

Benefits in kind include general medical assistance, 100 percent coverage for medicine, appliances and healthcare, and certain free dental treatments that are connected with the sickness or injury.

6.4.5   Other benefits

The family support system: This is a universal system, meaning that every citizen who meets the requirements is entitled to family support. Every citizen who has a child up to a certain age may be entitled to various family support benefits. The family support benefits are operated and administered by the Hungarian State Treasury (Magyar Államkincstár) and the National Health Insurance Fund (Országos Egészségbiztosítási Pénztár).

Social assistance: This means tested system is managed by the local governments and the district offices. Various social assistance benefits are granted by the local governments.

The unemployment scheme: This is also insurance-based, to which both employers and employees must contribute. There are both active and passive labour market measures to promote employment and to provide for the unemployed. Placement services are open to every resident including EEA nationals, irrespective of the insurance relationship. ①

6.4.6   Social security for foreigners

Social security coverage of international assignees from EEA countries is governed by EC Regulations 883/2004 & 987/2009 (or in certain cases by EC Regulations 1408/71 & 574/72). Third-country nationals assigned to Hungary become subject to Hungarian social security if the length of their assignment exceeds two years, unless a bilateral social security agreement stipulates otherwise. ②

---

① http://ec. europa. eu/employment _ social/empl _ portal/SSRinEU/Your% 20social% 20security% 20rights% 20in% 20Hungary_en. pdf.

② http://www. pwc. com/hu/hu/publications/investing-in-hungary/assets/investing _ guide _ en _2014. pdf.

Chapter 7   Environmental Law in Hungary

Erika Farkas Csamangó and Péter Hegyes

The overall social and economic changes following the democratic transformation and privatisation, environmental problems inherited from the previous period, and the requirements of the EU integration made it necessary for the state in the 1990s to undertake significant tasks in environmental protection. The conditions of the environment did not meet the requirements of the EU in many fields and the accession(2004) raised a large number of tasks to be solved, for example, concerning the canalisation of settlements, sewage disposal, and waste management. As a result of measures taken in the last few decades, there has been a significant improvement in several fields. [1]

With implementation concerns despite an adequate legal framework, Hungary has reached the upper-middle ranks internationally in the area of environmental policies. [2]

The country has a comprehensive set of environmental laws, strongly influenced by EU policies. However, enforcement has suffered from the country's tight budgets, and the responsibility for environmental enforcement was downgraded in 2010 from the ministry level to departmental level leaving it in the hands of a department in the Agriculture Ministry.

Internationally, the country has stressed its commitment to global efforts and supports EU policy, but does not initiate reforms independently. [3]

7.1   The main sources of environment protection law

The right to a healthy environment is long established in Hungarian constitutional law. Article XXI(1) of the Fundamental Law provides that "Hungary shall

---

[1]   http://elib. kkf. hu/hungary/magyar/environment/EN. htm.

[2]   http://www. sgi-network. org/2014/Hungary/Environmental_Policies.

[3]   Ibid.

recognise and give effect to the right of everyone to a healthy environment. "① The Constitutional Court has construed the right to a healthy environment as a fundamental right, which is at least on an equal footing with other values.

The main, general environmental protection rules are laid down in Act LIII of 1995 on the General Rules of Environmental Protection (Environment Act). This piece of legislation lays down, among others, the fundamental principles of environmental protection; deals with the responsibilities for environmental damage; and defines the main tasks of the parliament, the national government and the local governments in respect of environmental protection. In accordance with the Environment Act, special rules in the individual fields of environmental protection (water management, waste management, hazardous materials, arable land protection, etc.) are set forth in separate legislation. The enforcement of environmental law is carried out by the government's environmental bodies, which must act in accordance with the regulations of the Environment Act and other specialised legislation regulating the respective field of environmental protection. ②

Act LIII of 1996 on Nature Conservation considers natural heritage forms and areas to be irretrievable part of the national wealth and provides that its conservation as natural resources for future generations in its biodiversity must be made in compliance with Hungary's international obligations.

Supervisory powers in relation to environment protection belong to the National Inspectorate for Environment and Nature. The inspectorate is the environment and nature authority as defined in law. ③

---

① The Hungarian Constitution of 2011 incorporated "green" values providing a strong legal basis for environmental policy. There are in place comprehensive environmental regulations and the EU continues to serve as an important driver of policy formulation. However, environmental policy has suffered from the country's tight budgetary situation and the lack of a separate Ministry of Environment. In the third Orbán government, environmental issues have been dealt with by a Ministry of Agriculture department led by a deputy state secretary. While there is a certain awareness of the importance of environmental policy, the government has failed to address pressing issues such as the ragweed allergy that has been a big problem for many Hungarians, or the mismanagement of water levels in Lake Balaton, which has caused serious flooding in the neighboring region. (Source: Antal Attila, "Strong Constitutional Basis, Weak Environmental Policy," Paper Prepared for the 3rd UNITAR-Yale Conference on Environmental Governance and Democracy, 5 – 7 September 2014, New Haven (http://www. academia. edu/8117004/Strong_Constitutional_Basis_Weak_Environmental_Policy_The_Case_ of_Hungary).

② http://sz-k-t. hu/wp-content/uploads/2012/03/ICLG_Environment_Law_Hungary_2010. pdf.

③ http://www. eubusiness. com/europe/hungary/environmental-rules.

According to Article 12 of the Environment Act, everyone has the right to have access to environmental information which is considered data of public interest. Governmental agencies, local governments and other agencies dealing with environment-related obligations must monitor the status of the environment and its impact on human health, and provide access to and make available the environmental information that is available. [1]

7.2   Protection against air pollution

The transport sector occupies a prominent position with regard to environmental protection. Some 10 percent of the environmental pressure within the transport sector may be linked to infrastructure. Thus, sustainability can be interpreted in respect of carriageway structures and it must meet the requirements arising from development and growth; however, it is expected to decrease the negative effects on the environment and the utilisation of natural resources. Sustainable roads are part of sustainable transport.

Vehicle emissions causing significant environmental nuisance are closely associated with road traffic. Air is among the protected values in the Hungarian Fundamental Law. The Environmental Protection Act contains provisions on the protection of the air quality. The Act provides for the protection of the climate as well. In Hungary, international and EU rules and programs play a paramount role with regard to climate protection. The Hungarian regulation is closely modelled on the EU counterpart. The most important source of law is Act CCXVII of 2012 on the Participation in the Scheme for Greenhouse Gas Emission Allowance Trading within the Community.

Detailed regulation on the protection of the air is contained in government decrees and ministerial ordinances, the most important among them being Government Decree No. 306/2010(XII. 23). The current regulation on air pollutant emission activities sets out general requirements and allows for prescribing specific requirements during the authorisation procedure. The legislation emphatically prohibits smell emissions offending the population as well as emissions causing air pollution, exceeding certain prescribed limits. Limit values, air protection requirements and technical

---

[1]   http://sz-k-t. hu/wp-content/uploads/2012/03/ICLG_Environment_Law_Hungary_2010. pdf.

measures must be established concerning activities that strain or pollute the air. It is an important element of the regulation that air pollution requirements must be effected on the impact area of the air polluting source and, as a result, it is unnecessary to designate a protection zone. Based on the rate of pollutant emission levels and analysis threshold values, air pollution agglomerations or zones must be designated on the territory of Hungary. Decree No. 4/2002 (X. 7) of the Ministry of Environment Protection and Water Management divides the country's territory into air pollution agglomerations and zones by designating zone groups according to priority air pollutants.

With regard to mobile pollutants (road and rail vehicles, watercraft and aircraft), linear transport facilities, roads and railway and air pollution impacts of the vehicles travelling there must be examined. Establishing linear transport facilities is subject to authorisation. On the initiative of the environment protection authority, the transport authority may impose measures restricting traffic organisation or take other technical measures in case of frequent and permanent air pollution caused by the line source.

Particulate matter pollution ranks among the greatest environmental problems in Hungary. Among others, soot particles from the combustion of two-stroke engines and diesel engine fuel may be regarded as the main source of pollution. Based on Government Decree No. 306/2010 (XII. 23) on the protection of the air, a smog alert scheme must be devised and executed in settlements where there is a calculated risk of smog formation and the conditions for continuous measurement must be fulfilled.

7. 3   Protection from noise emission

Noise emission from traffic and road traffic affects a considerable section of the population. Therefore, the environmental protection authority pays special attention to traffic noise protection aspects of investments. In Hungary, protection against noise and vibration covers artificially triggered energy emissions which can cause causing disturbing, unpleasant, endangering or damaging sonorous or vibration strain. Detailed regulation on activities as well as facilities causing environmental noise and vibration is found in Government Decree No. 284/2007 (X. 29) on certain rules of protection against environmental noise and vibration. Prior to completing a planned road transport facility, it is necessary to establish the degree of the noise notwithstanding the completion of an investment ("white noise") known as "zero state". This value aids in determining the noise emission limit value.

Legislation differentiates between the limit values of sonorous and vibration strain of areas used for different purposes and allows significantly disturbing effects of noise to be declared as dangerous. Concerning areas to be protected from noise and the limit values of sonorous strain generated by traffic may be found in Appendix 3 of Joint Decree No. 27/2008 (XII. 3) of the Ministry of Environmental Protection and Water Management and the Ministry of Health on the Determination of Sonorous and Vibration Strain Limit Values. Areas to be protected must be designated to meet the criteria for sonorous strain limit values. Furthermore, transport facilities must be planned in such a way that the sonorous strain caused by them does not exceed the limit values. The limit values are values expressed in assessment levels where the assessment period is four hours during daytime (from 6 am to 10 am) and eight hours during night time (from 10 pm to 6 am).

In order to verify compliance with noise protection requirements, the environmental protection authority may carry out measurements, calculations or examinations. What is more, it may obligate the operator of the noise source to carry out measurements or calculations. Decree No. 93/2007 (XII. 18) of the Ministry of Environmental Protection and Water Management has standardised the checking method and mode of determination of noise emission limit values. This ordinance prescribes the method, the content and formal requirements of the control procedure, namely, the notification, application, limit values, decisions.

If noise pollution caused by an existing transport noise source is above the limit value, a specific solution plan (dealing with how to reduce noise such as by authorising the modernisation of routes or facilities or by the extension of road capacity), and a programmed implementation plan must be prepared. The requirement for the condition following the modernisation of existing transport routes or facilities and the extension of road capacity must be at least equal to the noise pollution prior to the change if exceeding the value limit is justified by the calculations or measurements for the conditions prior to the change.

Government Decree No. 280/2004 (X. 20) is about the assessment and management of ambient noise. The regulation has designated certain regions where specific survey and specific measures must be initiated to decrease ambient noise. The regulation tackles the problem of ambient noise in a complex manner due to the increase in noise emission mainly of traffic origin in big cities and their surroundings.

The decree applies mainly to noise effects of traffic origin triggered in Budapest and its catchment area, cities with a population of more than 100,000 and specially protected areas. The purpose of the regulation is to take exact assessment of noise effects of high-traffic airports, roads, railroads and transport facilities and to take necessary preventive or remedial measures. Based on the decree, strategic, noise pollution and conflict maps must be prepared and, as for areas exceeding limit values, action plans are prescribed. It is the local municipalities that are responsible for preparing the noise maps or having them prepared.

7.4   Protection of water resources, integrated, sustainable water management

The European Commission's communication on the protection of water resources is supposed to lay the groundwork for the strategic directions of a community water policy which is sustainable on the long term and which serves the interests of European citizens.

Hungary wished to participate actively in the preparation of the EU's water policy document, in order to assert and manifest interests in preserving the unique Hungarian water resources. In the field of climate change and water policy, Hungary considers it important to have an integrated approach to managing extreme water-related events, like droughts and the water scarcity; furthermore it wishes to emphasize the role of eco-services provided by water eco-systems. [1]

The legal basis for national programmes created in the areas of improving the quality of drinking water and removing and cleaning waste water has been formed by later amendments of the Water Management Act. [2]

The protection of water resources is also a principle objective in Hungary. Improving waste water treatment, modernising landfills, implementing the nitrate action programme and the Act CCIX of 2011 on Water Supply all contribute to a reduction in adverse effects on waters and the realisation of sustainable water management. Basic elements of the Act are principles of protection of natural resources and of recovery of costs, and the "polluter-pays" principle. The continued improvement of

---

[1]   http://eu.kormany.hu/environment.

[2]   Act LVII of 1995 on Water Management.

natural water retention, and reservation technologies also play an important role in climate change adaptation.

7.5　Waste management

Waste is defined in Act XLIII of 2000 on Waste Management(Waste Management Act) as any substance or object in the categories set out in Annex 1 of the Act which the holder discards or intends or is required to discard. Annex 1 provides a list of the waste categories such as unusable parts(e. g. discharged batteries, exhausted catalysts), and machining and finishing residues(e. g. lathe turnings).

The Waste Management Act identifies three special types of waste, which may involve additional duties: hazardous waste, municipal waste and liquid waste. According to Article 3 of the Waste Management Act:

(a) "hazardous waste" means waste displaying one or more of the properties listed in Annex 2 of the Waste Management Act and/or containing such substances or components, hazardous to health and/or the environment because of its origin, composition or concentration. Annex 2 provides a list of the hazardous features(e. g. toxic, flammable, etc.);

(b) "municipal waste" means waste from households or other waste which, because of its nature or composition, is similar to waste from households and can be managed together with the latter; and

(c) "liquid waste" means liquids that became waste and are not drained and discharged into sewerage systems or sewage treatment plants.

The detailed rules regarding activities related to hazardous waste are set out in Government Decree 98/2001 (VI. 15) on the Conditions of Activities Related to Hazardous Waste(Decree on Hazardous Waste). According to the Decree, hazardous waste may be handled only by an operator who has obtained an environmental permit(subject to a few exceptions). The operator has certain recording, reporting and disclosure obligations. According to Article 47 of the Waste Management Act, certain operators handling a certain quantity of waste are obliged to provide security in exchange for their activities; furthermore, they may be obliged to have special insurance as well.

The special rules on handling municipal waste(collecting, disposal, conditions of operation, etc.) are set forth in Government Decree 213/2001 (XI. 14) on the

Conditions of Activities Related to Municipal Waste. ①

7.6   Protecting biodiversity

The decline of biodiversity is one of the prominent global environmental challenges. EU efforts aimed at stopping the decline of species richness and the deterioration of ecosystems yielded little results until 2010.

The Nagoya Protocol, adopted in October 2010 and signed during the Hungarian EU Presidency on behalf of the EU, regulates access to genetic resources and the fair and equitable sharing of benefits arising from their use, while the Nagoya-Kuala Lumpur Supplementary Protocol regulates issues on liability and redress. The ratification and implementation of the two documents, an integrated approach to biodiversity protection and its inclusion into related sectoral policies are of key importance from both EU and national perspectives.

Hungary supports and urges for the earliest ratification of the Nagoya Protocol, and wishes to actively participate in preparing the implementation of the EU Biodiversity Protection Strategy. ②

7.7   Genetically modified organisms(GMO)

Gene technology continues to be a subject of heated debate in Hungary. The first Hungarian law on biotechnology activities(Act No. XXVII of 1998) was passed by the Hungarian Parliament in March 1998, and entered into force in January 1999. The Act covers all kind of genetically modified organisms with the exception of humans. The act is a framework-law, which is complemented by several decrees of the competent ministries.

In 2006, the five parliamentary parties formulated Hungary's GMO-free strategy and the process of implementation aimed at its realisation in complete agreement. Since then, this strategy has not been changed, moreover the new Fundamental Law of Hungary, which has been in force since 1 January 2012, includes the pursuit of a GMO-free agriculture. According to the Article XX of the Fundamental Law of Hungary: " (1) Everyone shall have the right to physical and mental health. (2)

---

① http://sz-k-t. hu/wp-content/uploads/2012/03/ICLG_Environment_Law_Hungary_2010. pdf.

② http://eu. kormany. hu/environment.

Hungary shall promote the effective application of the right referred to in Paragraph
(1) by an agriculture free of genetically modified organisms, by ensuring access to
healthy food and drinking water, by organising safety at work and healthcare provision, by supporting sports and regular physical exercise, as well as by ensuring the
protection of the environment. "

7.8   Green public procurement

Public procurement is considered green public procurement where the contracting entity takes environmental aspects into consideration in each phase of the procurement process, and promotes the distribution of environmentally friendly technologies and the production of environmentally friendly products by searching and prioritising solutions that affect the environment as little as possible during their life
cycles. In Hungary, it is a principal objective of the Public Procurement Authority to
help contracting entities and tenderers with information to go green. Paragraph 20 of
Article 182 (1) on Act CVIII of 2011 on Public Procurement authorises the Government to set out in a decree the detailed rules on environmental protection, sustainability and energy efficiency requirements covering all stages of the contract award
procedure, ways of ensuring fairness during the bidding process.

7.9   Authorisation procedures

Perhaps the most important aspect of environmental law is the part that regulatory legislation plays in environmental protection through a network of permissions,
licences, permits and authorizations. Authorization is a principal method of preventing activities that damage and jeopardize the environment. The Act on Environmental Protection sets out the general framework of environmental use authorization procedures. According to Article 66 of the Act, any use of the environment may commence or be carried out only after the permit or resolution set in the Environment
Act has become effective.

In addition, Government Decree 314/2005 (XII. 25) on the Environmental Impact Assessment and Consolidated Environmental Use Permit (Decree on Impact Assessment and Consolidated Environmental Use Permit) sets out a detailed list on the
activities which require an environment impact assessment (e. g. oil exploitation,
mining of ores) or a consolidated environmental use permit (e. g. energy industry,

processing of metals, waste management). It also defines the scope of activities where the environmental authority, i. e. the inspectorate must decide whether or not an assessment is necessary.

The activities in Appendix 1 of the Government Decree No. 314/2005 (XII. 25) on Environmental Impact Assessment and the Uniform Environmental Use Authorization Procedure are subject to an environmental impact assessment, thus including public roads and private roads not closed for public traffic in point 37. These include the construction of carriageways(motorways and dual carriageways) together with junction elements, roads with four or more lanes for a length of at least 10 km from continuous new carriageways (if they are not included in the previous point). Included also is any extension of existing roads to four or more lanes on the existing or modified tracks for a length of at least 10 km from continuous intervention. Depending on the decision reached by the inspectorate, the activities in Appendix 3 are subject to environmental impact assessment, thus including public roads and private roads not closed for public traffic in point 87 insofar as they are not included in Appendix 1. These activities include the construction of national roads, the improvement thereof from a length of 1 km and national roads, local roads, private roads not closed for public traffic, cycle routes on protected areas, on Natura 2000 areas and in the protected zones of caves with no size restrictions not included in the previous point.

The Environmental Act provides for different regulation regarding certain top priority investments. For instance, the Government's decision is sufficient for the authorization procedures of motorways and dual carriageways for the sake of accelerating and simplifying them. Act LIII of 2006 contains provisions on the acceleration and simplification of carrying out investments that are given top priority from a national economic aspect. In a matter of prioritised significance, the application must be examined as a matter of urgency and excluding exceptions, the processing time may not exceed 42 days. Choosing from cases of prioritised significance, the Government may designate cases that correlate to transport infrastructure investments of top priority from a national economic aspect with respect to the public interest of significantly accelerated realisation of the transport infrastructure investment. Appendix 1 to Government Decree No. 345/2012(XII. 6) contains the list of national road transport projects and the investments of prioritised significance in a national economic sense that are linked to them.

7.10　Issues of liability

Article 101 of the Environment Act provides that a polluter of the environment will be liable for the impact of his/her activities on the environment according to the Environment Act, as well as according to criminal and civil law, and regulatory and administrative provisions. Besides their obligation to mitigate damage and the obligation to inform the authorities of the pollution, the polluter must, *inter alia*, refrain from engaging in any activity which poses an imminent threat or damage to the environment, and must cease such activity. They must accept responsibility for the environmental damage caused, and cover the costs of prevention and rehabilitation. If the polluter fails to comply with these obligations, such as to refrain from polluting or to finance the rehabilitation of the polluted area, the environmental authority, or the authority that has granted the relevant authorisation at the request of the environmental authority, or the court may, depending on the degree of threat to the environment or the level of environmental damage, limit the activity that poses an imminent threat to the environment or causes damage to the environment, or may suspend or prohibit the activity in question until the conditions established by the authority are met. Besides this, certain environment users, such as hazardous waste operators, are obliged to provide security in exchange for their activities. [1]

Besides the liabilities set out in the Environment Act, polluters have civil law liability. They may be obliged by the competent court at the suit of the victim of the pollution to pay for all damage caused by the pollution, in accordance with the Civil Code of Hungary.

Criminal liability may arise if the breach of environmental law/permit is such that regulations of the Criminal Code become applicable.

---

[1]　http://sz-k-t. hu/wp-content/uploads/2012/03/ICLG_Environment_Law_Hungary_2010. pdf.

Chapter 8   Laws Relating to Resolution of Disputes Concerning Foreign Entities

József Hajdú

8.1   Introduction to the dispute resolution framework

Hungary's legal system is greatly influenced by continental legal principles and traditions. It is within its civil law system that Hungarian courts interpret and apply provisions of relevant legislation.

Within the framework of procedural law courts resolve disputes, rule on conflicts between local ordinances and other legislation if necessary making a declaration of invalidity, and decide whether a local government has failed to carry out its statutory obligations .

8.2   Litigation and the Hungarian court system

The Hungarian court system is a four-tier system: (1) the district and local courts; (2) the metropolitan and county courts; (3) the five regional courts of appeal[①] and (4) the Curia(Supreme Court). Although there is no system of binding judicial precedent in Hungary, the Curia sets guidelines, which are binding on all courts in Hungary. [②]The only special courts in Hungary are the "Administrative and Labour Courts". [③]

Judges and lay(non-professional)judges are independent. They render their de-

---

① The high appeals courts have regional jurisdiction, with seats in Budapest and four other cities(Debrecen, Győr, Pécs, Szeged). They consider appeals against resolutions of the metropolitan and county courts.

② Zoltán Balázs Kovács and Dávid Kerpel, "Hungary" in Richard Clark, *The Dispute Resolution Review* (Law Business Research: London, 2nd ed, April 2010). See http://www. szecskay. hu/dynamic/DRR_HU. pdf.

③ There are 20 administrative and labour courts located on the seat of regional courts. Administrative and labour courts shall proceed in the first instance in cases reviewing administrative decisions, and in cases regarding employment relationships and legal relationships of an employment nature. Administrative and labour courts are led by the President, but they are not legal entities. Groups may be established at administrative and labour courts to handle certain types of cases.

cisions based on the law and in accordance with their convictions. Non-professional judges may participate in judicial proceedings as assessors in certain cases and under conditions prescribed by law, but only professional judges may act as a single judge or presidents of council.

Professional judges are appointed by the President of the Republic and may be removed from office only on the grounds, and in accordance with the procedures, specified by law. Judges are independent and subject only to the law, and they may not be members of political parties or involved in political activities.

The composition of a court depends on its level. For instance, district courts u-sually consist of one judge, but a three-judge panel is convened in cases such as those concerning trademarks and patents (a three judge-panel decides by majority vote). The court of second instance consists of three judges. The Supreme Court convenes a three-judge panel when it conducts a supervisory proceeding and a five-judge panel in extremely complicated cases.

Trials are held in public, subject to certain statutory exceptions. The court an-nounces its decision in public. The court must give reasons for its decision, unless otherwise provided by law. There is a right of appeal against court decisions, unless otherwise provided by law. ①

According to Hungarian legislation a court of first instance is a trial court of o-riginal or primary jurisdiction. The court of second instance (county court) exercises jurisdiction to hear a case *de novo*, or its appellate jurisdiction to hear an appeal, from the court of first instance in which the matter was first litigated. Appeals from first instance decisions in labour matters are made to the ordinary county courts. The third instance courts are the regional courts of appeal. There are five Regional courts of appeal in Hungary. It reviews appeals—in second or third instance—submitted a-gainst the decisions of district courts or regional courts and proceeds in other cases referred to its jurisdiction.

8.2.1　District(Local) courts

There are 111 district courts in Hungary located in major cities. District courts are courts of first instance in all actions which are not reserved to regional courts. District courts are led by the President of the District Court. ②

---

① http://birosag. hu/en/information/grounds-court-procedures.
② http://birosag. hu/en/information/hungarian-judicial-system.

8. 2. 2 Regional(metropolitan and county) courts

There is a regional court in each of the 19 counties of Hungary and in Budapest (Budapest-Capital Regional Court).

The regional court proceeds as the first instance court in cases defined by law,[1] and act as a second instance court when considering appeals lodged against the decisions of district courts, administrative courts and labour courts.

Chambers, groups as well as (a) criminal, (b) civil, (c) economic and (d) administrative and labour judicial colleges operate at the regional court. [2]

Local courts have general jurisdiction; however, the metropolitan and county courts have jurisdiction over cases with a value exceeding five million Forints and in defined matters such as, for example, cases relating to patents, trademarks or copyright, international delivery of goods, securities and unfair contractual terms.

8. 2. 3 Regional courts of appeal

There are five regional courts of appeal in Hungary. The regional court of appeal reviews appeals in second or third instance submitted against the decisions of district courts or regional courts and proceeds in other cases referred to its jurisdiction. The regional court of appeal operates chambers as well as criminal and civil judicial colleges. [3]

8. 2. 4 The Curia(Hungarian Supreme Court)

The Curia is the highest judicial authority in Hungary. Under the authority of its President it has three departments: criminal, civil and administrative and labour law. [4] Each department has various chambers. [5] A decision of the Curia on uniform jurisdiction, that is a decision on a matter of great and general importance, is binding on other courts.

The responsibilities of the Curia are the following: (a) examining appeals sub-

---

[1]   Act of Civil Procedure and Act of Criminal Procedure.

[2]   http://birosag. hu/en/information/hungarian-judicial-system.

[3]   Ibid.

[4]   Within the framework of the departments, the judges administer justice in chambers consisting of three judges. A chamber adopting uniformity decisions consists of five judges chaired by the head of the section/department concerned. Where the collaboration of several sections/departments is required, the number of members increases to seven.

[5]   These are: (a) chambers hearing appellate cases, (b) chambers passing uniformity decisions, (c) chambers issuing decisions on principles, as well as(d) working groups examining judicial practice.

mitted against the decisions of the regional courts and the regional courts of appeal; (b) reviewing final decisions if these are challenged through an extraordinary reme- dy; (c) adopting uniformity decisions, which are binding on all other courts, analy- sing final decisions to examine and explore judicial practice; (d) publishing deci- sions on principles; (e) determining cases where a local government decree is alleg- ed to violate the law; (f) determining cases where the local government is alleged to have failed to legislate as required by the Act on Local Governments, and (g) per- forming any other duties conferred on it by law. ①

8. 2. 5   The Constitutional Court

The Constitutional Court has shaped the legal framework of Hungary since 1990. Its members② are elected by Parliament from among the country's legal schol- ars and legal practitioners. ③ Since 2010, the government has narrowed the scope of the Constitutional Court's jurisdiction. ④ The new Constitution⑤ abolished the right of citizens to initiate an abstract constitutional review, or *actio popularis*, but intro- duced a new competence for the Constitutional Court to review constitutionality of judicial decisions. The Constitutional Court has been relatively restrained in its use of this new power to protect individual rights. ⑥

8. 3   The Civil law courts procedure

8. 3. 1   Courts of first instance in civil law cases

A. District courts

They have first instance jurisdiction in all actions which are not reserved by law for the regional courts. Civil cases which are frequently litigated in district

---

①   http://birosag. hu/en/information/hungarian-judicial-system.

②   In 2011, the parliamentary majority increased the court's membership from 11 to 15 judges, and by the end of 2014, a total of 11 judges had been appointed by the ruling coalition. The Constitutional Court consists of 15 judges.

③   https://freedomhouse. org/report/nations-transit/2015/hungary.

④   For example, with extremely limited exceptions, the current rules exclude the possibility of a constitu- tional review regarding financial and tax measures which link to the central budget.

⑤   Officially it is called: Fundamental Law.

⑥   Az Alkotmánybíróság Határozatai [Constitutional Court Decisions], "2014. évi Alkotmánybíróság Határozatai" [Decisions of the Constitutional Court 2014], http://www. kozlonyok. hu/kozlonyok/index. php? m = 2&p = 0280&k = 1.

courts are: (a) legal disputes under property and assets law, where the value of the claim does not exceed HUF 30,000,000; (b) legal disputes relating to condominiums; (c) legal disputes relating to inheritance law; (d) legal disputes relating to damages; (e) legal disputes relating to contracts where the value of the claim does not exceed HUF 30, 000, 000 and (f) legal disputes relating to consumer contracts. ①

B. Administrative and labour courts

The administrative and labour courts proceed in the first instance (a) in cases reviewing administrative decisions and (b) in cases dealing with employment relationships and legal relationships of an employment nature. ②

C. Regional(Metropolitan and County) courts

The following actions fall under the jurisdiction of regional courts acting in the first instance:

(a) actions relating to rights in property and assets, where the amount of the claim exceeds HUF 30,000,000 (with the exception of actions relating to rights in property arising out of a matrimonial relationship if opened in conjunction with or in the course of matrimonial proceedings) ;

(b) actions for compensation for damage caused by persons in an official capacity within their administrative authority ;

(c) actions relating to copyright and related rights, as well as actions relating to the protection of industrial property rights ;

(d) actions relating to contracts for the international carriage of goods and forwarding contracts ;

(e) corporate actions(e. g. ruling of registration by a court of registry, the judicial review of resolutions passed by the bodies of a company, acquisition of control in a business association, etc.) ;

(f) civil rights actions filed in connection with claims for personal injury ;

(g) actions in connection with a legal relationship arising from securities ;

(h) actions for rectification ;

(i) actions brought for the annulment of unfair contractual terms ;

(j) actions relating to financing contracts concluded with healthcare serv-

---

① http://birosag. hu/en/information/civil-procedure.
② Ibid.

ice providers; and

(k) actions delegated under the competence of regional courts by law.

D. Special non-dispute procedures

There are certain special non-dispute resolution procedures that take place in first instance. In regional courts there are special Company Registry Courts and special divisions for liquidation and bankruptcy procedures and registration of civil organisations. In district courts there are special divisions for execution.

In civil cases, the court proceedings are set in motion by a petition. Such a petition or request, unless otherwise provided for by law, may only be submitted by a party to the dispute. Unless otherwise prescribed by law, the requests and legal statements made by the parties must be binding upon the court.

Unless otherwise prescribed by law, the court must adjudge civil cases in public. Court proceedings are conducted in the Hungarian language. No one may suffer any disadvantage for not being able to understand the Hungarian language. In court proceedings, to the extent provided for by international agreement, parties must be entitled to use their native language, or the language of their region or ethnic minority. The court is required to use an interpreter where necessary. ①

In principle the court decides about the claim in its judgment, which must be delivered publicly.

8.3.2　Proceeding in second instance in civil law cases

The decisions (judgment) of the court of the first instance may be appealed, unless legislation excludes the right of appeal. An appeal may be lodged by the party, the intervener and, by any person to whom any provision of the decision may be of concern.

Jurisdiction in second instance is exercised by (1) regional courts in cases decided by district courts, administrative courts and labour courts in first instance; and by (2) regional courts of appeal in cases decided by Regional courts in the exercise of first instance jurisdiction; and (3) by the Curia (Supreme court) in exceptional cases.

The judgment of the second instance court is a final judgment and may not be appealed against. A final judgment may be reviewed by way of an exceptional rem-

---

① http://birosag. hu/en/information/civil-procedure.

edy. ①

8.3.3   Exceptional remedies

Exceptional remedies in civil cases are retrial and judicial review.

8.3.3.1   Retrial

A motion for retrial may be submitted against a final judgment if:

(a) a party presents any fact or evidence, or any binding court or other official decision that the court of first instance did not take into consideration during the hearing, provided that it would have been to his/her benefit had it been considered originally;

(b) a party lost the action in the court of first instance in consequence of any offence committed by a judge who took part in rendering the judgment, or by the opposing party or any other person, contrary to the law;

(c) a final judgment has previously been adopted relating to the same right; or

(d) the statement of claim or any other document was delivered to the party.

If a retrial is found to be justified, the case must be reopened and heard. The court, relying on the findings of the retrial, may either sustain the contested judgment, or may decide to overrule the judgment in whole or in part and render a decision in place of the overruled decision or part of the decision. The court must proceed to hear the retrial in accordance with the general provisions. ②

8.3.3.2   Judicial review

A motion for the review of a final judgment or a final ruling adopted on the merits of the case may be submitted to the Curia by a party, an intervener, or by any person to whom any provision of the decision may be of concern.

The Curia decides the petition for review without a formal hearing, unless either of the parties request a hearing, or if the Curia considers it necessary to conduct a hearing. In a review no evidence is taken. The Curia decides the review application on the basis of the available documents.

If the decision reviewed is found to be in compliance with the relevant legislation, or a breach of procedural regulation that has occurred has no impact on the outcome of the case, the Curia must uphold the decision of the inferior court.

---

① Ibid.

② Ibid.

If a decision is found to be unlawful, the Curia invalidates it in whole or in part, and if the facts needed for a decision can be ascertained, it may render a new decision instead. In any other case the curia must instruct the competent court of the first or second instance to reopen the case and render a new decision (see Figure 2). ①

8.3.4　Court mediation

The aim of court mediation is to facilitate settlement of disputes speedily and expeditiously to the satisfaction of the parties to the dispute. Court mediation was adopted in second half of 2012. ② The goal is to make court mediation directly available for clients in all courts which employ more than seven judges. This could be an important instrument in ensuring the timely administration of justice and spreading a new culture of resolving disputes. In mediation proceedings the parties can settle their disputes in a responsible and amicable manner after taking into account various possible solutions. ③

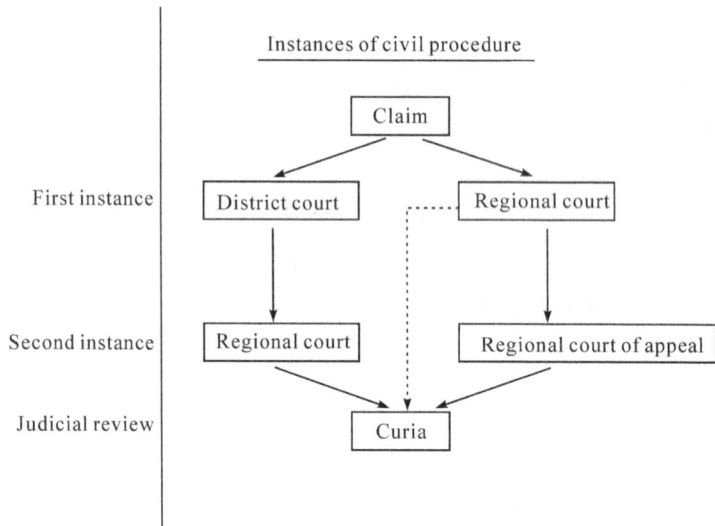

Figure 2. Instances of Civil Procedure

Source: www. birosag. hu.

---

① http://birosag. hu/en/information/civil-procedure.

② At the end of the first half of 2014 in 24 courts there were 70 court mediators (55 court clerks and 15 judges who were appointed as court mediators). 700 clients were received and 273 mediation procedures were conducted, out of which 176 procedures, that is, nearly 65 percent of all procedures were concluded with an agreement.

③ http://birosag. hu/en/information/court-mediation.

8.4　Overview of the civil court procedure

As a general rule, civil law disputes are submitted to the jurisdiction of the ordinary courts. [1] In Hungary, litigation is still the most common method of dispute
resolution. The main rules governing court litigation are laid down in the Civil Procedure Code(hereinafter, "CPC").

Before submitting the statement of claims, the plaintiff must attempt amicable
settlement of the dispute by communicating his/her legal or factual standpoint to the
defendant, indicating his/her evidence or other relevant documents in the case. If
parties are unable to reach an amicable settlement, the statement of claim may be
submitted to the competent court. If the plaintiff is a foreign entity, it may be o-
bliged, at the request of the defendant, to provide security for court costs, the a-
mount of which is stipulated by the court.

The CPC is based upon the principle of freedom of evidence; the court is entitled to accept all kinds of evidence regardless of their form. [2]

The procedural costs are borne by the defeated party. Certain costs(e. g. costs
of evidence) are advanced by the parties during litigation. [3] Procedures aimed at the
initiation of enforcement of foreign decisions as per EU Regulations No. 44/2001,
805/2004 and 2201/2003 are exempt from duty.

The length of a judicial procedure may vary for many reasons, such as the
number of parties, the complexity of the case, the quantity of evidence required,
etc. [4]

Since 1 July 2010, payment orders(i. e. creditors' requests either for payment
of a certain amount or another specific service, which may be final and enforceable
provided that the debtor fails to contest it in due time) are handled by notaries public
and not by the courts. If the debtor contests the payment order in due time, the mat-

---

　① http://www. bakermckenzie. com/files/Uploads/Documents/Global% 20Dispute% 20Resolution/
Dispute% 20Resolution% 20Around% 20the% 20World/dratw_hungary_2012. pdf.

　② The Civil Procedure Act explicitly mentions witness testimonies, expert opinions, inspections, documents and other forms of evidence(such as photos, audio or video recordings).

　③ The plaintiff must pay a fee prior to filing the statement of claim, which generally amounts to about six
percent of the value of claim.

　④ It is worth pointing out that litigation may take as long as one-and-a-half to two years or even more
depending on the circumstances. A procedure at the second instance may also take a year or more.

ter must proceed to litigation.

Monetary claims involving less than one million Forints may only be enforced through a payment order, provided that the debtor has a domestic residence (or registered seat) and the claim does not arise from the employment, public service, service outside worker or cooperative membership relationship. This provision does not prevent the creditor from enforcing its claim on the basis of EU Regulation No. 861/2007 of the European Parliament and the Council on the European Small Claims Procedure, or by way of an arbitration procedure. ①

8.4.1　Procedures and time frames

Within 30 days of submission, the court must examine whether a statement of claim meets the legal requirements or is in need of any supplements. If the court finds that the claim complies with the provisions of the CPC, it sets the date for the first trial within 30 days of receipt of the statement of claim. ②

Parties must attend the trial. If a plaintiff fails to appear on the first day of trial, the court may, upon the request of the defendant, terminate the proceedings. If the defendant fails to appear at the first hearing, the court may, at the plaintiff's request, condemn the defendant in accordance with the statement of claims. If the parties miss the trial held on a later date, the court only holds the hearing upon the request of any party, or may adjourn the hearing and impose a fine on the missing party. The parties must present their claims or counterclaims on the first day of the trial. The court may summon witnesses or experts if necessary, and the parties also have the right to initiate this measure. The court holds hearings until there is sufficient data and information to make a decision on the case. There is no provision in the CPC setting a maximum time frame for a procedure.

An appeal may be lodged against a first-instance decision within 15 days from

---

① Zoltán Balázs Kovács and Dávid Kerpel, "Hungary" in Richard Clark, *The Dispute Resolution Review* (Law Business Research; London, 2nd ed, April 2010). See http://www. szecskay. hu/dynamic/DRR_HU. pdf.

② The date of the first trial must be scheduled for no later than four months (or nine months in special cases) from the receipt of the statement of claims. Any subsequent trials must also be scheduled so that four months do not pass between two consequent trials. This rule does not apply if a summons is to be served on a party in a foreign country and the delivery process prolongs the date of the trial.

its communication. ①

The CPC also provides for urgent applications. ②

8.4.2   Class actions

There are numerous cases where the law permits the submission of a class action:

(a) The Civil Code provides that a third party③ is entitled to challenge an unfair term of contract. If the court rules that the condition is unfair, it may declare it null and void as regards all the parties who are in a contractual relationship with the party applying the condition.

(b) The Hungarian Competition Office(hereinafter, "HCO") may file a claim on behalf of consumers against a business entity engaged in any infringement of the provisions of the Act on the Prohibition of Unfair Trading Practices and Unfair Competition or the provisions of the UCPA, ④ falling within the competence of the HCO, where such illegal action results in a grievance that affects a wide range of unknown consumers, but whose identity can be established based on the circumstances of the infringement.

(c) Class actions may also be brought on the basis of the Consumer Protection Act⑤ according to which the consumer protection authority, non-governmental organisation for the protection of consumers' interests, or the public prosecutor may file charges against any party causing substantial harm to a wide range of consumers by infringing consumer rights.

Class actions are becoming increasingly popular in the field of consumer protection, but there have not been a large number of procedures initiated by class ac-

---

① The court examines the appeal, and if the appeal complies with the legal requirements, it delivers the documents to the competent court of second instance. The hearing must be scheduled so that four months do not pass from the receipt of the documents by the court of second instance.

② Zoltán Balázs Kovács and Dávid Kerpel, "Hungary" in Richard Clark, *The Dispute Resolution Review* (Law Business Research:London,2nd ed, April 2010).

See http://www.szecskay.hu/dynamic/DRR_HU.pdf.

③ Such parties are:(1)prosecutor,(2)minister or head of an office with a national jurisdiction,(3)notary and chief notary,(4)commercial or professional chambers,(5)social organisation protecting the interests of consumers,(6)organisation established in any of the member states of the EEA registered in accordance with Article 4(3)of Council Directive 98/27.

④ Act XLVII of 2008 on the Prohibition of Unfair Business-to-Consumer Commercial Practices which Implemented the Unfair Commercial Practices Directive(Directive 2005/29/EC).

⑤ Act CLV of 1997.

tions to date. ①

8.4.3   Representation in proceedings

As a general rule, litigants may represent themselves in every proceeding before the local or county courts. Legal representation② is mandatory before the Court of Appeal for a party submitting an appeal against a judgment or against an order made on the merits of the case. Legal representation is also mandatory before the Curia(Supreme Court) for a party filing a specific appeal or petition for review. ③

8.4.4   Mutual judicial assistance

The Taking of Evidence Regulation(Council Regulation 1206/2001/EC) is directly applicable in Hungary as well, by which the courts of the Member States(except for Denmark) may request assistance in taking evidences in another Member State, or may take evidence themselves. A foreign court's request must be made in the form attached to the regulation and must include the name of the requesting and the designated court, the name and address of the persons participating in the litigation and their legal representatives, a short description of the case, a short description of the evidencing procedure requested, and data of the persons to be interrogated.

As for cooperation with courts in non-EU states, Hungary is a member of the Hague Convention of 1970 on the Taking of Evidence Abroad in Civil or Commercial Matters. A foreign court's request must include the same information as indicated supra. ④

8.5   Alternatives to litigation

---

① Zoltán Balázs Kovács and Dávid Kerpel, "Hungary" in Richard Clark, *The Dispute Resolution Review*, Law Business Research: London, 2nd ed, April 2010. See http://www. szecskay. hu/dynamic/DRR_HU. pdf.

② Attorneys, law firms and legal counsel of a legal entity and patent agents are regarded as legal representatives. In matters where legal representation is mandatory, lawyers qualifying and registered with the competent bar association as European Community lawyers may only proceed as legal representatives if they have concluded a collaboration agreement for that purpose with a Hungarian attorney or law firm.

③ Zoltán Balázs Kovács and Dávid Kerpel, "Hungary" in Richard Clark, *The Dispute Resolution Review*, Law Business Research: London, 2nd ed, April 2010. See http://www. szecskay. hu/dynamic/DRR_HU. pdf.

④ Ibid.

8.5.1   Overview of alternative dispute resolution in Hungary

Since the beginning of the 1990s, arbitration and international arbitration have had an expanding role in dispute resolution. The Hungarian Bar Association published a set of arbitration rules which may be adopted on a voluntary basis in ad hoc arbitration cases. ①

There are three main types of alternative dispute resolutions in Hungary: arbitration, mediation and conciliation. ②

8.5.2   Arbitration

8.5.2.1   Hungary-based arbitration

Arbitration proceedings in Hungary are governed mainly by Act LXXI of 1994 on Arbitration(hereinafter, "Arbitration Act") and the European Convention on International Commercial Arbitration of 21 April 1961. The Arbitration Act basically covers: arbitration clauses, the formation, jurisdiction and procedure of the arbitration trial, procedure in international arbitration cases and the role of ordinary courts.

The main Hungary-based permanent courts of arbitration are as follows: (1) the Court of Arbitration attached to the Hungarian Chamber of Commerce and Industry; ③(2) the Money and Capital Markets Arbitration Tribunal; ④ and(3) the Permanent Court of Arbitration for Telecommunications. ⑤

The award of the arbitration tribunal has the same effect as that of a binding court resolution; therefore, it is not possible to appeal against the award. Within 60 days after receipt of the award, the party may file a request for annulment through a

---

①   The main ADR mechanism in Hungary is arbitration. The main advantage of arbitration as opposed to litigation is that the procedure is usually more expedient. The drawback is that arbitration is more expensive than ordinary court procedures. Other alternative dispute resolution methods such as mediation, expert determinations and referees are rarely used.

②   Zoltán Balázs Kovács and Dávid Kerpel, "Hungary", in Richard Clark, *The Dispute Resolution Review* (Law Business Research: London, 2nd ed, April 2010). See http://www. szecskay. hu/dynamic/DRR_HU. pdf.

③   This is the most important arbitration tribunal in Hungary which has been designed to resolve large commercial disputes.

④   If the parties agree to the jurisdiction, it has a broad jurisdiction to settle disputes in matters relating to financial and capital markets.

⑤   This body was founded by the Council of the National Telecommunications Authority and may also conduct mediation proceedings between the parties in accordance with the rules of Act LV of 2002 on Mediation.

statement of claims with the competent county court or the Metropolitan Court. ①
Failure to meet the 60-day deadline results in the forfeiture of rights.

In addition to the above, the court may suspend the enforcement of the award
at the request of the relevant party. The court may not revise the award on the merits
of the case. Instead, the court's role is to establish whether any of the grounds for
annulment applies. Although no appeal may be lodged against the decision of the
court, a petition for review is allowed.

8.5.2.2   International arbitration

Hungary has accepted binding international arbitration in cases where the resolution of disputes between foreign investors and the state is unsuccessful. ② First, the
court adopts a confirmation of enforcement in which it confirms that the foreign arbitral award is enforceable under Hungarian law in the same way as Hungarian arbitral awards or judicial decisions.

According to the reservation made by Hungary, the New York Convention③
applies only to recognition and enforcement of awards made in the territory of another contracting state and only to differences arising out of legal relationships,
whether contractual or not, that are considered commercial under Hungarian law.

---

① An arbitral award may be annulled any of the following grounds: (a) the party who concluded the arbitration agreement did not have legal capacity under the applicable law to act; (b) the submission to arbitration
is not valid under the applicable law; (c) the party was not given proper notice of the appointment of an arbitrator or the holding of the arbitration proceeding or was otherwise unable to present its case before the arbitration
tribunal; (d) the award concerns a dispute not covered by or not falling within the terms of the submission to arbitration; if the award contains a decision on matters beyond the scope of the submission to arbitration, provided
that the decision on matters submitted to arbitration can be separated from those not covered by the submission
to arbitration, annulment may only be requested in regard of that decision that is not covered by the submission
to arbitration; (e) the composition of the arbitration tribunal or the conduct of the arbitration procedure was not
in accordance with the agreement of the parties(except where such agreement is contrary to a mandatory provision of the Arbitration Act) or, in the absence of such an agreement, with the provisions of the Arbitration Act;
(f) the subject matter of the dispute may not be subject to arbitration under Hungarian law; or(g) the award violates Hungarian public policy. See Zoltán Balázs Kovács and Dávid Kerpel, "Hungary" in Richard Clark, *The
Dispute Resolution Review*(Law Business Research: London, 2nd ed, April 2010). See http://www. szecskay.
hu/dynamic/DRR_HU. pdf.

② In Hungary, foreign arbitral awards may be enforced by way of judicial enforcement in accordance
with the provisions of Act LIII of 1994 on Judicial Enforcement(the Judicial Enforcement Act).

③ Hungary is also a signatory to the 1958 New York Convention on the Recognition and Enforcement of
Foreign Arbitral Awards. In the last few years mediation has become a tool of increasing importance for dispute
settlement to avoid lengthy court procedures.

Pursuant to the New York Convention, recognition and enforcement of an arbitral award may be refused if, for example: (a) the subject matter of the dispute may not be subject to arbitration under Hungarian law; or (b) recognition or enforcement of the award would violate the public policy of Hungary. ①

There are domestic arbitration bodies within the Hungarian Chamber of Commerce, and local municipal governments. Hungary is a member of the International Center for the Settlement of Investment Disputes (ICSID).

In addition to the above courts of arbitration, it is worth noting that the International Court of Arbitration of the International Chamber of Commerce is the best known international arbitral tribunal in Hungary. When it comes to dispute resolution, arbitration is not too common and is typically used by certain players of the Hungarian business field. Mainly foreign-owned business organisations and large Hungarian-controlled companies submit their legal disputes to arbitration tribunals.

8.5.3   Mediation

The Mediation Act② contains the main rules governing mediation proceedings in Hungary. According to the Mediation Act, mediation is a special, non-litigious procedure which provides an alternative to court proceedings. Mediation is possible where the parties involved voluntarily submit the case to a mediator with a view to reaching a written agreement. Under the Mediation Act, the parties (natural persons, legal persons, business entities without legal personality or other organisations) to a civil dispute connected with their personal and pecuniary rights may, if they so agree and if the law does not limit their right of disposition, use a mediation procedure. They may initiate such a procedure by calling on the services of a mediator. The Act specifies the range of civil legal actions in which mediation is not possible and where its provisions cannot apply to mediation and conciliation proceedings governed by other acts or to mediation in arbitration proceedings. The Ministry of Justice publishes the register of mediators on its website.

Both natural persons and legal entities with legal personality may become mediators provided that they meet all the statutory requirements laid down in the Mediation Act. It is worth noting that an agreement reached during mediation has no effect of any kind on the parties' right to assert their claims before an ordinary court

---

① Case BH 2007/130.
② Act LV of 2002 on Mediation.

or a court of arbitration. In Hungary mediation is rarely used as a method of dispute resolution in the business field and we are not aware of any fact or development that would suggest that this may change in the future. ①

8.5.4 Other forms of alternative dispute resolution

With a view to enforcing consumer rights, the Consumer Protection Act established conciliatory bodies attached to the regional economic chambers. The conciliatory bodies deal primarily with the out-of-court settlement of disputes arising between consumers and undertakings in connection with the quality and safety of goods, the application of the rules relating to product liability, the quality of services and the conclusion and performance of contracts. The aim of the conciliatory procedure is to settle disputes between consumers and undertakings by way of reaching an agreement, and in the absence thereof, to make a resolution to enforce consumers' rights in an expedient, effective and simple way. Conciliatory proceedings are initiated at the request of the consumer or, if more consumers are concerned, by the competent organisation representing consumers' interests. In the absence of an amicable settlement, the decision of the conciliatory body is binding on the undertaking only if the same has previously made a declaration pursuant to which the undertaking would consider the decision of the conciliatory body as binding. ②

Based on the Labour Code, one can distinguish between two categories of collective labour disputes. On the one hand there are disputes arising as a result of a conflict of interests (non-legal disputes) ; on the other hand there are disputes arising from the violation or non-performance of rights or obligations, or disputes on the existence or non-existence of certain rights or obligations (collective legal law disputes). The Labour Code③ determines two kinds of conciliation procedures for solving collective labour disputes: conciliation [committee] and arbitration. ④

---

① Zoltán Balázs Kovács and Dávid Kerpel, "Hungary" in Richard Clark, *The Dispute Resolution Review* (Law Business Research; London, 2nd ed, April 2010). See http://www. szecskay. hu/dynamic/DRR_HU. pdf.

② Ibid.

③ Articles 291 – 292.

④ To promote effective and expeditious resolution of industrial disputes the state and the social partners agreed to establish the Labour Mediation and Arbitration Service (in Hungarian: *Munkaügyi Közvetítői és Döntőbírói Szolgálat*, MKDSZ) in 1996. Its role is to facilitate the peaceful resolution of collective interest related industrial (non-legal) disputes between employer(s) and employees' representatives by providing third party mediation and arbitration.

Norway

Professor Berte-Elen Reinertsen Konow

About the Authors

Berte-Elen Konow is professor and vice dean at the Faculty of Law, University of Bergen in Norway. Her authorship includes works from different areas of private law such as contract law, international sale of goods, secured transactions, comparative law and conflict of laws.

Introduction[1]

Geography, history and demography

Norway is situated in Northern Europe on the Scandinavian Peninsula. To the east, Norway has a long border with Sweden. Northeast in Norway there are also borders with Finland and Russia. South of Norway there is a rather small sea called Skagerak, facing Denmark on the other side.

Norway has the second longest coastline in the world after Canada, with a length of 100,915 km including all the islands. In the north, Norway faces the Barents Sea, the North Sea in the west and skagerak in the south.

In the northern region of Europe one often comes across the words Scandinavia and Nordic countries. Scandinavia refers to Norway, Sweden and Denmark, while the Nordic countries refer to Norway, Denmark, Sweden, Finland and Iceland. The Nordic countries share close historical links. Except for Finland, the Nordic countries are also closely linked by similarities in their languages.

The population of Norway is approximately 5.1 million. The life expectancy is 84 years for women and 80 years for men. Norway is ranked 6th among the countries on life expectancy.

The area of Norway is 385,170 km^2, including Svalbard and Jan Mayen. Norway has also an interest in Antarctica, the Bouvet Island, Peter I's Island and Queen Maud Land.

State form and judicial system

Norway is a monarchical democracy. The Norwegian Constitution dates back to 1814.

---

[1]   Key facts about Norway are provided by the Norwegian Central Bureau of Statistics. An overview is presented in a brochure that can be downloaded from the bureau's website, see https://www.ssb.no/befolkning/artikler-og-publikasjoner/_attachment/225814? _ts=14d005aeb20.

The Norwegian Constitution was adopted on 17 May 1814 and is the second oldest written constitution in the world. It was originally founded on the principles of sovereignty of the people; separation of powers; and human rights. The Constitution establishes three branches of government: legislative, budgetary and supervisory power is vested in the Storting (Parliament); executive power is vested in King in Council (Government); and judicial power is vested in the Supreme Courts and the subordinate courts, and the Court of Impeachment (Riksretten).

The ordinary court system consists of local Courts of First Instance (tingrett), Courts of Appeal for bigger regions in Norway and the Supreme Court.

Norway has a long tradition of Alternative Dispute Resolution in consumer disputes. Most of the Consumer Complaints Boards are set up by agreement between the industry associations and the Norwegian Consumer Council. Each Complaints Board is made up of representatives from the Norwegian Consumer Council and the relevant industry association, with a neutral chairman—usually a judge or an expert in the particular branch of jurisprudence from a law school. Most of the Norwegian Complaints Boards are notified to the European Commission.

The economy

According to the World Bank, Norway is considered as a high-income OECD country. [1]

Main sources of revenue in Norway

Because of its long coastline, fisheries have traditionally been important for the Norwegian economy. Agriculture and forestry have also been important sources of income, often in combination with fisheries for people living along the coast. The climate in Norway is rough, and many people have to struggle for their income.

The shipping industry is also an industry with a long tradition in Norway. The shipping industry is still important for the Norwegian society.

The industrialisation of Norway happened especially from 1880 and onwards. Many waterfalls are now being used to build hydropower plants, and heavy industry has been allocated to small areas close to the waterfalls but also with access to sea,

---

[1] See http://data. worldbank. org/country/norway.

such as Odda, Sauda and Høyanger. A major change in Norway's sources of income occurred when oil was discovered outside the coast of Norway in 1969. Since then, the petroleum industry has been of the utmost importance for the Norwegian economy. Today Norway is a big producer of energy both from the petroleum sector and from hydropower.

Norway's major revenue derives from a combination of taxes and fees plus income from the petroleum sector and other industries. The industries outside the petroleum sector include important sectors such as fisheries, fish farming and shipping. The figure below shows that income from taxes on income and property, VAT, employer taxes and contributions to the National Insurance Scheme contributes up to 62 percent of the revenue; 26 percent of the Norwegian state's income comes from the petroleum sector and the remaining 13 percent is created in other areas.

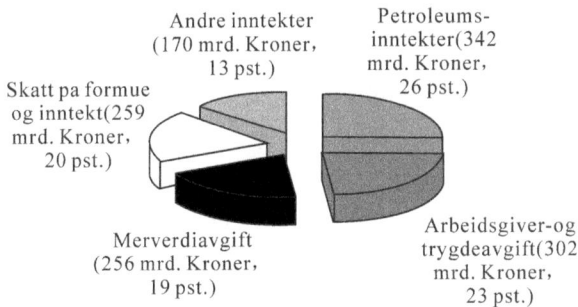

Figure 1. Breakdown of Norway's Revenue by Sectors

Source: http://www. statsbudsjettet. no/Upload/Statsbudsjett_2015/dokumenter/pdf/budget_2015. pdf. Information in Norwegian.

Taxes

As seen from Figure 1, taxes comprise the main income for the public sector in Norway. The taxes are spent on public services such as healthcare(hospitals, nursing homes), education(schools, colleges, universities), transport and communications (roads, railroads, airports). In addition to covering joint expenses, taxes are designed to contribute to greater equality between individuals. ①

The most important taxes to be paid are income tax, property tax, employment

---

① See: https://www. skatteetaten. no/en/International-pages/If-you-work-in-Norway-you-need-to/Are-you-working-for-a-foreign-employer/Are-you-working-for-a-foreign-employer/Articles/Tax-in-Norway/.

taxes and contributions to the National Insurance Scheme. VAT(value-added tax) is a tax on sale of goods or services. The general rate is 25 percent, but the VAT is lower for means of nutrition(15 percent).

Import and export

In parallel with the drop in oil price, the Norwegian Krone weakened against major international currencies. This has increased the value of Norwegian exports but has at the same time made Norwegian imports more expensive. This effect manifests itself in mainland exports, which rose by 5.1 percent in 2014 and amounted to NOK 406.2 billion in 2015. Natural gas exports increased in contrast to the dramatic drop in oil exports. Exports of natural gas amounted to NOK 227.9 billion in 2015; 1.9 percent more than in 2014. The trade balance went down from NOK 347.7 billion in 2014 to NOK 233.7 billion in 2015; a decline of NOK 114 billion. The sharp fall in the trade surplus is caused by both lower exports and an increase in imports. ①

Except for exports stemming from the petroleum sector, Norway exports goods made of metal, instruments and devices, machines, chemical products, fish and fisheries products, raw materials and paper. Member states of the EU are by far the most important exporting countries for the Norwegian industry. It is reported that the exportation to China and South Korea has increased.

As regards imports, member states of the EU also are the most important. Sweden and Germany are the two countries that Norway has the highest rate of import from. But imports from Asia, especially China, have increased substantially. Food, beverages, electronics and cars are some major imports.

Foreign direct investment

There has been an increased growth in direct investment in Norway. The stock of Norwegian foreign direct investment amounted to NOK 1,216 billion at the end of 2014, which was an increase of nine percent from 2013. The stock of foreign direct investment in Norway was NOK 1,297 billion; an increase of 10 percent.

The Norwegian direct investment abroad was dominated by investments in

---

①　Information about import and export can be found here: https://www.ssb.no/en/utenriksokonomi/ statistikker/muh/aar-forelopige/2016 − 01 − 15.

equity capital, which totalled NOK 1,200 billion. Foreign investment in equity capital in Norway amounted to NOK 764 billion; the remaining NOK 533 billion being other capital.

The geographical breakdown shows that 66 percent of the Norwegian foreign direct investment went to Europe, 16 percent to North and South America and 11 percent to Asian countries.

European direct investment in Norway accounted for 74 percent of the total investment. Direct investment from North and South America and Asia accounted for 15 and five percent respectively.

Trade agreements

Norway has joined several international trade agreements and conventions which are directly relevant to import and export.

Norway has been a WTO member since 1 January 1995 and a member of GATT since 10 July 1948. Norway is a member of the European Free Trade Association (EFTA). This organisation was established in 1960① and originally covered seven European states: Austria, Denmark, Norway, Portugal, Sweden, Switzerland and the United Kingdom. Later, Finland, Iceland and Lichtenstein joined the organisation. However, most of the EFTA states left the organisation to become members of the European Union (EU). Today there are four state members of the EFTA: Iceland, Lichtenstein, Switzerland and Norway. The EFTA Convention forms the legal basis for free trade between the EFTA countries (intra-EFTA trade).

As most of the former EFTA states have joined the EU, it became important to have an agreement with EU in order to secure free trade and smooth interaction between persons and businesses in Europe. In 1994 the European Economic Area was created by the so-called EEA Agreement. Switzerland chose not to join the EEA Agreement. Through the EEA Agreement, Norway, Iceland and Lichtenstein are practically part of the EU internal market.

The EEA Agreement provides for the inclusion of EU legislation covering the four freedoms—the free movement of goods, services, persons and capital. Norway is a party to the Schengen Agreement. ② This agreement secures free movement of

① The EFTA Convention was signed in Stockholm on 4 January 1960. A revised Convention, the Vaduz Convention, was signed on 21 June 2001 and entered into force on 1 June 2002.

② Convention Implementing the Schengen Agreement, 4 June 1985, amended 1 June 2009.

persons within the Schengen area while maintaining joint protection of the external borders. The Schengen Information System (SIS) is a compensatory measure to the abolition of checks at the internal borders. Norway joined the SIS on 1 January 2001. [1]

In order to ensure homogeneity of legislation in the EEA area, in line with the EU legal regime, relevant EU acts are continuously incorporated into the EEA Agreement. Due to the EEA Agreement, Norway is bound by EU legislation covering the scope of the EEA Agreement. This development is of high importance to understand Norwegian law in general.

The EFTA states have also made free trade agreements with non-European states (third countries). As of January 2016 there were 25 free trade agreements in existence with 36 third countries. There are ongoing negotiations with 10 more states among them India, Russia, Thailand and Vietnam. See the map that illustrates the extent of free trade agreements that Norway is party to, in its capacity as a member of the EFTA (taken from the EFTA website: http://www. efta. int/). This site gives further information about the EFTA organisation and also about the relationship between EFTA and the EU.

---

[1]   For more information about the Schengen cooperation, see https://www. politi. no.

Chapter 1   Customs System and Law

1. 1   Legal framework

The most important Norwegian regulations when it comes to questions related to customs in import-export trading of goods are:

(ⅰ) The 2007 Act on Customs Duties and Movement of Goods (Customs Act);[1]

(ⅱ) Regulations to the Customs Act(Customs regulations);

(ⅲ) The VAT Act;[2]

(ⅳ) The Norwegian Customs Tariff(annual);[3] and

(ⅴ) Special legislation regarding specific taxes, for example alcohol, tobacco, medicines, etc.

The Norwegian Customs Authority gives information in English on legislation and practical procedures at http://toll. no/en/. Information from this website is used in this report.

1. 2   Customs authorities and their powers

The Norwegian Customs Authority is an entity governed by the Ministry of Finance. The Customs Authority is organised by way of a Directorate and six regional subdivisions. There are approximately 1, 900 people employed by the Norwegian Customs Authority.

Norwegian Customs Authority is primarily a control agency. But at the same time the Customs Authority's goal is to be a service-minded agency and partner to the business community and to private individuals who comply with the regulations.

---

[1]   Act on Customs Duties and Movement of Goods, No. 119 of 21 December 2007.

[2]   Act on VAT, No. 58 of 19 June 2006.

[3]   The Norwegian Customs Tariff is based on the Harmonised Commodity Description and Coding System, done at Brussels on 14 June 1983, and its subsequent amending protocols.

The Authority strives to strike the right balance between the need to enforce controls and simplification of service procedures. ①

It is the main responsibility of the Norwegian Customs Authority to

(i) prevent the illegal importation and exportation of goods; and

(ii) ensure that customs duties are correctly declared, assessed and paid on time.

The main tasks of the Customs Authority include border control in order to stop illegal import and export of goods, assess the correct excise and customs duties, secure timely payment of excise and customs duties and provide a good service for the users.

At Norway's borders, Norwegian Customs Authority carries out not only its own tasks, but also tasks on behalf of more than 20 other authorities. The Customs Authority cooperates with the police, the Norwegian Tax Administration, the Norwegian Public Roads Administration, the Norwegian Climate and Pollution Agency, the Norwegian Food Safety Authority, the Norwegian Coast Guard, the Norwegian Coastal Administration, the Norwegian Maritime Directorate, the Norwegian Agricultural Authority, Statistics Norway, the Directorate of Fisheries and others. The Customs Authority seeks cooperation with other authorities where it can contribute to better results or greater efficiency.

The Norwegian Customs Authority also cooperates with foreign customs and police authorities, as well as international organisations such as the EU, EFTA, WCO and WTO.

The Customs Authority is managed by the Director General for Customs. The Directorate of Customs deals with issues at national and international levels. The Directorate is also responsible for infrastructure, for example modern and effective digital solutions for serving the authorities and the general public. There are six regional subdivisions responsible for border controls that take place in airports, harbours, border crossing by roads, etc. The regional offices are also responsible for control activities regarding imports/exports and payment of customs and taxes. Some national responsibilities have been delegated to the regional offices, for greater efficiency. For example the region for Mid-Norway has the national responsibility

---

① A Strategy Plan for the Norwegian Customs Authority can be found on the Customs' website, see http://www. toll. no/en/about-norwegian-customs/about-us/strategy-plan/.

for the Currency Register and also for Climate Quotas Businesses.

From 1 January 2016 some tasks and powers have been transferred from the Customs Authority to the Tax Authority, and now the Tax Authority is responsible for administering and enforcing the payment of VAT and special taxes. Customs declaration is the responsibility of the Customs Authority whereas VAT and special taxes are now the responsibility of the Tax Authority.

The powers of the Customs Authority are closely linked to the Authority's main tasks of preventing illegal importation and exportation of goods, and ensuring that customs duties are correctly declared, assessed and paid. What follows is a brief account of the Authority's powers in connection with (i) custom control, (ii) retention of goods presumed to infringe intellectual property rights and (iii) criminal and other sanctions.

1. 3   The powers of the Customs Authority in customs control

The relevant provisions are found in Chapter 13 of the 2007 Customs Act. Section 13-1 of the Act provides that in order to ascertain whether there has been any evasion of customs control in respect of goods or whether an attempt has been made to evade such control, the customs authorities may conduct a search (a) outdoors when the search takes place in direct connection with the pursuit of a matter which is believed to involve such evasion of control, (b) outdoors in areas where unloading or loading takes place or is believed to have taken place, or (c) in warehouses or other buildings or places where unloading or loading takes place or has taken place, or (d) on trains in the customs territory. The Customs Authority may also search persons who are travelling to or from the boundary of the customs territory; persons who are in or on their way to or from a means of transport which is on its way to or from the boundary of the customs territory; persons who are leaving a place of storage for goods not cleared for free circulation; persons who are in or are on their way to or from a place of call for vessels or a landing place for aircraft servicing international routes; or persons who are in such place and under such circumstances that the customs authorities may conduct if they are suspected of evading control of goods. Section 13-2 provides that the Ministry may make regulations concerning the customs authorities' control activities pursuant to this section.

Chapter 15 of the Customs Act contains special provisions to protect intellectual property rights. If the Customs Authority observe infringements of intellectual property rights, or if they have a reasonable suspicion to believe that an intellectual property right is violated, the Authority may retain the goods in question, see Section 15-1(1). In these cases the Customs Authority can(but is not obliged to) give notice to the holder of the intellectual property right. The goods may be retained up to a maximum of 10 days. Within this time the holder of the intellectual property right will have time to inspect the goods, and there will also normally be time to go to court and claim a preliminary order to stop the goods from entering into the Norwegian market. The consignee or the representative of the consignee will also be given notice in such cases, see Section 15-1(2).

Section 13-5 provides that the customs authorities shall at all times have unimpeded access to any area or building that is approved as a customs warehouse, and to other places approved by the customs authorities for the storage of goods not cleared for free circulation. The customs authorities may conduct any search that is considered necessary.

Where the Customs Authority suspects that there is a violation of the customs regulations or finds that such a violation has occurred, the Customs Authority has the power to

(a) stop the import or export of goods(Sec 4-2, Chapter 15 and 16);

(b) require additional customs duty(Sec 16-10)give a fine(Sec 16-9);

(c) retain goods violating intellectual property rights(Sec 15-1);

(d) decide forfeiture of the goods or a sum of money corresponding to the value of the goods(Sec 16-9(2)and Sec 16-8(1));

(e) detain goods to secure claims for customs(Sec 16-12);

(f) decide seizure and arrest(Sec 16-13).

Section 12-3 (1) of the Customs Act provides that the police and military authorities must provide the customs authorities with the necessary assistance and protection during the performance of customs services. Any port authority official, lighthouse keeper or state pilot who in the performance of his duties or in an official capacity becomes aware of a contravention of the legislation governing customs and movement of goods or of circumstances indicating that such a contravention is intended must seek to prevent the contravention, and must without undue delay notify the customs authorities or the prosecuting authority(12-3(2)).

Payment of custom duties in cases of physical import/export must be submitted to the Customs Authority at the point of entering or leaving Norway. If goods are sent by post or courier, the forwarding agent is obliged to send the Custom Declaration Form to the nearest customs region within five days. The power to enforce unpaid customs duties has been transferred to the Tax Authority, with effect from 1 January 2016.

Illegal movement of goods, handling illegally imported goods, breaking a lock or seal, etc. are prohibited under Section 16-2 to 16-6 and are demeanours (Section 16-4). A fine or imprisonment for a term not exceeding six months, or both, may be imposed on any person who contravenes or attempts to contravene any of these provisions, negligently or wilfully. Where such contravention, or attempt, is particularly gross, the penalty is a fine or imprisonment for a term not exceeding two years, but imprisonment for a term not exceeding six years in the case of wilful or grossly negligent contravention (Section 16-7). Where the owner of goods in respect of which a contravention has been committed under Chapter 16 is not known or has no known abode in Norway, and the offender is not known or has no known abode in Norway, the goods shall pass to the public treasury provided that the owner has not come forward within one month after the goods came into the possession of the authorities. Section 16-10 provides that a customs debtor may be required to pay additional customs duty not exceeding 60 percent of the customs duty laid down pursuant to the Customs Act and the Storting's resolution on customs duties if he has wilfully or negligently contravened the Act or regulations made pursuant thereto, and the public treasury has or might have been deprived of customs duty. [1]

Customs officers are be empowered to issue summary fines in lieu of prosecution in the less severe cases according to Section 16-9. The more severe cases are however handled by the Prosecution Authority (Police Lawyers and State Attorneys) following standard criminal procedure[2].

1.4   Import and export checking procedures and standards

In import and export trade towards Norway, the Customs Authority's checking

---

[1]   See generally Chapter 16 of the Norwegian Customs Act.

[2]   Act No 25. of 22 May 1981 on Criminal Procedure. Section 55 describes who has the power acting as Prosecution Authority.

procedure and routines are developed in order to make sure that

(ⅰ) No illegal goods enter into Norway;

(ⅱ) Customs duties and other taxes are paid correctly;

(ⅲ) Currency restrictions are not flouted; and

(ⅳ) Preferential treatment is given to persons or companies covered by Free Trade Agreements. ①

In order to make customs declaration and control as smooth as possible, the Norwegian authorities make use of special prescribed forms. The Customs Authority has developed an electronic customs declaration scheme(TVINN).

As for import and export procedures and standards, Norway has by and large the same procedures as in the EU. Through Protocol 10 of the EEA Agreement, Norway and the European Union have established an equivalent measure of security on goods entering or leaving the external borders of their customs territories(see Art. 9b of Protocol 10 on general provisions on security).

Traders are under obligation to provide the customs with advance electronic information for security purposes in bilateral trade between Norway and the EU. These rules have been applied since 2009.

The EEA agreement foresees that, in its trade with third countries, Norway implements customs security measures that are equivalent to those applied by the EU, which has been followed up from Norwegian side. This implies mutual recognition of systems of risk analysis and management, and of systems to facilitate reliable traders(the so-called EU AEO certificate). This will ensure both smooth trade flows between Norway and the EU and a high level of security of the supply chain.

All movements of goods between Norway and third countries other than member states of the European Union need to be accompanied by an Entry or Exit Summary Declaration(see Art. 9c(3) of Protocol 10 of the EEA Agreement).

1. 5   Measures relating to documentation

As of 1 January 2011 it is mandatory for a transporter to electronically lodge a

---

① See the site: toll. no for an overview of Free Trade Agreements that Norway is a party to. Information is also given about the Generalised System of Preference(GSP) providing exporters from developing countries duty relief when exporting goods to Norway.

summary declaration for goods entering or leaving the external customs territories of Norway and the European Union.

The system in use for lodging a summary declaration to Norwegian customs authorities is the New Computerised Transit System (NCTS). The data to be included is listed in Annex 30A of Regulation(EC) No. 648/2005.

As there is no system in place for exchange of security data between Norway and member states of the European Union, the summary declaration needs to be lodged at the office of exit in the case of indirect transport, and not at the office of departure, as is the case within the EU. ①

There are exceptions to the duty to lodge a summary declaration. Here are some examples where an entry or exit summary declaration is not required(the list is not exhaustive) : electrical energy; goods entering or leaving by pipeline; letters, postcards and printed matter, including on electronic media; goods moved under the rules of the Universal Postal Union Convention; goods for which an oral customs declaration or a declaration by simple crossing the border is permitted in accordance with the legislation of the contracting parties except for pallets, containers and means of road, rail, air, sea or inland waterway transport carried under a transport contract; and goods contained in travellers' personal luggage.

A prescribed form regarding means of payment must be completed in all cases of import or export of goods to Norway. ②

The Norwegian Customs Authority has to be notified if a person carries with him currency with a value corresponding to more than NOK 25,000 to or from Norway. Where such notification is not given, the person will be fined 20 percent of the entire amount and may be reported to the police.

---

① The information is taken from http://www. toll. no/en.

② The form RD-0026E(means of payment) can be downloaded from the Custom Authority's website http://www. toll. no/en.

Chapter 2   Foreign Trade System and Law

2. 1   Licensing system and procedures regarding trade in goods

The Norwegian Customs Authority and the entity called Innovation Norway (Innovasjon Norge) have both gathered information that is useful for businesses importing goods to Norway. Innovation Norway is the Norwegian Government's most important agency for innovation and development of Norwegian enterprises and industry[1] The information is to be read together with information given by the Norwegian Customs Authority as described in Chapter 1.

An import licence is required for only a few types of goods such as agriculture products, certain kinds of food or nutritional products, weapons and explosives. Import of any product containing alcohol or nicotine without having permission is forbidden. The term "nutritional product" includes any food, drinking water or beverages meant for human consumption, but medicals are excluded from the definition. [2]

Import restrictions have been imposed on certain types of goods and there are different reasons for these restrictions. Not only are there different legal justifications for such different categories of goods, there are also different authorities administering applications of import permissions and licences. Information concerning which body of authority to contact in order to gain import permission or licence is given at the Customs Authority's website. Table 1 is a list of the authorities involved in importation of goods that require an import licence or permission. [3]

---

①   See http://www. toll. no/en/ and http://www. innovasjonnorge. no/en/start-page/.

②   See the preparatory works to Sec. 2 of the Food Act, Ot. pop. 100(2002 – 2003), p 135. The Food Act is Act No. 124 of 19 December 2003.

③   The information is taken from the Customs Authority's website http://www. toll. no/en.

Table 1. Authorities Involved in Importation of Goods

Restricted Goods	Responsible Authority
Alcohol	Tax and Health Administration
Tobacco	Health Administration
Food, animals, plants, seed	Norwegian Food Safety Authority
Endangered Species of Wild Fauna and Flora (CITES-goods)	Norwegian Environment Agency
Pharmaceuticals	Norwegian Medicines Agency
Waste	Norwegian Environment Agency
Explosives, fireworks, hazardous substances	Norwegian Directorate for Civil Protection
Weapons, weapons spare parts, ammunition	Police Force
Cultural property, antiques	Directorate for Cultural Heritage

2. 2   Rules of origin of goods

As mentioned in Chapter 1, the question of whether or not imported goods are covered by taxes or customs duties, and the amount to be paid, is dependent upon the existence of a Free Trade Agreement between Norway and the exporting country.

There is free movement of goods within the EEA area. [1] Requirements for information on origin of goods was originally governed by Protocol 4 to the EEA Agreement, but the rules in this Protocol have been replaced by a decision by the EEA Committee dated 20 March 2015. Norway thus has the same rules when it comes to determining the origin of goods as the rules in the European Union.

By offering Generalised System of Preference (GSP) country status, Norway offers exporters from under-developed countries certain measures of relief in customs duty in respect of types of goods that are coved by the scheme of GSP. As the main rule, a product must be either wholly obtained or sufficiently processed in a GSP-country in order to satisfy originating status and in turn preferential treatment.

A declaration of origin of goods must be made with the customs declaration,

---

[1]   See the EEA Agreement Art. 8.

most often by entering the information in the Customs Authority's digitalised application system. The information given regarding origin of goods will be monitored by the Customs Authority as part of its routine work.

Rules of origin of goods are relevant not only in determining the liability for customs duty but also for reasons of health and safety, as in the case of weapons.

Several nutritional products also attract import restrictions, and sometimes the importer will need a special permission from the Norwegian Food Safety Authority in order to legally import such products to Norway. This is for example the case when importing food containing meat, fish or milk originating from a country outside the EEA area. Any commercial importer bringing food or nutritional products into Norway must be registered and approved by the Norwegian Food Safety Authority before starting import activity. Because there are different rules regarding import/export depending on whether the import/export is connected to the EEA area or not, the Norwegian Food Safety Authority requires information about the origin. As the main rule, the Norwegian Food Safety Authority requires information beforehand about any food or nutritional products that will be imported from a country outside the EEA area, with some exceptions for fresh fruits and vegetables.

When it comes to importing animals, plants and seed, the Norwegian Food Safety Authority requires information about the country of origin in order to prevent import of unwanted species, or to prevent bringing diseases to Norway.

Commercial importation of weapons and ammunition is strictly regulated. Such import is covered by specific provisions in the Weapon Act and the Weapon Regulation. Approval of the Police Authority is necessary to import weapons. ①

2. 3　Sanitary and phytosanitary measures

The Norwegian Food Safety Authority is responsible for ensuring the population's safety regarding food. This Authority is also responsible for animal health and plant health.

In cases of import of food, animals, plants and seeds, some rules are the same as in the EU whereas some rules have been developed especially for Norway. It is

---

①　See Sec. 23 of the Weapon Act, Act No 1 of 19 June 1961. For more information, see https://www. politi. no/.

the responsibility of the importer that the imported foodstuff is safe for human consumption and that the labelling and the content comply with Norwegian food regulations.

In addition to EU legislation given effect in Norway through the EEA Agreement, the legal framework regarding sanitary or phytosanitary measures consists of the following Norwegian acts:

(i) The Animal Welfare Act, No. 97 of 19 June 2009;

(ii) The Cosmetics Act, No. 126 of 21 December 2005;

(iii) Act on Food Production and Food Safety, No. 124 of 19 December 2003;

(iv) Act on Plant Breeder's Rights, No. 32 of 12 March 1993.

Any food imported into Norway must comply with Norwegian food regulations. Because of the EEA Agreement, Norwegian food legislation is harmonised with the EU law, and Norway is obliged to follow the EU legislation in the food and veterinary area. Regulations about requirements, prohibited substances not allowed for use in food products, quality requirements etc. are the same as in the EU. If the product does not comply with Norwegian food regulations, the Norwegian Food Safety Authority (NFSA) may refuse their import into Norway and sale on the Norwegian market.

Import of living animals or food products of animal origin must be registered in the same way as in the EU. The Norwegian Food Safety Authority uses the same electronic registry that is used in EU member states, a system called TRACES (Trade Control and Expert System). The procedure for registering food or living animals originating from a country outside the EEA area is the same as for the EU member states.

Food products of animal origin imported from a third country will be inspected at a veterinary border inspection post (BIP) before being imported into Norway, under its authorisation. Consignments must be notified in TRACES before the physical arrival of the consignment on EEA territory. The purpose of the veterinary border control is to prevent the spread of contagious animal diseases to Norway and the EU, and to ensure that the imported foods are safe for human consumption.

Sanitary requirements apply to cosmetics commercially imported into Norway. The Norwegian Food Safety Authority is responsible for the control of import of cosmetics. The Norwegian legislation is nearly identical to the European cosmetics regulation, EU Regulation No. 1223/2009. There are only a few exceptions.

Norway has national requirements when it comes to language. Information must be in Norwegian and the products labelled in Norwegian, or a language which is similar to Norwegian in spelling and meaning (in practice Danish or Swedish).

Norway has for a long time had restrictions on the use of a variety of substances in cosmetics which have been allowed in the EU. Many of these compounds are active ingredients in pharmaceuticals, and may have adverse effects. Because of EU regulatory framework for cosmetics and Norway's commitment under the EEA Agreement, Norway could no longer maintain the national restrictions on these substances in cosmetics. The Norwegian Food Safety Authority has assessed the safety of a wide variety of these substances. Without restrictions on use, these substances may cause a variety of adverse effects, such as cancer, organ damage, malformation of foetuses and skin irritation and sensitisation. The substances are collected in a list that is provided on the website of the Norwegian Food Safety Authority[1]. The Norwegian Food Safety Authority urges industry to respect the recommendations on the safe use of these pharmacological active ingredients.

Further information regarding sanitary and phytosanitary measures when importing goods into Norway can be found at the website of the Norwegian Food Safety Authority. [2]

2.4   Anti-dumping and countervailing duties law

As a WTO member Norway is also a member of the WTO Anti-dumping Agreement. Anti-dumping and countervailing duties are also covered by the EEA Agreement and the EEA Act. [3] In practice this means that the rules of anti-dumping and countervailing in Norway are similar to those operative in EU member states. In addition to the WTO Anti-dumping Agreement and the EEA Agreement, the legal basis for anti-dumping measures can also be found in Free Trade Agreements that Norway is a party to.

---

[1]   See http://www.mattilsynet.no/language/english/cosmetics/.

[2]   See http://www.mattilsynet.no/language/english/.

[3]   See the EEA Agreement Art. 26. See also more details in the Norwegian regulation dated 21 December 2011.

The importance of the duties and responsibilities that Norway has taken upon itself under binding public international agreements is reflected in the preparatory work of the Norwegian Customs Act. [1]

More detailed rules regarding anti-dumping measures, special countervailing duties and emergency measures are given in the 2007 Norwegian Customs Act in particular in Chapters 10 and 12. [2]

The Ministry of Finance has the formal responsibility under the Norwegian Customs Act.

Section 10-1 of the Customs Act provides as follows: " If the Ministry determines that dumping has taken place, and that the dumping causes or threatens to cause significant injury to an industry in the customs territory or significantly delays the establishment of such an industry, the King may, within the limitations that follow from an agreement with a foreign state or an international organisation, or from international law, implement an anti-dumping measure. Such measure may also be implemented at the request of a third country where the dumping causes or threatens to cause significant injury to an industry in that country. "This means that a decision upon whether or not to implement anti-dumping measurements will be taken by the government after the question has been prepared by the Ministry.

In practice, anti-dumping measures will be taken either by way of a Custom Duty Order or by what is called a " Price Agreement". A Price Agreement (sometimes also called a Price Promise) is a statement from an exporter or group of exporters that commit themselves to maintaining a minimum price level.

According to the Customs Act Section 10-1 (3) the anti-dumping measure shall remain in force only as long as it is necessary to counteract injury resulting from the dumping, and the measure shall be reduced if called for by a further review. Where there are reasons for doing so, the authorities shall on their own initiative or on request consider whether, after a certain period, it is necessary to uphold the measure. An anti-dumping measure only lasts as long as it is needed in order to prevent damage caused by the dumping.

Section 10-3 of the Norwegian Customs Act provides as follows: " If the Ministry determines that there exists direct or indirect subsidisation of goods that are

---

[1] See Ot. prp. nr 58(2006 – 2007) comments to Section 10-1.

[2] Act No. 119 of 21 December 2007.

exported to Norway, and that the subsidisation causes or threatens to cause significant injury, the King may, within the limitations that follow from an agreement with a foreign state or an international organisation, or from international law, implement a countervailing measure. " As for anti-dumping, a decision regarding countervailing is also taken by the government after it has been prepared by the Ministry. In practice the countervailing measure will be by way of a countervailing custom duty.

In extraordinary situations there may be a need to take measures to protect the Norwegian market, for example Norwegian producers of certain products. Section 10-5 provides that if the Ministry determines that, as a result of an unforeseen development, goods are being imported in such increased quantities and under such conditions as to cause, or threaten to cause, serious injury to Norwegian producers of similar or competing goods, the King may within the limitations that follow from an agreement with a foreign state or an international organisation, or from international law, implement a safeguard measure. Section 10-6 provides that of the imported quantity of agricultural goods exceeds a specified reference level, or the import price for such goods falls below a specified reference price, the King may, within the framework of an agreement with a foreign state or an international organisation, implement a special safeguard measure, including the imposition of a special customs duty on the goods concerned in addition to ordinary customs duty.

Emergency measures under the Norwegian Customs Act in order to limit imports temporarily are taken by way of a special Customs Duty. This Customs Duty will be given regardless of the country of origin of the goods in question, and also regardless of any quota agreement. Emergency Customs duty under Section 10-5 is temporal by nature. Section 10-3(5) provides that a safeguard measure shall not be applied beyond a period of four years, unless it is again determined that the measure continues to be necessary. A provisional safeguard measure of up to 200 days' duration may be implemented.

To protect Norwegian agriculture, Section 10-6 gives more detailed criteria for emergency measures to be taken: " If the imported quantity of agricultural goods exceeds a specified reference level, or the import price for such goods falls below a specified reference price, the King may, within the framework of an agreement with a foreign state or an international organisation, implement a special safeguard measure, including the imposition of a special customs duty on the goods concerned in addition to ordinary customs duty. " Section 10-6 must be understood as a provision that implements the WTO Agreement on Agriculture, Article 5 (Special Safeguards, SSG). ①

The Norwegian Customs Act also contains provisions regarding inspections to be made, duty to inform and proceedings, see Sections 12-5 to 12-9.

2.5   Technical barriers

Norway is part of the Trade in Services Agreement(TISA) negotiations and has been so since the negotiations formally started in 2013. The negotiations seek to find solutions to make a TISA Agreement compatible with the WTO's General Agreement on Trade in Services(GATS). It is important from a Norwegian point of view to reach agreement for an international legal framework that is adjusted to the developments in international trade since the GATS agreement was reached in 1995.

Technical regulations and standards are important, but they vary from country to country, creating a myriad of challenges for producers and exporters. It is of course important to recognise a country's right to adopt the standards considered necessary for example for human, animal or plant life or health, for the protection of the environment or to meet other consumer interests. For Norway it is important that governments apply international standards, which is why Norway is participating in the TISA negotiations. It is also important to Norwegian exporters of services that national regulations do not discriminate against foreign service providers.

When it comes to international trade, the services industry takes an increasingly bigger part of Norwegian export. Trade in services is important for economic growth and employment in Norway. ②The branches of trade in services most important to Norway are services in maritime sector, telecommunications, services related to energy and also financial services.

In general Norway has fewer trade barriers related to services than many other countries. The GATS agreement and the bilateral free trade agreements that Norway is a party to, show that Norway has an open trade regime. Norway is ranked as

---

① See Ot. prp. 58(2006 – 2007), comment to Section 10-6.

② Statistics found on the WTO website, https://www. wto. org/english/res_e/statis_e/tradeserv_stat_e. htm.

number 9 out of 189 in 2015 in the "Ease of Doing Business, 2016". ①

2.5.1   Market access in general

By virtue of the EEA Agreement, Norway is part of the internal market. This means that Norway in general will have access to the market in any EU/EFTA member state and vice versa.

Outside the EEA area, Norway has bilateral agreements with many third countries. By these agreements Norwegian businesses will have access to the market in foreign countries, whereas businesses from the reciprocating country will have access to the Norwegian market. It depends however on the particular branch or sector if there are any particular hindrances for market access.

2.5.2   Rules on financial services

Foreign entities doing business in Norway in the financial sector are governed by the 2015 Act on Financial Companies and Financial Groups (the Financial Business Act). ②The act is applicable to foreign companies doing business through a branch in Norway, or through cross-border finance activity. The purpose of this Act is to contribute to financial stability, and to ensure that banks and financial institutions function in an appropriate and satisfactory manner. Financial stability entails that the financial system is sufficiently robust to receive deposits and other repayable funds from the public, channel funds, execute payments and redistribute risk in a satisfactory manner. Chapter 5 of the Act gives more detailed rules concerning Foreign Finance Companies' activities in Norway.

The Act covers financial businesses such as banks, credit institutions, finance and mortgage companies, insurance companies, pension companies and holding companies in financial groups.

In order to be allowed to do business in Norway, a financial business entity needs permission(concession) from the Financial Supervisory Authority of Norway (Finanstilsynet). Provisions on concessions exist to secure adequate competition in the financial markets, while at the same time securing the necessary financial stability.

Norway has been part of the internal market for financial services since the

---

① http://www. doingbusiness. orgdataexploreeconomies/norway, http://globaledge. msu. edu/countries/norway/.

② Act No. 17 of 10 April 2015.

EEA Agreement came into force in 1994. As a result, Norway regularly implements legislation developed in the EU system. This is also true of the legal framework for financial services. A Norwegian branch of a Financial Company with the centre of main interest situated in another EEA member state, is subject to more liberal rules regarding doing business in Norway compared to financial companies from a state outside the EEA area. [1]

2.5.3 Telecommunications

The telecommunication sector is covered by the EEA Agreement. The 2003 Act on Electronic Communication strives to harmonise EU law and Norwegian law in this sector. [2]

The Norwegian company Telenor has a dominant position in the Norwegian market. This has however not hindered foreign companies from establishing businesses in Norway. Being a strong actor in the telecommunication sector, Telenor is doing business in many other jurisdictions. In the GATS negotiations Norway originally worked to remove specific requirements regarding establishment or performance, but the Norwegian government withdrew its demand in 2005 to meet the needs of the least developed countries.

---

[1] See Chapter 5 of the Financial Business Act of 2015.

[2] Act on Electronic Communication No. 83 of 4 July 2003.

Chapter 3   Foreign Direct Investment System and Law

3. 1   Admission of foreign direct investment

What we consider in this Part is the extent to which a foreign person or company is allowed to investment in Norway. In practice this is a question of producing something or doing business in Norway. Foreign direct investment as understood here as being about controlling ownership in a business enterprise in Norway by an entity based in another country. It may also be a question of a foreigner buying a Norwegian company or expanding a business already established in Norway. Foreign direct investment is distinguished from portfolio foreign investment, a passive investment in the securities of another country such as public stocks and bonds. These issues will not be commented upon. It will not be possible to answer all questions related to foreign direct investments in detail, so only the most important main rules and restrictions will be mentioned in the following text.

Commenting upon direct investments and doing business in Norway will in the following be structured under the headings of: (i) organisation of business activity, (ii) representation by an agent, (iii) VAT and(iv) special concessions or permissions needed in some branches of industry. ①

3. 1. 1   Organisation of business activity

In Norway the industries are largely divided into regional clusters, and there are many different organisations and service providers ready to offer their assistance. ②

In practice, doing business in Norway by a foreigner often will happen in the framework of a company. Alternatively business can be carried out through a trade agent or other representative.

---

① General information regarding doing business in Norway is given at this website http://www.innovasjonnorge. no/en.

② For more information about the business regions in Norway, see http://www. nortrade. com/invest/map/.

When it comes to the legislative framework of companies, there are basically three main types of companies each governed by a separate act: Unlimited liability partnerships and limited partnerships (The Partnerships Act 1985), [1] limited liability companies (Limited Liability Companies Act 1997) [2] and public limited liability companies (Public Limited Liability Companies Act 1997). [3] The limited liability companies are the most common form of organising the business.

The biggest companies will be public limited liability companies. The minimum share capital for these companies is NOK 1,000,000. Unless the company's owners decide the company to be a public limited liability company, it will be treated as an ordinary limited company. Very many of the provisions in the Public Limited Liability Companies Act are comparable to those in the Limited Liability Companies Act. All limited liability companies must be registered in the Norwegian Register called the Brønnøysund Register Centre. [4]

Before 1997 there were criteria in the 1976 Limited Liability Company's Act regarding a stock holder's domicile. Because of the EEA agreement, exceptions had to be made for the benefit of citizens domiciled within the EEA area. When new legislation was enacted in 1997, a general requirement relating to domicile or citizenship was abandoned. Today neither the Limited Liability Companies Act nor the Public Limited Liability Companies Act demands that any of the founders of the company must be resident or previously have had domicile in Norway.

It is also important to underline that neither the Limited Liability Companies Act nor the Public Limited Liability Companies Act have any requirement of Norwegian citizenship. As a general principle a foreigner may just as a Norwegian start or join a limited liability company in Norway. There are however exceptions to this general starting point, and a person or a company from another jurisdiction is advised to make thorough investigations to find out how it could get best possible legal protection.

Franchising is also a business concept that foreign companies use when doing business in Norway. There is no legislation specifically designated for franchising. Business activity by way of franchising must comply with the ordinary legal

[1] Act No. 83 of 21 June 1985.
[2] Act No. 44 of 13 June 1997.
[3] Act No. 45 of 13 June 1997.
[4] See https://www.brreg.nohome.

framework for business activities in Norway.

3.1.2 Representation by an agent

Doing business in Norway can also be done by being represented by an agent. Agency agreements are partly covered by the 1918 Contracts Act① and partly by the 1992 Agency Act. ② This area of law has been developed in close cooperation between the Nordic countries, meaning that Norwegian law by and large will be similar to the law in Denmark and Sweden. The Agency Act has also been adjusted to the EU Directive 86/653 on commercial agents.

There are no formal requirements regarding the validity of an agency contract. Choice of law can be decided between the principal and the agent, and such a choice of law clause is frequently being used in international relations. Norway has no legislation covering conflict of laws in contractual matters in general or agency contracts in particular, so conflict of laws questions will be dealt with by case law if the parties have not dealt with it in their agreement. See Chapters 8.2 and 8.3 of this report for more information about Norwegian private international law.

Chapter 3 of the Agency Act contains some provisions that are mandatory in favour of the agent. These provisions must be read together with Section 3 which states that " a provision that is mandatory in this act cannot be set aside to the detriment of a commercial agent or a commercial traveller, through an agreement that the agency relationship is to be governed by foreign law if, in the absence of such an agreement, the relationship will be governed by Norwegian law. "

It is a fundamental duty of a commercial agent to look after the principal's interests. The commercial agent must comply with(lawful) instructions given by the principal. Normally an agency contract implies that the agent will work to procure orders and also conclude contracts. The details of the duties of the agent are determined by the contract. The agent also has a duty to take proper care of goods that belong to the principal. The duty to take care of the goods also includes a duty to keep the goods insured to the degree that is customary in that branch of business.

The principal is obliged to act dutifully and in good faith towards the agent, be supportive of the agent so he is able to carry out his/her work.

---

① Act No. 4 of 31 May 1918.

② Act No. 56 of 19 June 1992 relating to Commercial Agents and Commercial Travellers (The Agency Act).

The mandatory provisions in the Agency Act give the agent protection particularly in cases of termination of the agency agreement. According to Section 25 of the Agency Act notice of termination must be given to the agent. The notice period varies from one month up to six months depending upon how long the agent has been working for the principal. The agent has the right to commission as normal during the notice period. In case of termination, the commercial agent is entitled to indemnity to the extent that the agent has brought new customers to the principal or significantly has increased the volume of the business. The level of indemnity is dependent upon the overall discretionary assessment by the court.

3.1.3   VAT on sales and services

VAT is a sales tax on the final consumption of goods and services. In principle, VAT shall be calculated on all sales. This means that all goods and services being sold in Norway are liable to VAT unless they have been specifically exempted from VAT. A business shall be registered in the VAT Register when the total value of sales and withdrawals that fall under the scope of the Norwegian VAT Act exceeds NOK 50,000 during a 12-month period. [1] A foreign company must be registered by an agent being domiciled or having the place of business in Norway.

3.1.4   Concessions and permissions

When it comes to specific branches of industry, it might be special provisions restricting the access for foreigners. The petroleum sector and fisheries are examples of branches of industry where special permissions from the authorities are needed. Due to the EEA Agreement and the overarching principle of non-discrimination, many restrictions have been abandoned over the years.

3.2   Preferential treatment measures

Norway has introduced several preferential treatment measures in order to improve the amount of international trade with businesses originating from the least developed countries(LDCs).

The least developed countries can basically export their goods into Norway free of duty. The Norwegian GSP-scheme provides exporters from developing countries duty relief when exporting goods to Norway. The GSP-scheme under the WTO

---

① Act No. 58 of 19 June 2009.

Agreement has been implemented for about 90 countries and territories, of which 35 are ranked among the LDCs. LDCs benefit from more preferential treatment than other countries included in the system, the so-called GSP + or ordinary GSP-countries.

As a rule, goods must be transported directly from the GSP-country to Norway upon request by an identified Norwegian importer (a Norwegian consignee). However, goods may be transported through one or more other countries on the condition that they have remained under customs surveillance during transit or storage. Further, when shipping GSP-products through the European Community or Switzerland, re-exportation of GSP-products, either as a whole or split consignment, is also allowed. As such, in order to save transport costs, whole shiploads may be shipped from a GSP-country to a central store in the European Community for later distribution to other consignees in Europe.

To obtain GSP preferential treatment for a product on exportation to Norway, the originating status must be proven by a satisfactory proof of origin.

Norway is part of the LDC Service Waiver under WTO 2011. Norway has thus used the possibility under Article XVI of the GATS to implement preferential treatment related to market access. Preferential treatment is subject to approval by the Council, and Norway has notified the Services Council about joining the Service Waiver.

The aim of increasing the participation of developing countries in trade in services is enshrined in the preamble to the WTO's General Agreement on Trade in Services. At the Eighth Ministerial Conference in 2011, WTO members adopted a waiver to allow preferential treatment for services and service suppliers from least-developed countries. As stated above, Norway is a party to the Service Waiver. [1]

3. 3   The relationship between bilateral investment treaties and Norwegian law

Norway has 18 bilateral investment treaties under the UNCTAD umbrella(The United Nations Conference on Trade and Development). These agreements are

---

[1]   More information about Preferential Treatment Measures can be found at the Norwegian Customs website http://www. toll. no/en/corporate/import/free-trade/gsp—generalized-system-of-preference/. On this site a Draft Bilateral Agreement Version 130515 can also be found.

made in the spirit of the UNCTAD definition of a Bilateral Investment Treaty "for the reciprocal encouragement, promotion and protection of investments in each other's territories by companies based in either country". Norway's BITs follow the pattern of the development when it comes to the containment of the BITs. Originally the investment treaties focused on investment protection as the core issue together with matters reflecting public policy concerns(e. g. health, safety, essential security or environmental protection). In recent years protection of environment has more frequently been incorporated into BITs.

The government (the Solberg administration) has stated that they have an intention of increasing the number of bilateral investment agreements for Norway. Before the Solberg administration came to power in October 2013 Norway had not entered into bilateral investment treaties since the 1990s. The main reason for the increased use of bilateral investment agreements is to make sure that Norwegians investing in other countries will gain better protection and be able to better compete in business. But of course, since these agreements are bilateral, foreign investors will also be given better conditions when making investments in Norway. The draft bilateral agreement dated 13 May 2015 sought, at the same time as giving protecting to foreign investors, to balance the agreement by taking into account the host state's need to execute legitimate state power. ①

The Draft Bilateral Agreement, Version 130515, contains clauses that

- secure investor access to the market;
- give protection after the investment is made;
- acknowledge the legitimate need for the host state to maintain or regulate investment activity so as to be sensitive to health, safety, human rights, labour rights, resource management or environmental concerns;
- afford the host country(Norway) opportunity to make exceptions regarding environment, health, security issues, consideration of financial matters or exceptions related to protecting culture;
- give investor the opportunity to present a dispute before an international arbitration tribune, for so-called Investor-State Dispute Solution(ISDS).

There are ethical guidelines that must be followed by the members of the

---

① https://www. regjeringen. no/notemanaringsliv/handel/nfd—innsiktsartikler/frihandelsavtaler/ investeringsavtaler/id438845/.

ISDS. The procedure will secure openness and transparency.

3.4　Expropriation and compensation

A BIT will in practice also contain a clause regarding expropriation. See for example Art. 6 of the Norwegian Draft Bilateral Investment Agreement, Version 130515. The main principles stated in the article are:

　1. A Party shall not nationalise or expropriate an investment except:

　　ⅰ. for a public purpose,

　　ⅱ. under due process of law,

　　ⅲ. in a non-discriminatory manner, and

　　ⅳ. against payment of prompt, adequate and effective compensation.

　2. The preceding paragraph shall not, however, in any way impair the right of a Party to enforce such laws as it deems necessary to control the use of property in accordance with the general interest or to secure the payment of taxes or other contributions or penalties.

　3. Compensation pursuant to subparagraph 1(ⅳ) of this Article shall amount to the value that could be obtained by selling the investment on the market (market value) or, if this results in a higher compensation, the value of the return the investor would have obtained from the investment if it had not been nationalised or expropriated (exploitation value). Compensation based on the market value shall be determined on the basis of the amount that it is likely that ordinary buyers would have offered for the investment in a voluntary sale process.

　These principles are basically in line with the main principles applicable also in domestic cases of expropriation and compensation. Property rights are protected by Art. 105 of the Norwegian Constitution since 1814:

　If the welfare of the state requires that any person shall surrender their movable or immovable property for the public use, they shall receive full compensation from the Treasury.

　If, due to consideration of the need of the society, the Authorities will have to expropriate private property, the owner's right to get compensation is protected by the Constitution. Not only rights of real property but also rights in immovable property will be compensated in case of expropriation. In practice government "takings" of property are generally limited to non-discriminatory land and property condemnation for public purposes (road construction, etc.).

This rather short provision in Art 105. has over the years been interpreted by the Norwegian Supreme Court. This court practice is important when trying to understand Norwegian law on expropriation and compensation.

The property protection clause in Art. 105 was (as was the Constitution in general) inspired by both the North American and the French constitutional documents of the late 18th century. In recent years, Art. 105 on protection of property rights and the right to compensation in cases of expropriation, is to be interpreted and understood in the light of modern human rights principles as stated in Art. 1 in Protocol 1 of the European Human Rights Convention Art. 1 :

When it comes to compensation, the Norwegian tradition has been that only economic losses caused by the expropriation will be compensated. Also in tort law cases and in cases of compensation in matters of contract, the general principle under Norwegian law is that only economic losses will be compensated. The rather strict approach to what can be compensated in cases of expropriation is in line with the general understanding in Norwegian legal tradition of how to calculate the losses to be compensated. The Norwegian legal tradition in these matters deviates for example from the legal tradition in the US where large amounts of money can be at stake because of the tradition in the US of also including "punitive damages".

Chapter 4   Monetary and Banking System and Law

4. 1   Banking system and essential rules on banking operation

The legislative framework of the Norwegian banking system and banking operations consists of some essential acts. These acts are supplemented by acts that are important also outside the financial sector, for example questions regarding payment, mortgages or security interests in movable or immovable property or for trading in securities. Norway has revised the regulations relating to financial institutions as a result of the EEA Agreement. With respect to financial services, the EEA Agreement provides for full adaptation of EU regulations.

Although Norway is not a member state in the EU, the principles of free movement of capital and the right to establish a business are stated in the EEA Agreement (see Articles 40 and 31). Article 46 of the EEA Agreement states that "The Contracting Parties shall exchange views and information concerning the implementation of this Agreement and the impact of the integration on economic activities and on the conduct of economic and monetary policies. " Furthermore, they may discuss macro-economic situations, policies and prospects. This exchange of views and information shall take place on a non-binding basis. EU law is thus incorporated into Norwegian legislation.

There are many acts covering the Norwegian banking system, banking operations and payment, and this list is not exhaustive. Important legislations are:

• The Act of Finance Businesses and Finance Groups (Finance Businesses Act);[1]

• The Financial Contracts Act, No. 46 of 25 June 1999 ;

• The Guarantee Scheme Act, No. 75 of 6 December 1996;

• The Promissory Note Act, No. 1 of 17 February 1939;

---

[1]   Act of April 10 2015, in force Since 1 January 2016.

- The Act of Mortgages and other Security Interests, No. 2 of 8 February 1980;
- The Stock Exchange Act, No. 74 of 26 June 2007;
- The Financial Supervision Act, No. 1 of 7 February 1956;
- The Act on Norges Bank (Central Bank) and the Monetary System, No. 28 of 24 May 1985;
- The Securities Trading Act, No. 75 of 29 June 2007;
- The Security Register Act, No. 64 of 5 July 2002;
- The Money Laundering Act, No. 41 of 20 June 2003;
- Late Payment Interest Act, No. 100 of 17 December 1979;
- The Act on Limitation Period for Claims, No. 18 of 18 May 1979.

All banks and financial institutions are under supervision of the Financial Supervisory Authority in Norway (Finanstilsynet).[1] The Financial Supervisory Authority in Norway is thus responsible for the supervision of banks, finance companies, mortgage companies, insurance companies, pension funds, investment firms, securities fund management and market conduct in the securities market, stock exchanges and authorised market places, settlement centres and securities registers, estate agencies, debt collection agencies, external accountants and auditors.

The Central Bank of Norway (Norges Bank) is organised as a share-issuing company, but the government owns all the shares. It is the executive and advisory entity for monetary, credit and exchange policy. It is the sole bank of currency issue.[2]

The 2015 Finance Businesses Act repealed the Commercial Banking Act and the Savings Bank Act, as from 1961. Banking activities are now covered by the 2015 Finance Businesses Act. This Act also covers other financial activities such as insurance, pension, credit institutions, finance companies and mortgage companies.

Even though the 2015 Financial Businesses Act repealed, with effect from 1961, the statutes regarding Commercial Banks and Saving Banks, the banks in Norway may still be organised as saving banks or commercial banks. Commercial banks enjoy a very close relationship with trade and industry. Savings banks have a long tradition in Norway and also cover a substantial part of the local credit

---

[1] See the 1956 Act on the Supervision of Financial Institutions etc. (Financial Supervision Act).

[2] See http://www. norges-bank. no/english.

requirements. While saving banks primarily focus on loans for individuals to buy a family home or for small to medium-sized businesses, and commercial banks are more into large scale financing of bigger companies, this is not a static picture. Commercial banks have private persons as customers and give loan to finance private homes, while saving banks may also have big companies among their customers. Despite the organisation in saving banks and commercial banks, the banks more or less compete in the same market for the same customers. When it comes to financing bigger companies, it will be the bigger commercial banks that have specialised departments covering the areas generally regarded as typical of merchant banking such as for example financing the shipping industry.

In Norway there are also some special banks for fisheries, agriculture, shipping, industry, house building, and export finance. The State, to varying degrees, plays a role in these banks as they are related to policy considerations.

Table 2 shows statistics from Norges Bank over the banks established in Norway in 2015:

Table 2. Banks Established in Norway in 2015

Number of banks	137
Saving banks	107
Commercial banks	18
Number of foreign bank branches in Norway	12

4.2　Monetary system and payment in Norway

Payment in Norway is nowadays normally done electronically. This is so regardless of whether it is a question of payment in ordinary daily shopping situations, paying a contract party in an advanced sales contract or contract of services, or settling a loan. Statistics from the Norwegian State Bank (Norges Bank) show that the number of notes and coins in circulation has been relatively stable over the last decade. But since the use of money (money spent) has increased during the same period, the demand for cash has decreased (see Table 3). ①

---

①　The statistic is taken from:

http://www. norges-bank. no/pages/68197/notes_coins_statistics_2015. htm .

Table 3. Notes and Coins in Circulation 2006 – 2015

Year	Coins	Notes	Total
2006	4,695,1	44,522,8	49,217,9
2007	4,581,3	45,857,9	50,439,2
2008	4,574,8	45,838,5	50,413,3
2009	4,651,4	45,704,0	50,355,4
2010	4,773,6	45,676,0	50,449,6
2011	4,851,8	45,463,0	50,314,8
2012	4,800,0	46,378,3	51,178,3
2013	4,253,9	45,508,5	49,762,4
2014	4,357,3	44,995,0	49,352,3
2015	4,463,1	45,604,7	50,067,8

Notes: Annual average

Figures in millions of NOK

Payment services can only be done by banks, credit institutions, payment and e-payment institutions or by finance institutions that have permission from the Financial Supervisory Authority in Norway. Payment services may be carried out by foreign credit institutions or payment or e-payment institutions if they have permission to do such business in Norway. [1]

Norges Bank plays an important role in order to make the Norwegian banking and payment system functioning smoothly and with little risk for the society. Norges Bank settles interbank payments in banks' accounts at Norges Bank, and supplies the society with banknotes and coins in a manner that promotes payment system efficiency. Norges Bank also supervises Norwegian payment systems with the aim of strengthening financial stability by promoting the robustness and efficiency of the systems. While this work is primarily aimed at minimising risk in interbank clearing and settlement systems, Norges Bank also monitors important trends in payment systems as a whole.

Norges Bank is the ultimate settlement bank for interbank payments in Norway. This task is related to Norges Bank's responsibility under the Norges Bank

---

[1] See Section 2-3 of the 2015 Finance Businesses Act.

Act to promote an efficient payment system in Norway and with other countries, and to banks' right to hold accounts and raise loans at Norges Bank. Because the central bank issues money, central bank deposits do not involve credit or liquidity risk for banks. The interest rate on central bank deposits therefore provides a basis for interest rate formation throughout the economy. [1]

The most common forms of payment in Norway are bank cards (debit and credit cards), internet banking or payment by "cell phone bank". Although the payment system in Norway is highly automated and computerised, some parts of the basic legal framework covering rules of payment are quite old. Many of the rights and duties of the debtor and creditor are still based on the rules in the 1939 Promissory Notes Act, by analogy. Section 14 of the Norges Bank Act provides that Norwegian currency must be accepted by the creditor as means of payment. In practice, however, the use of coins and bills have decreased, and payment is done by using payment cards or transferring money to the creditor's bank account.

Usually, interest is charged if payment is late. The level of late payment interest is a certain percentage above the basic interest rate of Norges Bank. See Section 3 of the 1979 Interest of Late Payments Act. The level of the late payment interest is decided upon by the Ministry of Finance. By April 2016 it was 8. 75 percent.

The normal limitation period for a money claim under Norwegian law is three years (see the 1979 Limitation of Clams Act, Section 2) According to Section 3 (1), the limitation period runs from the date on which the creditor first acquired the right to demand performance. For claims arising from breach of contract, the limitation period runs from the date when the breach occurred. The limitation period is three years also for claims for damages in non-contractual relationships (see Section 9). In these cases the limitation period runs from the date on which the injured party obtained or should have acquired necessary knowledge of the damage. The limitation period may be extended by one year at a time, up to 10 years, if the creditor did not have the knowledge to make a claim previously (see Sections 10 (1) and (4)). In cases of claims for damage in non-contractual relationships, the limitation period can be extended to a maximum of 20 years.

Securing a money claim by way of mortgage or other types of security interests

---

[1] For more information regarding the role of Norges Bank, see http://www. norges-bank. no/en/ about/Mandate-and-core-responsibilities/Payment-systems-and-settlement-system/.

is mainly covered by the 1980 Act of Mortgages and Security Interest. It is important to be aware that Norwegian law follows a strict principle of legality: A mortgage or any kind of security interest can only be created in compliance with the 1980 Mortgage Act or special legislation for example given in the Maritime Code or in the Aviation Act (see the Mortgage Act Section 1-2(2)). It is unlawful to make an overall mortgage or security interest covering all the debtor's belongings (see Section 1-3(1)).

Security interests over real estates are created by way of mortgage. A security interest in real estate must be registered in the Norwegian Land Register. This register is centralised and covers all real estates in Norway. Registration of the mortgage is necessary in order for the creditor to be protected against the debtor becoming bankrupt or against third parties with a competing interest on the property.

When it comes to security interests in movable (tangible) goods, there are several possible ways to secure the creditor. The traditional way of taking the movable out of the possession of the debtor is one possibility, but is seldom used in practice (see Section 3-2 on the "Faustpfand" rule). In the process of buying or selling an item, the seller's lien (purchase money security interest) is often used (see Section 3-14). Under Norwegian law, a retention of title clause is treated as an agreement of a seller's lien. This follows from Section 3-22. It is not possible under Norwegian law to create a security interest in one single item and let the owner keep possession except by way of a seller's lien. This means that it is not possible to raise credit on a single item unless the item is taken out of the debtor's possession, or the security interest is made a condition in connection to a sales contract.

Business entities have the possibility of creating a security interest in classes of the debtor's assets. These security interests have similarities with floating charges, but the security interest cannot be created in one go covering all the debtor's belongings. Security interest can be created in inventory (Section 3-4) or in equipment such as operating machinery and plant (Section 3-11). Security interests in inventory or in operating machinery etc. must be registered in the Brønnøysund Register Centre in order to gain protection against bankruptcy or against third parties with competing interests.

Security interests can also be established in money claims, either by transactions connected to one single claim or to a class of claims under a factoring agreement. Security interests by way of factoring must be perfected by registration in the Brønnøysund Register Centre(Section 4-10).

Some intellectual property rights are included in the security interest in machinery and plant, such as patents rights or trademarks(Section 3-4). Since 2015 it is possible to create a security interest in a patent right separately (see Section 4-11).

4.3   Restrictions on foreign banks and foreign financial institutions

The 2015 Finance Businesses Act is applicable to banking activities in Norway as well as financial activities abroad done by Norwegian financial enterprises. This means that banking activities done by a foreign registered bank will be covered by the 2015 Act. This Act will also govern banking activities done by a branch of a foreign registered financial entity(Section 1-2).

Doing professional financial business in Norway requires special permission given by the Financial Supervisory Authority in Norway. Financial business can thus only be done by banks, credit institutions or financial institutions that have such permission. Financial business may be carried out in Norway by a foreign financial institution if it has been granted permission by the Norwegian Financial Supervisory Authority. [1] Since 1985, foreign banks have been allowed to establish subsidiaries in Norway. Since the implementation of the EEA Agreement in January 1994, foreign banks may also establish branches in Norway.

To qualify for a licence, banking activity in Norway requires an initial capital (equity capital or ownerless capital)amounting to at least the equivalent of EUR 5 million in Norwegian Kroner. The bank's capital must be sufficient to undertake the type of banking in question. Members of the Board, the CEO or any other person directly in charge of the bank must also be fit and proper for the position. The bank must meet all legal requirements that govern its operations. [2]

Once a bank is licensed to operate in one EEA state it may lawfully operate in another EEA state, provided it notifies that country of its intention to do so. Requirements to be met by banks from elsewhere in the EEA that intend to operate

---

[1]   See Section 2-1 of the 2015 Finance Businesses Act.

[2]   See information concerning licensing at the website of the Financial Supervisory Authority in Norway: http://www. finanstilsynet. no/en/Banking—Finance/Banks/Supervision—Licensing/Licensing/.

in Norway, and by Norwegian banks that intend to operate elsewhere in the EEA are regulated by Chapters 4 and 5 of the Financial Businesses Act. ①

A licence application must be sent to the Financial Supervisory Authority which either prepares a response for final decision by the Ministry of Finance or makes a decision itself under powers delegated to it by the ministry. Applications relating to institutions of major importance, or in cases likely to create a precedent, are decided by the Ministry of Finance.

Chapter 5 of the 2015 Financial Businesses Act gives more detailed rules regarding the activity in Norway of foreign financial enterprises.

4.4　Foreign exchange system

Norway has in principle no currency restrictions. Foreign exchange controls were abolished in 1990 and no licence is required for foreign exchange activities. The only requirement is a reporting requirement for international payments and financial transactions. The transaction bank generally takes care of this reporting.

As part of its monetary policy, the government has set an inflation target in Norway. The operational target is consumer price inflation of close to 2.5 percent over time. Monetary policy shall also contribute to stabilising output and employment. The interest rate on banks' deposits with the Central Bank of Norway (the sight deposit rate) is the most important monetary policy instrument.

Norges Bank purchases foreign currency from the State's Direct Financial Interest(SDFI) each month. If the government's net cash flow from petroleum activities exceeds the non-oil budget deficit, some of the foreign exchange purchased from the SDFI is transferred to the Government Pension Fund Global (GPFG). Norges Bank sells the remaining amount in the market.

If the government's net cash flow from petroleum activities is insufficient to cover the non oil budget deficit, foreign exchange will be transferred from the GPFG to cover some of the budget deficit. Norges Bank will then sell foreign exchange from the GPFG, as well as the foreign exchange from the SDFI, in the

---

① See Regulation No. 326 of 2 May 1994 as amended last 29 June 2007 on branches of banks and other credit institutions having their head offices in another state in the European Economic Area, etc.

market. Norges Bank performs this task on behalf of the government. ①

4. 5   Rules on movement of funds

Within the EU there should be no restriction on free movement of capital. Under Article 63 of the Treaty on the Functioning of the European Union(TFEU) , all restrictions on movement of capital and payments between Member States shall be prohibited. This main principle is also found in the EEA Agreement. Freedom of movement of funds is stated in the EEA Agreement Art. 1(2)(e) and regulated in more detail in Arts. 40 – 45.

Undertakings for Collective Investment in Transferrable Securities(UCITS) are investment funds regulated at European Union level. They account for around 75 percent of all collective investments by small investors in Europe. The legislative instrument covering these funds is Directive 2014/91/EU amending the Directive 2009/65/EC. UCITS established in another EEA state may be marketed in Norway once the supervisory authority in the UCITS's home state has been given to the Financial Supervisory Authority of Norway. Notification of marketing must be in accordance with the Securities Funds Act, Section 9-3.

Companies authorised to carry on activities under the Securities Trading Act, Securities Funds Act, Central Securities Depository Act and Stock Exchange Act are under supervision by Norwegian Financial Supervisory Authority. Important areas of supervision are the market players' financial position and operations and their compliance with rules governing their activities. Supervision also covers compliance with a number of general rules of conduct laid down in the Securities Trading Act. The supervision also covers fund management and movement of funds.

---

① For further information, see Foreign exchange for the Government Pension Fund Global http://www. norges-bank. no/en/Liquidity-and-markets/Foreign-exchange-purchases-for-GPFG/.

Chapter 5   Laws Relating to Construction of Infrastructure

5. 1   Infrastructure in Norway

The World Bank provides a ranking of the quality of a country's infrastructure. ①Norway ranks 20th on the list. Information in this chapter is mainly found in the WTO website and in national reports from Norway submitted to the WTO. ②

In the following sections only a few aspects of infrastructure and investments in infrastructure will be treated. The selection is made in order to show different policy considerations to be made when answering the questions: (i) who has the responsibility of building the infrastructure and (ii) who can invest? It is questions of infrastructure related to roads, railways, water and energy that will be commented upon.

5. 2   Roads, roadbuilding and financing

Basically questions of planning, building, repairing, maintenance and operations of roads in Norway are governed by the Roads Act, No. 23 of 21 June 1963. This Act continues a tradition of legislation from the 1824 Roads Act.

The ownership of the roads in Norway is basically divided into four sub-categories:

 (i)State owned roads(including European highways) ;

 (ii)Roads owned by the counties;

 (iii)Roads owned by the municipalities;

 (iv)Privately owned roads.

Also car ferries may be considered as part of the road network in Norway.

---

①   See http://www. worldbank. org.

②   See http://www. wto. org.

The Norwegian Public Roads Administration is responsible for planning, construction and operation of the national and county roads network. According to Section 10 of the 1963 Roads Act, Norway is divided into five regions; the northern, central, western, southern and eastern region. [1] Today the Norwegian Public Roads Authority is the largest construction client in Norway, with around 7,000 employees all over the country.

According to Section 20 of the Road Act, the Norwegian state is responsible for the expenses related to planning, building, repair, maintenance and operation of roads owned by the state, the county pays for roads owned by the county and each municipality is economically responsible for roads owned by the municipality. As provided by Section 27 of the Roads Act, toll can be demanded only after the approval of the Parliament. This right to demand toll may be used as a tool to finance a road. According to Section 27(3), the right may be used as the basis for a security interest.

Under the public private partnership (PPP) model, a private company is given full responsibility for a road section for a period of 20 – 30 years. The company is responsible for financing, design, development, operation and maintenance. The company's task is to make sure that the road is open and available for public travel, and that it conforms to the agreed standard.

The Norwegian Public Roads Authority and PwC Norge AS have entered into an agreement, effective March 2016, by which PwC Norge AS will act as a financial advisor for the procurement of new PPP projects. This framework agreement lasts until 2018 and may be prolonged for two more years.

The role of the Norwegian Public Roads Administration under the PPP agreement regime is the planning up to and including the preparation of the zoning plan, and ensuring that all contractual requirements are adhered to. At the end of the operating period, the road shall be handed over to the Norwegian Public Roads Administration.

A PPP contract stipulates the annual amount the private company will be paid, and any deduction mechanisms and bonus schemes that are contingent on the quality and performance of the road section.

---

[1] For more information about the Norwegian Public Roads Authority, see http://www. vegvesen. no/ en/Home.

On the public procurement procedure, see Section 5. 6 of this chapter below.

5. 3   **Railways**

Activity related to railways is by and large covered by the Railroad Act, No. 100 of 11 June 1993. The Norwegian National Rail Administration (Jernbaneverket) is responsible for the management of the national railway network, on behalf of the Ministry of Transport and Communication.

The Norwegian Parliament determines the annual funding through the national budget. Long-term planning is dealt with through Norsk Transportplan (the Norwegian Transport Plan), in which the Parliament draws up the economic framework for the four year period. This means that the railway activity basically happens through public funding and with socio-economic perspectives.

Until 1996 the state owned company NSB was responsible for all aspects of railroads activity. The company was split in 1996. Now the Norwegian National Rail Administration (Jernbaneverket) is responsible for developing and operating the rail network, railway stations and terminals, timetabling, traffic management, regulation of the public network and making studies and plans for the railway sector. The transportation of passengers is the task and responsibility of the NSB. [1] A few railroad distances is operated by private companies, the foremost example being the line between Oslo and Gardermoen Airport operated by Flytoget (the Airport Express Train).

The Ministry of Transportation is responsible when it comes to all permissions and licences necessary to carry out railway activity. According to Sections 8a – 8g the Ministry of Transportation will provide for competition by way of public procurement. For more information regarding the public procurement regime, see Chapter 5. 6.

The Norwegian National Rail Administration is spending a total of about NOK 13 billion or about EUR 1. 5 billion. The major part is spent on construction work. The Norwegian National Rail Administration is related to requirements from the Ministry of Government Administration and Reform in connection with the

---

[1]   More information about the Norwegian Public Rail Administration and NSB can be found on the companies' websites, see http://www. jernbaneverket. no/en/startpage1/ and http://www. nsbkonsernet. no/en/.

"strategy and actions for use of electronic business processes (e)-commerce in the public sector".

The main requirement is that 25 percent of the expenditure shall be completely or partially provided through competitions based on electronic processes for interaction with industry.

5.4 Drinking water and water supply to industry

Norway is blessed with enough water to supply the inhabitants and the industrial activity in Norway.

The Norwegian Food Safety Authority(Mattilsynet) is responsible for approval and supervision of the quality of the water, the water supply systems and the water treatment products. The authority also develops regulations and guidelines. The Norwegian Food Safety Authority works closely with other authorities in order to achieve a safe and stable supply of drinking water. ①

The legislative framework for drinking water is found in the Food Act(No. 124 of 19 December 2003) together with more detailed rules in the Drinking Water Regulation(No. 100 of 4 December 2001). When it comes to legislation covering the right to access and use of the water, the legislation is the same as when use of water is for energy purposes. The Water Resources Act No. 82 of 24 November 2000 is of great importance for these questions, and so is the so-called Industry Concession Act, No. 16 of 14 December 1917. Access to water can also be based upon an agreement with the owner (s) of the land, often in combination with concessions or permission from the authorities. The Expropriation Act, No. 81 of 6 April 1997, may also be used if necessary. See also Chapter 5.5.1 below on access to water for energy purposes. The EU Water Directive, Directive 2000/60/EC, is incorporated into Norwegian legislation through the EEA Agreement.

In Norway it is mainly the municipalities that distribute water to households and industry. Because of the geography in Norway, there are several small water plants in rural areas whereas there are large scale water plants closer to the bigger cities. But some big water plants are also situated in rural areas. As the main rule one can assume that the municipality owns the water pipes except pipes connecting

---

① See http://www. mattilsynet. no/language/english/food _ and _ water/drinkingwater/ and http://www. norskvann. no/index. php/om-norsk-vann/information-in-englishfor more information.

each house or building to the network. These small side-pipes are owned by the owner of the house, therefore these pipes will be owned by private persons or entities.

Much of the infrastructure for water distribution was built just after the end of World War II. This means that throughout Norway there is now a great need for changing and upgrading the distribution network. The cost will basically have to be carried by the municipalities, but some economic input from the Norwegian state will also be needed. It is to be expected that a lot of technically advanced equipment will be needed in this upgrading process. Competition between suppliers through processes of public procurement is also to be expected. [1]

5.5 Energy

5.5.1 Hydropower

Due to the combination of geographical condition and climate, there are a lot of waterfalls in Norway. Hydropower is by far the most important source of energy for Norway:99 percent of all power production in Norway comes from hydropower. [2]

In Norway the two main state owned companies in the hydropower market are Statkraft and Statnett. Statkraft is the energy producer, whereas Statnett owns the power lines. [3]It is also important to mention the Norwegian Water Resources and Energy Directorate(NVE). [4]The mandate of NVE is to ensure an integrated and environmentally sound management of the country's water resources, promote efficient energy markets and cost-effective energy systems and contribute to efficient energy use.

Statkraft produces hydropower, wind power, gas-fired power and district heating and is a global player in energy market operations.

Norway has a long history of using waterfalls to create hydropower. The pioneering period for using hydropower in a greater scale started in the late 1800s. At that time waterfalls were purchased and power plants rapidly developed. After a

---

[1] See http://kommunal-rapport. no/debatt/rent_vann_i_2030_krever_store_investeringer.

[2] See http://www. statkraft. com/energy-sources/hydropower/.

[3] For more information about the companies, see http://www. statkraft. com and http://www. statnett. no. See also Act on State-Owned Enterprises, No. 71 of 30 August 1991.

[4] See https://www. nve. no/english/.

while laws were enacted to secure national sovereignty over these new sources of wealth. The first time the Norwegian state acquired ownership to a waterfall was in 1895. It became important to secure national interests in the waterfalls. This led to legislation making it possible to avoid foreign takeover of ownership rights to waterfalls, and also legislation to preserve waterfalls for recreation and tourism. The 1917 Concession Act is important from this period of time, and the Act is still in force. ①The perception was that hydropower resources belong to society at large and that public ownership was the best way to ensure that everyone would benefit from them. Between 1907 and 1920, the Norwegian state bought waterfall rights for large sums of money and became northern Europe's largest owner of hydropower plants.

As for the legal framework, this was basically the same until the 1990s. At this time Norway had become a member state of the EEA and, through the EEA Agreement, the freedom of establishment, the freedom of movement of capital and the prohibition of discrimination had become part of Norwegian legislation. The EFTA Surveillance Authority (ESA) reacted upon the Norwegian practice of the "hjemfallsrett". By this practice a private company would have to give back the right to use the waterfall to the Norwegian state after 75 years (50 or 60 years under older legislation). The EFTA Court found that the "hjemfallsrett" contravened the EEA Agreement.

The EFTA Court found that it was not permissible to discriminate between public and private owners in the way it was done under the rules of the ' hjemfallsrett" and Norway had to change the way to follow this ruling. ②In the EFTA Court Judgement it was stated that "The Court holds that Article 125 EEA is to be interpreted to the effect that an EEA State's right to decide whether hydropower resources and related installations are in private or public ownership is, as such, not affected by the EEA Agreement." The corollary of this is that Norway may legitimately pursue the objective of establishing a system of public ownership over these properties, provided that the objective is pursued in a non-discriminatory and proportionate manner. After 2007 Norwegian Authorities have not given private parties concession to buy waterfalls or hydropower plants. However, private parties may still own up to one third of publicly owned hydropower plants.

---

① Act No. 16 of 14 December 1917.

② See Case E – 2/06 of the EFTA Court.

As the above brief historical overview shows, the system of licensing plays an important role in the Norwegian hydropower industry. It is a main task of NVE to processes licence applications for construction of power plants, building dams, power lines or other installations that need special permission.

5.5.2 Petroleum sector

Licences and permissions play an important role in the petroleum sector as well. Important legislation covering this sector is given in the Petroleum Act. [1] The 1990 Energy Act is not applicable to the Norwegian sea territory (see Section 1-1 (2)). [2]

The history of Norway as a provider of oil and gas is much shorter than that of hydropower. Oil was found offshore Norway in 1969, and from the mid-1970s the petroleum industry grew stronger and stronger. The petroleum industry has had a huge impact on the Norwegian economy. As for the petroleum, the Norwegian perception is that petroleum resources found on Norwegian territory belong to the Norwegian State.

It is stated in Section 1-1 of the Petroleum Act that "The Norwegian State has the proprietary right to subsea petroleum deposits and the exclusive right to resource management".

Searching for petroleum resources as well as drilling requires permission by way of a licence from Norwegian authorities. Such licences are issued by the Norwegian Petroleum Directorate after thorough and careful considerations. [3]

STATOIL is the largest operator on the Norwegian continental shelf, and a licence holder in numerous oil and gas fields. The company was formed in 1972, and was from the start owned 100 percent by the Norwegian State. Today the state owns 67 percent of the company's shares. [4]

In addition to the Petroleum Directorate being responsible for the licensing, the Petroleum Safety Authority should also be mentioned. [5] This authority is an independent government regulator with responsibility for safety, emergency

---

[1]   Act No. 72 of 29 November 1996.

[2]   Act No. 50 of 29 June 1990.

[3]   http://www. npd. no/en/.

[4]   http://www. statoil. com/en/about/history/pages/default3. aspx.

[5]   http://www. psa. no/role-and-area-of-responsibility/category916. html.

preparedness and the working environment in the Norwegian petroleum industry.

There are many foreign companies that are connected to the Norwegian petroleum sector, especially companies in the services and supply industry, and also in maritime industry connected to the petroleum sector. There are also some big and well known foreign companies acting as operators, such as ExxonMobil, BP and Total.

5.6   Public procurement and the DOFFIN regime

DOFFIN is the Norwegian Web-based database for notices of public procurement and procurement in the utility sector (water and energy supply, transport, and telecommunications) that are subject to the European Union regulations. ①

The purpose of the base of the procurement notices is:

● to ensure competition and openness about business opportunities;

● to forward all procurement notices for the announcement in TED when this is necessary;

● to ensure the control of procurement notices before publishing;

● to publish and distribute the procurement notices in a searchable format;

● to prepare relevant statistics in the public sector.

Trade policy and other elements of economic, social and structural policies are integral parts of a totality of government policies that not only stimulate growth and secure jobs, but also ensure decent working conditions and an equitable distribution of the benefits of trade and economic growth to its population. Similarly, the Norwegian government is committed to pursuing trade and environmental policies—including policies related to climate change—that are mutually supportive.

5.7   Government participation

Compared to many countries, the Norwegian State is involved in the Norwegian economy as owner. This is a historic fact that has become even more pronounced over the last 20 – 30 years due primarily to the way the income from the petroleum sector is distributed. A large part of savings in the Norwegian economy

---

① https://www.doffin.no/en.

takes place through the public sector. The Norwegian State and municipalities owned 33. 5 percent of the equity capital instruments at Oslo Stock Exchange capitalisation at the end of 2015. ①The State is a major shareholder in several of the larger commercial listed companies. The State acts as an active long-term owner, whose main aim is to contribute to the commercial companies' long-term value creation and industrial development.

Government policy is that the extent of state ownership should remain at approximately the current level. This does not imply that the Government will not privatise certain companies or participate in sensible industrial transactions. Decisions to buy or sell are taken on a case-by-case basis, and usually depend on parliamentary approval. ②

State ownership has undergone a number of reforms since the turn of the century. The Government has organised the management of its ownership in such a way as to keep the role of owner separate from the roles of policymaker, regulator and supervisor. The Minister of Trade and Industry exercises the ownership role in most commercial companies where the State is involved, and the ministry's coordinating role in managing ownership has been strengthened. The State's exercise of its ownership is based on generally accepted principles of corporate governance, and on the division of roles set out in Norwegian company legislation. Other important issues are corporate governance of state-owned entities, expectations concerning CSR (corporate social responsibility), expectations concerning remuneration and composition of Board of Directors.

To enhance the transparency of state ownership, the Norwegian Government publishes an annual report of state ownership. These ownership reports can be found on the webpage of the Ministry of Commerce and Fisheries. ③

---

① Statistics found at the website of Oslo Stock Exchange, see oslobors. no and statistics on shareholder structure.

② Information regarding state ownership is given by the Norwegian government here: https://www. regjeringen. no/en/topics/business-and-industry/state-ownership/statens-eierberetning-2013/id725446/. Here annual state ownership reports and policy documents can be found as well.

③ Information found https://www. wto. org/english/tratop_e/tpr_e/tp369_e. htm.

Chapter 6   Laws Relating to Labour
Management and Treatment

6. 1   Labour management and treatment: an overview

In general, a Norwegian employee is well educated. Wages are relatively high compared to other countries. The rate of unemployment in Norway is low. Registered unemployed workers by March 2016 were 3. 3 percent. The unemployment rate however varies within different parts of Norway, the south-west region being particularly badly affected by the decreased activity in the petroleum sector.

The 2005 Working Environment Act forms the core legal framework when it comes to employment and legal protection of employees. [1]The provisions of the Act are basically mandatory and provisions may not be departed from by agreement to the detriment of the employee unless this is expressly provided in the Act itself (Section 1 −9).

To get a broader picture of rights and duties of employees in Norway, the Working Employment Act must be read together with other legislation such as for example:

• The National Insurance Act, No. 19 of 28 February 1997;

• The Holidays Act, No. 21 of 29 April 1988;

• Certain sections of the Smoking Act, No. 14 of 9 March 1973.

There is a special authority with the main task of supervising business entities to make sure that they follow the provisions set out in the Working Environment Act: The Norwegian Labour Inspection Authority (Arbeidstilsynet), which is a governmental agency under the Ministry of Labour, mainly focused on occupational

---

[1]   Act No. 62 of 17 June 2005 relating to working environment, working hours and employment protection, etc. The act can be downloaded as a PDF document from the webpage of the Norwegian Labour Inspection Authority.

safety and health. ①

The Labour Inspection Authority has approximately 600 employees and consists of a central office, the Directorate, seven regional offices and 16 local offices throughout the country. The Directorate in Trondheim regulates the agency's overall strategy, programs and information. The district offices guide and supervise individual enterprises in local communities.

In dealing with enterprises that do not comply with the requirements of the Working Environment Act, the Labour Inspection Authority may respond with orders, coercive fines, shutdown of operations and/or report enterprises to the police.

6. 2   Employment contract, salary and protection of workers' rights

All employees must have a written contract of employment. See the Working Environment Act Section 14-5 regarding the duty to have a written contract and Section 14-6 regarding minimum requirements to the content of the contract. The duty to have a written contract of employment applies to all types of employment, both permanent and temporary. The requirement of a written contract is mandatory with no exceptions.

In Norway there is a strong tradition of using so-called "collective employment agreements", agreements that aim to establish conditions that are more or less equal to the same kind of positions in the entity. Individually negotiated employment agreements and collective agreements will often be read together when determining the rights and duties of the employer and the employee. Labour organisations and employer organisations have developed such collective employment agreements over many years, and these agreements are often much more detailed and advanced than what can be expected from an individually negotiated contract of employment.

There is no general minimum wage in Norway. Wages are subject to agreement between the employer and the employee as part of the written employment contract. Although there is no general minimum wage in Norway, minimum rates of pay have been introduced in certain sectors:

● Construction sites(for construction workers);

---

① http://www. arbeidstilsynet. no/working-conditions-in-norway. html? tid = 240097.

- The maritime construction industry;
- The agriculture and horticulture sector;
- Cleaning workers;
- Fish processing enterprises;
- Electricians;
- Freight transport by road;
- Passenger transport by tour bus.

In sectors with a minimum wage, the contractor at the top of the chain is liable for the obligation of contractors further down in the chain of contracts to pay the minimum wage(joint and several liability). This means that an employee can claim payment of the minimum wage all the way up to the contractor at the top of the chain.

Wages must be paid in accordance with the agreement. In Norway, it is usual to agree on payment of wages once or twice a month. The employer must provide the employee with a pay slip stating the wages paid, tax deducted and other deductions.

The Holidays Act safeguards the right of employees to annual holidays. Everyone should be able to take a holiday, and employees therefore have a right to "holiday pay" which is a way of calculating the wages to be paid. The Holidays Act applies to all employees in both public and private entities.

The Working Environment Act has provisions that give the employee protection of health and safety. In workplaces with 10 or more employees, a safety representative shall be elected. The safety representative shall safeguard the interests of the employees in working environment matters and ensure that the employer complies with the provisions of the Working Environment Act.

The Working Environment Act obliges the employer to provide all employees with the training necessary to carry out their work properly. Industrial undertakings and commercial and office undertakings with more than 10 employees shall have staff rules including code of conduct and working procedures.

The Working Environment Act also has provisions to protect the employee against unjustified termination of the employment contract. In cases of termination, notice must be given one month before the last day of work. The time limit is longer for employees who have been employed for many years at the same workplace. See Section 15-3 in the Working Environment Act regarding details for the period of notice.

An employee may not be dismissed without just cause and the employer must state the grounds for termination in writing. Membership of a union, for example, will not be considered as a just reason for dismissal under Norwegian law. Another example to be mentioned is that a woman may not be dismissed on the ground that she is pregnant.

6.3   Contribution to pension fund

The pension system in Norway consists of pensions from the national insurance scheme, to which everyone is entitled, and some supplementary pensions. The most important supplementary pensions are occupational pensions, i. e. pensions from pension schemes in employment relationships. There are also various early retirement schemes, i. e. pension benefits paid from the date of early retirement to the national insurance retirement age of 67. [1]

Contributions to pension funds under Norwegian law thus consist of public pension; flat rate basic pension; a special supplement; earnings-related pension; mandatory occupational pension; minimum occupational defined contribution pension; voluntarily occupational or private pension funds; individual pension schemes and annuities.

As a general rule, all persons who are either resident or working as employees in Norway or on permanent or movable installations on the Norwegian Continental Shelf, are compulsorily insured under the National Insurance Scheme. Citizens from EEA countries working on Norwegian ships, except hotel and restaurant staff on cruise ships registered in the Norwegian International Ship's Register are compulsorily insured. Foreign (non-EEA) citizens not resident in Norway or any other Nordic country, who are employed on ships in foreign trade, registered in the regular Norwegian Ship's Register, are compulsorily insured only with regard to entitlement to occupational injury benefits and funeral grants. Persons of the same category, but who are employed on ships in the Norwegian International Ship's Register, are not compulsorily insured for any contingency. Excluded from compulsory insurance are foreign citizens who are paid employees of a foreign state or of an international organisation.

---

[1] An overview of the Norwegian Social Insurance Scheme is given at the government's website, see https://www.regjeringen.no/en/dokumenter/det-norske-trygdesystemet-2016/id2478621/.

The National Insurance Scheme is financed by contributions from employees, self-employed persons and other members, employers' contributions and contributions from the state.

Employees and self-employed persons, earning more than a minimum pensionable income of NOK 49, 650 in 2016, must make a contribution to the Norwegian National Insurance Scheme. The contribution shall not exceed 25 percent of income exceeding this threshold amount.

The contribution rate for employees is 8.2 percent of the pensionable income (gross wage income). The contribution rate for a self-employed person is 11.4 percent of the pensionable income (income from self-employment). The contribution rate for other kinds of personal income (pensions etc.) is 5.1 percent.

The employers' contribution is assessed as a percentage of paid out wages. The employers' contributions are differentiated according to where the enterprises are established. There are regional zones based on the geographical situation and level of economic development. The employers' contribution rates in these zones vary from zero percent to 14.1 percent.

Non-EEA nationals must have minimum three years' service to qualify for a pension. In this case they will usually qualify for a pension from the Norwegian Public Service Pension Fund and need apply only to them.

In 2006 new legislation widened the obligation to provide certain minimum occupational pension plan requirements, which most large employers, in fact already had exceeded. It became a statutory duty for all employers to contribute to a pension plan for their employees (just a few exceptions). Already in 2007 the mandatory occupational pension system covered over 90 percent of the labour force. [1]

Companies bear the costs of administering plans. In addition to retirement pension plans, they must offer compulsory insurance policies that provide exemption from contributions during periods of disability (depending on the degree of disability).

The Norwegian Financial Supervisory Authority supervises the private pension system. [2]

---

[1]   Key information about the structure of the Norwegian pension system can be found on the webpage of OECD: www. oecd. org/daf/pensions/gps.

[2]   See http://www. kredittilsynet. no.

6.4   Compensation for casualties

The Working Environment Act requires employers to protect employees against injuries and to create a fully satisfactory working environment. The Act not only provides rules designed to prevent hazardous and strenuous work; it also gives employees the right to influence their own working situation.

To avoid accidents from happening, there are requirements for entities to have internal control procedures. Regulations regarding Internal Control require enterprises to have written objectives in relation to health, environment and safety activities. Roles and responsibilities regarding health and safety issues must be clarified. Risk analysis and assessment must be carried out, and plans of action made and carried out according to assessments.

The person responsible for the enterprise must ensure that internal control is introduced and performed in the enterprise and that this is done in collaboration with the employees and their representatives.

The Norwegian Labour Inspection Authority reviews enterprises' internal control systems to see whether regulations and procedures are being followed. An audit that takes place may last for several days.

All serious and life threatening accidents are investigated by the Norwegian Labour Inspection Authority.

Compensation for casualties may be given on the basis of different legal grounds. There is legislation in Norway making it a duty for entities to have occupational insurance covering the employee. General tort law may also be a basis for responsibility for economic loss due to work related casualties. In addition, the Norwegian National Insurance Scheme has special rules for occupational injury and illness. [1]

In cases of negligence, the entity will have responsibility to pay compensation. Negligence for entities will under Norwegian tort law also, in principle, cover bad routines or failures in routines of the entity.

Usually the entity will have insurance, so questions concerning compensation will often be dealt with as an insurance case. It is mandatory for employers to have

---

[1]   As for the occupational injuries and illness covered by the National Insurance Scheme (Folketrygden), see https://www.nav.no/423123/occupational-injury-and-illness.

occupational insurance that cover their employees. If work related injuries happen, the employee will have full economic compensation under the occupational insurance scheme regardless of whether the employer has been negligent or not. ① Because the rules of occupational insurance are mandatory, most of the employee groups are covered for occupational injury through their employment agreement. ② Foreign registered companies must have arrangements ensuring financial compensation for their workers in the event of occupational injuries. Self-employed persons and freelancers must take out voluntary occupational injury insurance in order to be entitled to occupational injury coverage.

Occupational injury is defined as a personal injury, illness or death resulting from an occupational accident. An illness may also be approved as an occupational illness if it is a result of a harmful influence from the working environment and is one of the illnesses mentioned in the regulations relating to occupational illnesses.

If an accident occurs in the workplace, the employer is obliged to send the claim form to NAV(the Norwegian Labour and Welfare Administration). ③Compensation is in addition claimed directly from the employer's insurance company. As the Occupational Injuries Insurance Act creates a separate compensation scheme outside the National Insurance Scheme, inquiries relating to the scheme are not made to NAV, but to the employer, his insurance company or the employee organisations. On the claim form to the National Insurance Scheme, the employer must state with which insurance company the company has taken out insurance in accordance with the Occupational Injuries Insurance Act.

6.5   Special rules for foreign entities

The 2005 Working Environment Act applies basically to all land-based operations with employees.

When foreign companies post workers to Norway, there are certain rules that

---

① See Act Relating to Industrial Injury Insurance, No. 65 of 16 June 1989, Section 2.

② Persons employed by the Norwegian state will not be covered. Municipalities in Norway may also, after approval from the Ministry of Local Government and Modernisation, have special solutions for their employees.

③ For more information about NAV, see http://nav. no .

apply depending on what the situation is. ① The regulations apply both when a Norwegian company posts employees to another EU/EEA country, and when foreign companies post workers to Norway to provide services here, provided that the worker is employed by the posting firm for the duration.

The regulations of the Working Environment Act concerning occupational safety and health apply to all employment in Norway, posted workers included. The regulations apply even if the worker is employed by a foreign company, is working in Norway on an assignment to provide services, and the stay is temporary.

Some acts and provisions in acts will apply to workers posted to Norway, regardless of in which country the posting is taking place from:

- The Working Environment Act Chapters 4, 10, 11, 13 and Section 12-9, Section 14-5, Section 14-6, Sections 14-12 to 14-14 and Section 15-9;
- The Annual Holidays Act;
- The Fishermen's Holiday Act Section 2, Sections 4 to 6, Sections 9 and 10;
- The Employment Act Section 27;
- The Gender Equality Act Sections 3 to 6.

Other regulations may also be of relevance, but their applicability may depend on whether the employment is primarily connected to Norway or another country.

There are no statutes regarding minimum wages in Norway. Posted workers can therefore work in Norway for the same wages they receive in their home country. However, if the area of employment is regulated by the general application of wage agreements, this agreement will apply regarding wages and working conditions. Neither the listed regulations regarding working conditions, nor the terms of a general wage agreement, apply if the posted worker has better terms in her/his own country, either by tariff or by law.

General application of collective agreements is one of a number of ways to prevent foreign workers from being given poorer pay and working conditions than are usual in Norway. The following sectors have generally applicable collective agreements(regulated in separate regulations):

- Construction sites(for construction workers);

---

① Regulations concerning posted workers are found in Regulations No. 1566 of 16 December 2005. This regulation is based on the Working Environment Act Section 1-7 about posted employees. The regulation may be downloaded from the webpage of the Norwegian Labour Inspection Authority.

- The maritime construction industry;
- The agriculture and horticulture sectors;
- Cleaning workers;
- Fish processing enterprises;
- Electricians;
- Freight transport by road

Undertakings that perform such work are responsible for ensuring compliance with these regulations. This also applies to any person managing the undertaking on the employer's behalf.

Chapter 7   Environmental Law

7.1   Essential policies

It is fair to say that the Norwegian people in general take a great interest in protecting the environment. In 1972, Norway was the first country in the world to have a ministry at cabinet level with a special responsibility for environmental issues. Being a country with a large export of oil and gas, it is difficult for Norway to substantially reduce the CO_2 emission. The balance between exploitation of natural resources and conservation of natural values is an important challenge for the Norwegian government. Norway actively participates in international environmental cooperation. Norway has also formulated ethical norms related to environment and human rights, to be used in governmental investments abroad.

The Norwegian Ministry of Climate and Environment has the main responsibility for ensuring governmental climate and environmental policies. Environmental considerations need to be made in all areas of the society. It is therefore in important task of the Ministry of Climate and Environment to act as promoter and coordinator to ensure that the authorities in the different sectors implement environmental policies in their particular areas.

The Ministry of Climate and Environment has four departments: the Norwegian Environment Agency, the Norwegian Polar Institute, the Directorate for Cultural Heritage and the Norwegian Cultural Heritage Fund. The Ministry of Justice and Public Security published in May 2016 a White Paper on the Future of Svalbard. [1]By strengthening research, tourism and the general businesses, the government will develop Svalbard further. But basically the essence of the White Paper is that the Norwegian policies regarding Svalbard remain unchanged.

When it comes to essential policies, the Ministry has pinpointed certain topics as

---

[1]   The White Paper can be downloaded from the Ministry's webpage: https://www. regjeringen. no/en/ aktuelt/white-paper-on-the-future-of-svalbard/id2500474/.

environmental targets; biodiversity, cultural heritage and cultural environment, outdoor recreation, pollution, climate and polar areas. The Norwegian Government has stated that the High North is Norway's most important foreign policy area. Environmental issues regarding this area is therefore of great importance.

The Norwegian Environment Agency has been created as an agency with special responsibility to manage Norwegian nature, prevent pollution and to supervise and support the work to reduce greenhouse gas emissions. ①

Norway's climate policy is based on agreements reached in the Parliament (Stortinget) in 2008 and 2012 between all the political parties with the exception of the Progress Party. The agreements are a result of the broad political consensus that Norway shall take responsibility for a reduction in greenhouse gas emissions through an active national policy. The agreement contains targets for emission reductions in 2020, including ambitions for national emission reductions and a long-term goal of restructuring Norway to a low-emission society. ②

Norway has also put forward suggestions to the UN Climate Convention for new goals for a Climate Commitment for 2030. This suggestion is based on a report to the Norwegian Parliament from February 2015. ③The Parliament gave its approval to the suggested climate policies in March 2015, and this report now forms the basis for the Norwegian climate policies.

Norway signed the Paris Agreement in New York on 22 April 2016 together with 174 other countries.

Under the 2015 Climate Agreement (based on the St. 13 (2014 – 2015) report to the Parliament) between the Norwegian Government and the Parliament, Norway makes a commitment to reduce global greenhouse gas emission with at least 40 percent compared to the emission from 1990 (the same primary goal as in EU). The Norwegian Government has pinpointed five areas of special importance in order to reach the goal of substantially reducing the greenhouse gas emission:

● Reduce emission from the transport sector;

---

① More information about the Norwegian Environment Agency can be found on this website: miljodirektoratet. no.

② See information given on the webpage of the Ministry of Climate and Environment, https://www. regjeringen. no/en/topics/climate-and-environment/climate/innsiktsartikler-klima/agreement-on-climate-policy/ id2076645/.

③ St. 13 (2014 – 2015).

● Develop low emission technology and clean technology for industry production;

● CO_2 capture and storage;

● Strengthen Norway's position as a provider of renewable energy;

● Environmental friendly shipping.

Some of the overarching climate goals from the agreement between the Government and the Parliament from 2012 are still relevant, but some are new and even more ambitious:[1]

● Norway will exceed its Kyoto commitment by 10 percentage points in the first commitment period;

● Norway will be a low-emission society in 2015;

● Norway will be carbon neutral in 2050;

● As part of a global and ambitious climate agreement where other industrialised countries also make major commitments, Norway will have a binding target of carbon neutrality by 2030 at the latest.

The first Norwegian agreement on climate policy was adopted in 2008. Through this agreement a number of basic principles were highlighted in order to form the basis for Norwegian climate policy: "the polluter pays" principle; the precautionary principle; general measures shall be key; the climate policy must substantially reduce emissions both in Norway and abroad; the opportunity to use other measures in addition to quotas and taxes.

The 2012 agreement on climate policy was based on a report from the Stoltenberg ministry describing key climate policy principles, goals for emission reductions and contains a review of the various sectors in the economy. The report builds on the first agreement on climate policy and includes follow-up of the specific items from the agreement in 2008. It is now the 2015 report from the Solberg ministry that forms the political platform for Norwegian climate policy(St. 13 (2014 – 2015)).

7. 2 Legislation possibly impacting on foreign direct investment and trade

There are many Norwegian acts and regulations that cover environmental issues

---

[1] The goals for Norway are also stated in the annual report for 2015 made by the Norwegian Environment Agency.

and that therefore may possibly affect foreign direct investment or trade. Some of the acts that most likely could have such an effect are:

- The Pollution Control Act, No. 6 of 13 May 1981;
- The Greenhouse Gas Emission Trading Act, No. 99 of 17 December 2004;
- Product Control Act, No. 79 of 11 June 1976;
- Gene Technology Act, No. 38 of 2 April 1993;
- Environmental Information Act, No. 31 of 9 March 2003.

To reach the ambitious climate policy goals explained above, Norway has made use of legislation to make necessary changes, for example Norway uses green taxes as a tool, Norway also has established a domestic emissions trading scheme and develops legislation.

The CO_2 tax introduced in 1991 is Norway's main instrument in environmental policy. In addition, a national emissions quota system for parts of the processing industry and the offshore sector was introduced in 2005 and was expanded from 2013. This means that there are targeted instruments for approximately 90 percent of Norwegian emissions. [1]

In 2003 Norway introduced taxes on the import and export of hydrofluorocarbons (HFCs) and perfluorocarbons (PFCs), followed by annually decreasing allowances of import. As of January 2010 Norway banned all import and export of all ozone depleting gases. Most of these gases are also greenhouse gases with a strong global warming potential.

In 2004 the Norwegian Parliament passed the Act on Climate Quotas. [2] Norway established a domestic emissions trading scheme in 2005. In 2008 this trading scheme became part of the European Trading Scheme (ETS), with harmonised legislation with the EU. From 2012 aviation was covered by the ETS.

The Norwegian Environment Agency produces monthly and annual reports and statistics covering greenhouse gas emission in Norway. [3] The annual report from 2015 shows that Norway had an increase of CO_2 emission in 2015 compared to previous years, despite the goals of substantial reduction of CO_2 emission.

---

[1]   Information is found at the webpage of the Norwegian Environment Agency, see http://www. environment. no/topics/climate/instruments-to-reduce-emissions/. See also the website of Norway's Ministry of Finance on *Existing green taxes* at www. regjeringen. no.

[2]   Greenhouse Gas Emission Trading Act, No. 99 of 17 December 2004.

[3]   See miljodirektoratet. no.

Some of the import restrictions for goods are also aimed at protecting the environment. Import restrictions of goods are treated in Chapter 2 of this report. ①

Because Norway has a very long coastline and is a country with long traditions in fisheries and exploiting marine resources, marine management is important to Norway. There are three management plans in existence: Management plan for the Barents Sea and Lofoten, Management plan for the Norwegian Sea and Management plan for the North Sea and Skagerak. The purpose of the management plans is to facilitate value creation while also maintaining natural diversity. The Ministry of Climate and Environment is responsible for the work related to the management plans. ②

The legal framework of importance for human activity on Svalbard consists of

- the Svalbard Treaty; ③
- the Svalbard Act; ④ and
- the Svalbard Environmental Protection Act. ⑤

The Antarctic contains some of the last vast undisturbed areas of nature in the world. The cooperation under the Antarctic Treaty is critical to safeguarding the preservation of the natural environment and cultural heritage. ⑥ The Antarctic Treaty entered into force in 1961 and sets out the legal framework for operations and environmental protection in the Antarctic. The treaty ensures that the entire treaty area south of 60° South Latitude shall be devoted to peace and science. In addition, 37 countries have signed the Protocol on Environmental Protection to the Antarctic Treaty. ⑦ According to this Protocol, environmental protection is one of the main pillars in the cooperation under the treaty. The protocol establishes stringent environmental requirements on all human activities in the treaty area and prohibits any activity relating to mineral resources for 50 years.

---

① See also information given on the webpage of the Norwegian Customs Authority: http://www. toll. no/ en/goods/.

② The management plans can be downloaded from the Ministry of Climate and Environment's webpage https://www. regjeringen. no/en/topics/climate-and-environment/biodiversity/id1298/.

③ Treaty of 9 February 1920.

④ Act No. 11 of 17 July 1925.

⑤ Act No. 79 Relating to the Protection of the Environment in Svalbard of 15 June 2001.

⑥ The Antarctic Treaty was signed in Washington on 1 December 1959.

⑦ The Protocol on Environmental Protection to the Antarctic Treaty was signed in Madrid on 4 October 1991 and entered into force in 1998.

Chapter 8   Laws Relating to Dispute Resolution Concerning Foreign Entities

8.1   The Norwegian court system: an overview

The Norwegian Constitution from 1814 has established three different branches of government: legislative, executive and judicial. The legislative, budgetary and supervisory power is vested in the Parliament; executive power is vested in the King in Council; and judicial power is vested in the Supreme Court and the subordinate courts, and also in the Court of Impeachment(Riksretten).

The 1915 Courts of Justice Act sets out the basic legal framework for the organisation of the ordinary courts in Norway. [1]

The ordinary courts in Norway operate at three levels:

- District courts;
- Courts of Appeal(with jury in serious criminal cases);
- The Supreme Court.

In addition, there are some administrative bodies somewhat similar to courts, but they are not formally courts. The courts in Norway are managed by the Norwegian Courts Administration. There is also a Supervisory Committee for Judges that handles complaints against judges. [2]

As the main rule, all court hearings in all three levels of the court system are held in public.

8.1.1   District courts

There are 66 district courts in Norway. A judicial district consists of one or more municipalities.

The district courts hear civil and criminal cases. The district courts will hear all types of legal disputes such as cases of enforcement, bankruptcy, debt settlement and

---

[1]   Act No. 5 of 13 August 1915 relating to the Courts of Justice [Courts of Justice Act].

[2]   For information regarding the Norwegian court system, see http://www. domstol. no/en/. Much of the information given here is taken from this website.

disputes over property rights or division of joint property. Legal disputes concerning divorce or succession are also often brought to the district courts. These courts also determine matters relating to official certification, licences and permissions.

There is no jury trial in criminal cases before a district court.

Many civil cases are handled by a Conciliation Board, which are mediation bodies that have a certain power to enter judgment as well. Every municipality will have such a Conciliation Board. If the parties are not able to resolve their dispute through conciliation, the dispute may be brought before the district court. If the parties to a civil dispute are legally represented, the case may also start directly in a district court.

8.1.2 Courts of Appeal

Decisions from the district courts can be appealed to a Court of Appeal. There are six Courts of Appeal in Norway, each covering a certain geographical area. The Courts of Appeal have jurisdiction in both civil and criminal matters.

Not every appeal will be tried by the Courts of Appeal. There is an Appeal Screening Committee which screens appeals and decides which cases that should proceed to a hearing before the appellant court. The Appeal Screening Committee may refuse an appeal if it considers that the appeal chance of success.

In cases where the maximum sentence exceeds six years, the Court of Appeal will sit with a jury (lagrette) consisting of 10 members (laymen). [1] In order to find the defendant guilty, at least six jurors must agree. [2] The level of punishment will be decided by four jurors and three professional judges. If the appeal concerns the sentence for an offence for which the maximum sentence does not exceed six years, the appeal will be determined by three professional judges, after an oral proceeding. [3]

An appeal in a civil cases generally tried by three professional judges. In certain types of cases lay judges must be appointed as well. The parties also have the opportunity to require that two to four lay judges must be empanelled.

Decisions regarding the question of guilt in criminal cases are finally decided upon by the Court of Appeal. These decisions cannot be appealed. In all other cases,

---

[1] See Sections 352 –355 of the Criminal Proceedings Act.

[2] See Section 372.

[3] See the Criminal Proceedings Act of 22 May 1981 No. 25.

decisions from the Court of Appeal can be appealed to the Supreme Court.

8.1.3   The Supreme Court

Section 88 of the Norwegian Constitution provides that the Supreme Court pronounces judgment in the final instance. The Supreme Court is the highest court in Norway and is situated in Oslo. The Norwegian Supreme Court began its activities in 1815. Since that time, both the caseload of the Court and the number of justices have, not surprisingly, increased. Today, there are a Chief Justice and 19 ordinary justices in the Supreme Court. The Chief Justice of the Supreme Court is ranked number four in the order precedence in Norway after the King, the President of the Parliament (Stortingspresidenten) and the Prime Minister. [1]

It is the function of the Supreme Court to ensure uniformity of legal processes and to contribute to the resolution of matters on which the law is unclear. The Supreme Court also has a responsibility for the development of law, for example, when required by new societal problems. Accordingly, leave to appeal to the Supreme Court is often granted in cases that raise important matters of principle.

A decision of the Supreme Court is final, and there is no appeal or complaint against it. The one special exception is for cases that can be brought before the European Court of Human Rights in Strasbourg.

The Supreme Court has authority in all areas of the law. The court thus considers both civil and criminal cases, and the Norwegian Supreme Court also tries cases concerning constitutional law. In criminal cases the question of guilt is finally determined by the Courts of Appeal, whereas the Supreme Court may make a ruling on matters of sentencing and the quality of the procedure.

An appeal to the Supreme Court from a decision of a district court or a Court of Appeal is first considered by the Supreme Court's appeals committee. This committee decides whether a case shall proceed to the Supreme Court. The Appeals Selection Committee functions as a filter for appeals against judgments made by lower courts. In issues whose significance extends beyond the case in question, or when it is urgent to reach a final verdict, the decision from first instance may be appealed directly to

---

[1]   Information about the Norwegian Supreme Court can, in addition to the site mentioned in the previous footnote, also be found at http://www. domstol. no/en/Enkelt-domstol/-Norges-Hoyesterett/The-Supreme-Court-of-Norway-/. Information on the Norwegian Supreme Court in this article is mostly taken from this site.

the Supreme Court if the Selection Committee approves. ① The Committee is constituted of three judges. Proceedings in the Appeals Committee are on paper (without hearing oral submissions), and the decision is made on the strength of the documents in the case.

A substantive hearing is normally held before five justices. To ease the workload, the Supreme Court works in two parallel and equal divisions. In some instances, however, cases are heard in Grand Chamber by eleven justices or by all of the justices sitting in plenary session.

Justices sit in the two divisions of the Supreme Court and on the Appeals Selection Committee in rotation.

The proceedings of the Supreme Court are almost always oral, and are generally conducted in open court. Unlike the district courts and the Court of Appeal, the Supreme Court does not hear evidence. Nor does the Supreme Court conduct site inspections, such as the scene of a crime.

The decisions of the Supreme Court and of the Appeals Selection Committee of the Supreme Court are published in the Norwegian Law Gazette (Norsk Retstidende) and the Lovdata Foundation legal information system. The most recent decisions are also available on Internet for a limited period of time after they have been delivered.

8.2 Jurisdiction of courts: the main rules

There are two sets of rules that are important when deciding whether or not the Norwegian court has jurisdiction in an international dispute in a commercial or civil matter:

- The 2007 Lugano Convention; ② and
- The 2005 Civil Proceedings Act. ③

The Norwegian legislation may contain special rules regarding venue or choice of law that is of importance in disputes involving foreign entities. See for example the Norwegian Customs Act Section 10-1 (6) which states that a dispute regarding the

---

① See Section 8 of the Criminal Proceedings Act and the Civil Procedure Act Section 30-2. This procedure is commonly known as "leapfrogging".

② Convention between Norway and EU as well as Denmark, Switzerland and Iceland concluded in Lugano, Switzerland of 30 October 2007.

③ Act No. 90 of 17 June 2005.

validity of an anti-dumping measure will be treated by the Oslo district court as appropriate for resolution in a court of first instance. It is also stated that the court is obliged to give such a case priority so that a timely judgement may be delivered. The same is true for countervailing measures(Section 10-3(5)).

Norway is not a member of the Hague Convention of 30 June 2005 on Choice of Court Agreements.

The Lugano Convention is applicable in cases which have a connection with the EEA area. The Lugano Convention is often called a parallel convention because it mirrors the Brussels I Regulation[①] which is applicable to EU member states only. The Lugano Convention is also called a double convention because, as for the Brussels I Regulation, the Lugano Convention consists of rules regarding jurisdiction as well as recognition and enforcement of judgements.

The 2005 Norwegian Civil Procedure Act was primarily drafted for national disputes. But the Act is also applicable to international disputes that are not governed by the Lugano Convention (Section 4-3). The Lugano Convention is regarded the primary source for international law cases having a close enough connection with the EEA area. Questions of jurisdiction in disputes where the case is not connected to the EEA area will be decided on the basis of the Norwegian Civil Proceedings Act.

The 2005 Act replaced the previous Civil Proceeding Act from 1915. During the preparations for the 2005 Act, the rules concerning jurisdiction were amended in order to make them as close as possible to the wording and content of the Lugano Convention. In most cases the rules on jurisdiction are the same in the Norwegian Civil Proceedings Act and the Lugano Convention. Yet, there are some differences between the Convention and the Act. Therefore it is important to be aware and to use the correct legal basis for jurisdiction when filing a case in an international dispute before a Norwegian court.

(a) *Agreement on jurisdiction.*

In international commercial cases, questions of jurisdiction are most often agreed upon in a jurisdiction clause in the parties' agreement. Both the Lugano Convention and the Norwegian Civil Proceedings Act acknowledge the parties' right to decide where to litigate. The party autonomy is recognised in Art. 23 of the Lugano

---

① Council Regulation(EC) No. 44/2001 of 22 December 2000 on jurisdiction and the recognition and enforcement of judgements in civil and commercial matters.

Convention and Section 4-6 in the Civil Proceedings Act.

It is stated in Section 4-6(2) of the Norwegian Civil Proceedings Act that an agreement that extends or limits the authority of the Norwegian courts, must be in writing. Under the Lugano Convention Art 23 an agreement on jurisdiction may be made orally but it must be confirmed in writing. It is also accepted that an agreement on jurisdiction is in conformity with established practice between the parties or with trade practices that the parties knew or ought to have known and that is commonly known and followed in similar branches of international trade (see Art. 23(1)(c)).

If the parties have made an agreement on jurisdiction, the court mentioned in the agreement will have exclusive jurisdiction unless the parties have agreed otherwise (Art. 23(1)). The wording is somewhat different in the Norwegian Civil Proceedings Act Section 4-6(1), but the result is the same. The Norwegian Civil Proceedings Act Section 4-6(1) says that an agreement on jurisdiction may either be exclusive or be treated as an addition to the alternative rules on jurisdiction. The solution must be found on an interpretation of the agreement.

There are limitations to the freedom of contract in relation to jurisdiction in consumer contracts under both the Lugano Convention and the Norwegian Civil Proceedings Act. Under both sets of rules the contract of jurisdiction must be in writing. Section 4-6(3) of the Norwegian Civil Proceedings Act provides that an agreement on jurisdiction entered into before the dispute arose is not binding on the consumer. There are also special rules for choice of court in matters of insurance and disputes regarding employment contracts. ①

(b) Main rule of jurisdiction—Place of domicile.

Both under the Lugano Convention and the Norwegian Civil proceedings Act the court of the defendant's domicile will have jurisdiction. ②If the parties have not made an agreement on the question of jurisdiction, the plaintiff may sue the defendant where the defendant is ordinarily resident. The plaintiff has to seek out the defendant.

It is the place of domicile (habitual residence), not the citizenship of the defendant that is decisive on jurisdiction of the court. This is in line with traditional private international law in Norway. Natural persons have domicile where they are

---

① See the Norwegian Civil Procedure Act Section 4-5(4) on employment contracts and Section 4-5(9) on jurisdiction in matters of insurance. Employment contracts are governed by the Lugano Convention Art. 18-21 whereas jurisdiction in insurance cases are dealt with in Art. 8-12.

② See the Lugano Convention Art. 2 and the Norwegian Civil Procedure Act Section 4-4.

ordinarily resident. Norwegian courts will make an overall assessment of all the relevant circumstances in order to decide whether or not a person is domiciled in Norway.

When a case, which has a connection with the EEA, is against a business entity, the question of the defendant's domicile is governed by Arts. 59 and 60 of the Lugano Convention. These rules are parallel to Arts. 62 and 63 of the Brussels I Regulation. [1] In domestic cases, a Norwegian company is domiciled where its registered main office is situated. [2]A foreign company with a branch or an agent in Norway is considered to be domiciled at his place of its business. [3]

In commercial disputes, the place of performance of the contractual obligation could be a better alternative than domicile in determining which court has jurisdiction. Where the Lugano Convention forms the legal basis for jurisdiction, it is Art. 5(1) that gives the criteria to be met in order to try the case before a court at the place of performance: "In matters relating to a contract, in the courts for the place of performance of the obligation in question; in matters relating to individual contracts of employment, this place is that where the employee habitually carries out his work, or if the employee does not habitually carry out his work in any one country, this place shall be the place of business through which he was engaged". Art. 5(1) in the Lugano Convention is parallel to Art. 5(1) of the Brussels I Regulation for the EU member states.

Jurisdiction at the place of performance is an alternative also under the Norwegian Civil Proceedings Act Section 4-5(2). This provision will be applicable in international disputes lacking the sufficient connection to the EEA area and thereby falling outside the scope of the Lugano Convention.

In international disputes where the place of performance is not agreed upon, the place of performance will be decided upon by the law applicable by virtue of private international law in the state where the court is situated. This is so according to Norwegian Supreme Court practice[4]as well as under EU law, and thereby under the

---

[1]   Regulation (EU) No. 1215/2012 of 12 December 2012 on jurisdiction and the recognition and enforcement of judgements in civil and commercial matters.

[2]   See the Norwegian Civil Procedure Act Section 4-4(3), first sentence.

[3]   See the Civil Proceedings Act, Section 4-4(3), second sentence.

[4]   See Rt 2006 p. 1008.

Lugano Convention. ①

The Norwegian Civil Proceedings Act Section 4-5(2) is meant to be in line with the Lugano Convention Art. 5(1). There is however an important difference when it comes to disputes regarding money claims. If the defendant is domiciled in Norway and the dispute in question is about a money claim, then the case cannot be tried in the court of the place of performance. The reason for having an exception in these cases is to prevent a creditor in a debt collection case from instituting action where the creditor is domiciled rather than seeking out the debtor.

(c) *Disputes regarding matters relating to tort, delict or quasi-delict.*

The appropriate court is the court that has jurisdiction in the place where the harmful event occurred or may occur. This is stated both in the Norwegian Civil Proceedings Act Section 4-5(3) and the Lugano Convention Art. 5(3). The wording of the Norwegian Civil Procedure Act Section 4-5(3) is somewhat extended compared to Art. 5(3) of the Lugano Convention, but it must be assumed that the Norwegian rule will be interpreted in line with the Lugano Convention Art. 5(3).

Jurisdiction of the court where the harmful event took place, is an alternative jurisdiction. For the purpose of filing action, the plaintiff may choose this place as an alternative to the defendant's domicile.

In commercial cases, it can sometimes be difficult to decide whether a claim for compensation is contractual or non-contractual. Disputes regarding product liability and pre-contractual liability will be considered as non-contractual so that the alternative jurisdiction will be decided under the Lugano Convention Art. 5 (3). Disputes regarding unjust enrichment or *negotiorum gestio* are also considered to be non-contractual. A claim for compensation for losses caused directly by a breach of contract will be considered as a contractual claim, whereas a claim for indirect losses will be treated as a non-contractual claim. ② According to practice of the European Court of Justice, a claim directly referable to a breach of contract is treated as a non-contractual claim. ③ Under domestic Norwegian law, a claim directly referable to a breach of contract is regarded as a contractual claim, the reasoning being that these claims cannot exist without a chain of contracts. The Supreme Court practice is to

---

① See Case C – 12/76 (Tessili).

② See Rt 2011 p. 897.

③ See Case C – 26/91 (Handte).

consider the place of performance as the correct venue. This practice may be referred to a domestic case predating Norway's accession to the Lugano Convention. At least in international cases, it is presumed that the Norwegian Civil Proceedings Act Section 4-5(3) and the Lugano Convention Art. 5(3) will be interpreted in line with EU law as regards direct action claims too.

Disputes regarding immovable property:

Jurisdiction in disputes regarding immovable property is treated somewhat differently in the Lugano Convention when compared to the Norwegian Civil Procedure Act. Under Art. 22 of the Lugano Convention disputes regarding rights *in rem* in immovable property or tenancies of immovable property, must be filed at the court where the property is situated. However, in proceedings which have as their object tenancies of immovable property concluded for temporary private use for a maximum period of six consecutive months, the courts of the state in which the defendant is domiciled shall also have jurisdiction, provided that the tenant is a natural person and that the landlord and the tenant are domiciled in the same state.

As for disputes regarding rights *in rem* in immovable property or long term tenancies of immovable property, the court in the state where the property is situated have exclusive jurisdiction under the Lugano Convention Art. 22. The case must be filed here regardless of where the defendant is domiciled or regardless of any agreement on jurisdiction that the parties have agreed upon. The exclusive jurisdiction under Art. 22 is however limited to "rights *in rem*". Dispute related to purely contractual matters is not covered by Art. 22.

Under the Norwegian Civil Procedure Act Section 4-5(1), jurisdiction regarding disputes over immovable property is not exclusive. The plaintiff may choose to file the case at the place where the defendant is domiciled. Section 4-5(1) differs from the Lugano Convention Art. 22 also in the sense that Section 4-5(1) does not draw a difference between rights *in rem* and purely contractual claims.

8.3   Choice of law: main rules

Private international law is not codified in Norway. There are however some choices of law-related Norwegian legislative acts which are relevant in international commercial cases. Norway adopted the 1955 Hague Convention on the Law Applicable to International Sale of Goods and incorporated it into Norwegian law by the Act on Applicable Law in International Sale of Goods No. 1 of 3 April 1964.

There is also an Act on Choice of Law in Insurance, No. 111 of 27 November 1992.

The leading case in Norwegian private international law is the *Irma Mignon* case[1] arising out of a collision in English waters between the two Norwegian ships, Irma and Mignon. The dispute regarding compensation for losses and cost of repair was brought before a Norwegian court. Under Norwegian law, the ship owner was responsible for mistakes made by the state pilot on board the ship, whereas English law did not have this rule at that time. The outcome of the dispute depended upon whether English or Norwegian law was applicable, and a choice of law had to be made. The Supreme Court took the opportunity to establish the principle that "a legal relationship is to be governed by the law of the country with which it is most closely connected," despite the fact that the collision had in fact occurred on English territory. This principle, known in Norway as "the Irma Mignon formula", is the same as the "principle of the closest connection" in Article 4(1) of the 1980 Rome Convention. The Irma Mignon formula has over the years been applied by Norwegian courts to disputes regarding contractual matters as well. [2]

Even though Norway is not a party to the Rome I Regulation, it is considered important that Norwegian non-codified private international law regarding contractual obligations is interpreted and practiced in line with European law in order to achieve uniformity. This has been stated by the Supreme Court (*obiter dicta*) and also expressed in legal doctrine and by the Norwegian Ministry of Justice.

The applicable law in matters of contract has traditionally been pointed out by an overall assessment of the case in order to find the state in which the contractual relationship has the closest connection. As long as the 1980 Rome Convention was applicable within the EU, it was relatively easy to adopt the Norwegian main rule of choice of law in contractual matters to EU private international law. The principle of the closest connection is however not that main rule under Act 4 of the Rome I Regulation. Rome I Art. 4(1) have a list of choice of law rules applicable to different types of contracts or different legal questions. It is not clear how close the Norwegian courts will follow the European legal instruments in detail, but it must be assumed that the Norwegian courts will interpret the principle of the closest connection in such

---

[1]   Rt. 1923 II s. 58.

[2]   See Rt 1931. 1185, Rt 1937. 888, Rt 1980. 243 and Rt 1982. 1294.

a way that the applicable law will be the same as under the Rome I Regulation. ①

The choice of law rules regarding tort law cases or disputes over compensation in non-contractual matters is also not codified. The two cases in which the Norwegian Supreme court has stated that Norwegian private international law should be applied in line with EU private international law related to compensation in non-contractual matters. ② The main choice of law rule for disputes regarding non-contractual obligation is that the law of the state in which the harmful event took place, will be applicable. This main rule is parallel to the Rome II Regulation Art. 4(1). ③ If the defendant and the plaintiff both were domiciled in the same state at the time the harmful event took place, the law of the country of common domicile is applicable according to Rome II Art. 4(2). If the case is manifestly more closely connected with a country other than where the harmful event took place or the country of common domicile, the law of the state with the closest connection to the dispute will apply; see Art. 4(3) of the Rome II Regulation: "Where it is clear from all the circumstances of the case that the tort/delict is manifestly more closely connected with a country other than that indicated in paragraphs 1 or 2, the law of that other country shall apply. A manifestly closer connection with another country might be based in particular on a pre-existing relationship between the parties, such as a contract, that is closely connected with the tort/delict in question. " The Norwegian court practice following the Irma Mignon formula makes it likely that choice of law under Norwegian law will be in line also with Arts. 4 (2) (where both parties have their habitual residence in the same country) and 4(3) (manifestly more closely connected with a country other than the country where the non-contractual loss occurred, or the country of habitual residence of both parties) of the Rome II Regulation. ④

Norwegian choice of law rules are not codified in relation to rights *in rem* too. There is no leading Supreme Court case in this area of law, but it can be deduced from the practice in courts of lower instance supported by legal literature that the

---

① See Rt 2009 p 1537, Rt 2011 p 531. See also Giuditta Cordero Moss, Internasjonal privatrett på formuerettens område, Oslo 2013 pp 45 – 48 and p 207, Giuditta Codero Moss, Lov og Rett, 2009, p. 67 and the hearing statement from the Ministry of Justice dated 13 June 2003.

② See Rt 2009 p. 1537 and Rt 2011 p. 1531.

③ Regulation(EC) No. 864/2007 on the law applicable to non-contractual obligations(Rome II).

④ As for Norwegian legal literature regarding choice of law on non-contractual obligations, see Lars Anders Heimdal, Rettsvalg for erstatning ved krenkende ytringer, Bergen 2011 and Giuditta Cordero Moss, Internasjonal privatrett på formuerettens område, Oslo 2013 pp. 327 – 359.

main rule is the principle of *lex rei sitae*: namely, that the law of the state in which the movable or immovable property is situated will be applicable to disputes regarding rights *in rem*. ①

The *lex concursus* principle applies to international disputes in matters regarding insolvency. If the core question of the legal dispute is considered to be a matter of insolvency, Norwegian courts will apply the law of the state where the insolvency proceedings opened. As for most of Norwegian private international law, this choice of law rule is also not codified.

Inter-Nordic cases, cases where the insolvency could have effect in another Nordic country, are governed by the 1933 Insolvency Convention. ②When insolvency opens in one of the Nordic countries, the insolvent estate will also include property situated in another Nordic State according to Art. 1 of the convention. Art. 1 thus makes it clear that even if the property is situated in another state than the state where the insolvency proceedings take place, the property will be included in the insolvency estate. The convention builds on the principle of universality for the treatment of the bankruptcy estate in cases of inter-Nordic insolvencies. This convention also has some choice of law rules. The convention also contains rules regarding recognition and enforcement. Even though this is an old convention, it is still in force and of practical importance when it comes to inter-Nordic insolvencies.

The EU Insolvency Regulation is not part of the EEA Agreement. Norway has no legislation that is parallel to this set of rule, such as the Lugano Convention in comparison to the Brussel I Regulation. Since matters of international insolvencies are not covered by the EEA Agreement, Norwegian law is basically the same regardless of whether the insolvency in question is connected to another EEA member state(but inter-Nordic insolvencies are treated by the 1933 Convention)or to a state outside the EEA.

As long as Norway has not entered into any agreement with another state or with the EU that is binding under public international law, an insolvency that happens in another state will not have any effect in Norway. The principle of territoriality will apply in these cases. This is stated by the Norwegian Supreme Court in a 2015 case

① See RG 1958 p. 646 and RG 1963 p. 528. See also Berte-Elen Reinertsen Konow, Løsørepant over landegrenser, Bergen 2006, Giuditta Cordero Moss, Internasjonal privatrett på formuerettens område, Oslo 2013 pp. 277 – 283.

② Convention between Norway, Denmark, Finland, Iceland and Sweden dated 7 November 1933.

and is also in line with Norwegian legal literature. ①

8. 4　Arbitration

The legal framework for international arbitration in Norway is found in:

- The Arbitration Act, No. 25 of 14 May 2005;
- The 1958 New York Convention.

The Norwegian Arbitration Act is based upon the UNCITRAL Model Law on International Commercial Arbitration. ②

Section 1 of the Arbitration Act provides that the act is applicable equally to domestic and international arbitration. Disputes concerning legal relations in respect of which the parties have an unrestricted right of disposition may be determined by arbitration(Section 9). Article 11 provides that an arbitration agreement to which a consumer is a party shall not be binding on the consumer if entered into prior to the dispute arising. In other cases, the parties may agree to submit to arbitration disputes which have arisen, as well as all or certain disputes which may arise in respect of a defined legal relationship.

The parties may decide in the agreement how many judges the court of arbitration will consist of. If there is no agreement about the number of judges, the arbitral tribunal will consist of three judges(Section 12).

It is up to the parties to nominate an ad hoc arbitral tribunal, or to use for example the Arbitration and Dispute Resolution Institute of the Oslo Chamber of Commerce as a facilitator for appointing an arbitration court.

The Arbitration and Dispute Resolution Institute is a body incorporated in the Oslo Chamber of Commerce. The institute can be of assistance in both national and international disputes and within different areas of commerce such as industry, trade of goods and services, shipping, offshore/onshore activities and other fields of business activity. Among arbitrators and mediators representing the institute are leading and most experienced commercial lawyers, judges and legal academics in

---

① See Rt 2015 p. 129. See also Mads Henry Andenæs` memorandum to the Norwegian Ministry of Justice dated October 2010(available on the website of the Ministry of Justice) and Berte-Elen R. Konow, International insolvencies and the classical struggle between the principle of universality and the principle of territoriality: a Norwegian perspective, A Tribute to Joseph Lookofsky, Copenhagen 2015.

② The Model Law can be found at the UNCITRAL website: http://uncitral. org.

Norway. For parties who so wish, the institute can act as the appointing authority and provide administrative assistance under the rules of the United Nations Commission on International Trade Law (UNCITRAL). ①

As regards recognition and enforcement in Norway of arbitral awards given by foreign arbitral tribunals, Norway is party to the 1958 UN Convention. ②The rules of the convention are incorporated in the Norwegian Arbitration Act. As stated in Section 45, an arbitral award, irrespective of the country in which it was made, shall be recognised and enforceable in Norway. Exceptions to this general rule follow basically the content of the New York Convention.

---

① For more information about Oslo Chamber of Commerce, see http://www. chamber. no.

② Convention on the Recognition and Enforcement of Foreign Arbitral Awards (New York, 1958). This Convention is frequently referred to as "The New York Convention".